DHARAVI

DHARAVI
The City Within

Edited by

JOSEPH CAMPANA

HarperCollins *Publishers* India

First published in India in 2013 by
HarperCollins *Publishers* India

Anthology copyright © HarperCollins *Publishers* India 2013
Introduction copyright © Joseph Campana
Copyright in individual pieces vests with the respective contributors

ISBN: 987-93-5029-399-7

2 4 6 8 10 9 7 5 3 1

HarperCollins *Publishers*
A-53, Sector 57, Noida, Uttar Pradesh 201301, India
77-85 Fulham Palace Road, London W6 8JB, United Kingdom
Hazelton Lanes, 55 Avenue Road, Suite 2900, Toronto, Ontario M5R 3L2
and 1995 Markham Road, Scarborough, Ontario M1B 5M8, Canada
25 Ryde Road, Pymble, Sydney, NSW 2073, Australia
31 View Road, Glenfield, Auckland 10, New Zealand
10 East 53rd Street, New York NY 10022, USA

Typeset in 12/14 Adobe Jenson Pro at
SÜRYA

Printed and bound at
Manipal Technologies Limited, Manipal

This book is dedicated to the people who have made Dharavi their home. May they continue to live there on their own terms.

CONTENTS

SECTION TWO: WORK AND MONEY

SECTION THREE: THE DAILY GRIND AND TIMEPASS

INTRODUCTION

Joseph Campana

Vinod Shetty, the head of ACORN India, an NGO that provides various services for the waste collectors and sorters in Dharavi's recycling district, came up with the idea for this book in February of 2009. At the time, all eyes were on Dharavi—or so it seemed. *Slumdog Millionaire* had just won numerous Golden Globe and BAFTA awards, and was primed to win an academy award for best picture. Articles appeared daily, both excoriating and defending the film, in national and international publications. The term 'poverty porn' was coined to describe Boyle's portrayal of slum life and viewers' fascination with what they saw.

Shetty thought the international attention had created an audience that would listen to the people of Dharavi speak about their families, their work, and what they felt about the changes that would be coming if the Dharavi Redevelopment Plan was implemented. He asked me to find journalists who would go into Dharavi and tell the stories of the people and the place. The writers would do this for free. 'You can have this book ready in a month,' he said. No problem, I told him.

There were, however, two problems. First, I knew exactly zero journalists in town. Second, I was not confident that anyone would have the time to participate. It was worth a shot, though. The first four people I contacted enthusiastically endorsed the book, told me it was an important project, and politely declined. Some politely declined numerous times. Then Dilip D'Souza and Sonia Faleiro endorsed the project—and agreed to provide material. Things began falling into place. Then in November 2010, HarperCollins came into the picture. Nearly four years later—after commissioning, selecting, and editing the articles—we finally have a book.

At the start, I conceived the book as an argument against the Dharavi Redevelopment Plan. Approved in 2004, the DRP amounted to an agreement between the Government of Maharashtra, managing planner Mukesh Mehta, and several consortia of builders to divide Dharavi into sectors, modernize its infrastructure, bulldoze the many hutments where people lived and worked, reinstall the residents in high-rises consisting of 300 sq. ft apartments, and construct upscale buildings on the freed-up space to be used as homes and offices by the city's rising middle class. In Mehta's words, Dharavi would be transformed into an 'integrated township', complete with schools, hospitals, green spaces and all the amenities anyone could want. Potters, jewellery makers, leather workers and garment makers would be trained to improve their work so they could sell their goods at higher prices to richer consumers. The idea was that Dharavi's indigent would be better off. The builders and the government, of course, would be better off, too. Builders would pay a fee to be involved. They'd also have to build new homes for the residents free of cost. They'd get their money back, in spades presumably, by selling off the new buildings to wealthy investors. Everyone would win.

The plan was nothing if not grand, financially as well as morally. In 2007, Mehta told a reporter from *Mint* that if people were to initiate his design elsewhere, 'the world could be slum free by 2025'. Mehta also made this promise to Bill Clinton, whose picture hangs proudly on the wall of Mehta's office, the former president smiling between the builder and his son.

Numerous activists railed against the project. They had many sound reasons for doing so, not all of which need to be enumerated here. Some do bear mentioning, though. First, only those residents who could prove that they'd lived in Dharavi since 2000 would be entitled to receive a free apartment. This meant that perhaps as many as half of Dharavi's 500,000-plus residents would be displaced. Second, those who did qualify would be housed in approximately 47 per cent of Dharavi's 1.7 sq. km surface area. The density would be unmanageable, no matter how high the new buildings were. Last, the majority of people in Dharavi I spoke to either had not heard of Mukesh Mehta and his plan or did not support it. To be fair, numerous residents fully endorsed the project and looked forward to a better life in a high-rise with a steady supply of water and a workable bathroom. Many sought the dignity that would come with having their own mailing address. I thought the book had a good case to make. But any argument against such a plan, sound as that argument may be, is still a negative argument. And negative arguments only take one so far.

I found a better argument, and a better method of putting the book together, after reading the work of Nobel-prize winning economist Amartya Sen. Sen opens *Development As Freedom*, a philosophical work concerned with social justice, with a parable about the limits of wealth. He graciously allowed me to reprint that story as the prologue to this book. In the parable, a woman named Maitreyee despairs when she learns that she cannot purchase immortality with her riches. Rather than pursuing the theological implications of Maitreyee's conundrum, Sen considers the worldly aspects of Maitreyee's wish to live forever. He focuses on the relationship between the money we have, the lives we live now, and the opportunities we have to improve our circumstances in the ways we see fit. Wealth is useful, Sen says, to the extent that it enlarges our freedom (which is, in Sen's words, 'the ability to live as we would like') without encroaching on the freedom of those with whom we live. By extension, development, or the increase of one's wealth, is only beneficial to the extent that it expands one's freedom. Wealth is only useful to the extent that it can be used to help us live as we would like to live.

Sen's parable raises questions that are relevant to the DRP. What about the freedom and the quality of life of residents who will be excluded from the new, integrated township? Furthermore, will residents who live gratis in a 300 sq. ft apartment be freer than they were before? Will they be living as they want to live? Will they be able to improve their living spaces as they could when they had their own place at ground level? They surely won't be able to add a second floor, as they could before. What happens when the elevator breaks, or the water gets cut off?

But those questions amount to arguments. What Sen's parable really teaches is that stories are richer than arguments.

This book is therefore a collection of stories about the people who live in Dharavi. All of them are true. The people you meet in twenty-three of the twenty-four chapters that follow Sen's prologue have acquired some measure of material wealth—and a great deal of self-sufficiency. In the opening chapter, Sonia Faleiro demonstrates that freedom, as Sen conceives of it, begins at home. Faleiro writes about two fathers and their daughters. The first of the fathers, Mohammad Rais Khan, acquires a sense of self and purpose in part by keeping his wife and daughter tethered to their home, safe from the dangers of the world—namely, men. The second, the late Dharavi-activist Waqar Khan, has shown his daughters how to be strong, ambitious individuals by encouraging them to go to school and pursue careers. As Faleiro shows, Khan has also taught his daughters how to participate in a community by restoring trust among Hindus and Muslims in the aftermath of the 1992–93 riots.

There are a lot of good people in Dharavi, but they're not all saints. S. Hussain Zaidi chronicles the life of D.K. Rao, Dharavi's most notorious gangster made famous by his Rasputin-like grip on life. Priyanka Pathak-Narain writes about an illegal lending scheme that some Dharavi residents have exploited to start businesses, and Freny Manecksha explains how the water mafia works. Jerry Pinto, who contributed three chapters, instills some charm in the narrative with his account of a milk carrier-cum-poet who texts a poem a day to over 400 adoring fans in Tamil Nadu. When he's late with his verse, his readers beckon him via text message. One reader responded to a poem with a marriage proposal. In one way or another, by means legal or illegal, the people in this book are seeking freedom—or the means to live as they would like. Several, including D.K. Rao, have done so at the expense of others. Most, however, live communally and have sought to improve themselves and others around them.

The stories in this book are separated into four parts. Section One, 'Arrival in Dharavi', chronicles the settlement patterns in Dharavi and explains how various groups of people have sustained themselves through a complex system of social networks that connect Dharavi to markets throughout India and across the globe. Saumya Roy and Aditya Kundalkar report on Koliwada and Kumbharwada—the fishers' and the potters' colonies—the oldest and most unified communities in Dharavi. Section Two, 'Work and Money', illustrates some of the many ways people there earn a living. Annie Zaidi documents the rise of several entrepreneurs, including Sayeed Khan Bucklewala, a brass foundry owner who made millions selling belt buckles, and L. Kannan, who irons clothes in a tiny shop. In 2010, Kannan's son was accepted into one of India's top IT schools, and Kannan irons clothes every day to make sure he graduates. In Section Three, 'Daily Struggles and Timepass', writers examine how the residents get through the day: how they make their marriages work; how some cope with shiftless and abusive spouses; how they get water; and how they ensure that their kids get a proper education. Most of the stories in Section Three focus on women. Sharmila Joshi, for example, gives an account of a single mother who lost her entire stock of recycled goods in a fire. Certain that it was arson, Hanumanti Kamble defied her tormentors by getting back to work the next day. In Section Four, 'Fixing Dharavi', Kalpana Sharma traces the history of redevelopment in Dharavi and Dilip D'Souza writes three accounts documenting what people stand to lose if the new plan is implemented.

Above I say that twenty-three of the twenty-four chapters contain stories. I reserved space at the end of the final section for Shirish Patel's argument against the sweeping changes the government and the builders plan for Dharavi. Ultimately, the book has to take a stand on one of the most pressing issues facing the city. The people living and working in Dharavi do so on some of the most expensive real estate on the planet. In most cases, they never bought the land. They just got there first and made it their own. With India's largest building conglomerates and some of its leading politicians threatening to crowd them out, Patel explains why the Dharavi residents have a right to stay where they are and continue living as they do.

The simplest reason Dharavi residents should be left alone is that they are far better off without outsiders interfering in their business. Grand schemes like Mukesh Mehta's invite too much corruption.

Here are two redevelopment stories I was told on my visits to Dharavi. In June of 2009 I met thirty-nine-year-old Santosh Narkar outside his building, located immediately south of Kumbharwada. It was an unbearably humid day. The rain was two weeks overdue. It was early evening and the smoke from the kilns in Kumbharwada was blowing over us.

Narkar is a well-dressed, athletic-looking gentleman with a thick, black moustache and a clean-shaven face. Every time I met him, he wore tight-fitting, dark dress pants and a white collared shirt, always neatly tucked in and wrinkle free. He kept three or four pens in his breast pocket. Narkar is the chairman of the Subosh Nagar Housing Society. He collects utility fees from the residents of the high-rise where he lives—about Rs 300 per month for water, power and trash removal—and supervises the workers who are putting up another high-rise building next to the one he lives in. From what I could tell,

Narkar spent the better part of his days hanging out with three or four other fellows trading stories.

Narkar was tight-lipped the first time I met him. I wanted his opinion on the redevelopment project, and all he would say was that he trusted the government. He encouraged me to walk through his building and speak to residents, which I did with my guide, Rajesh. The second time I met him, Narkar repeated, yet again, that he had faith in the government. However, while we were drinking tea, he sent a boy off to retrieve something. We continued with some idle chat and some talk about Narkar's family. The boy soon returned with a copy of *Mid Day* dated 10 July 2004. The headline read: 'He waited for four hours to kill himself and then . . .' There was a picture of an unconscious Santosh Narkar being carried off by several men.

Narkar had sat outside a city bureaucrat's office for so long because he wanted to know where his home was. Ten years prior, in 1994, Narkar and approximately 300 other people had reached an agreement with Shivshashi Punarvasan Prakalp Limited (SPPL), a local builder, whereby the residents agreed to turn over the land on which their hutments stood. In exchange, SPPL would build two seven-storey high-rises, one for the residents to live in rent free and a second which SPPL would sell at market value. The project was set to take between three and four years, during which time Narkar and his cohort would live in a nearby transit camp. Ten years later, the buildings weren't finished due to lack of funds, and SPPL was demanding that Narkar raise Rs 30 lakh to complete the job.

Narkar went to the government for help several times but was stymied. On 10 July 2004, after a four-hour wait in the halls of the Maharashtra Housing and Area Development Authority

(MHADA) building, Narkar poured kerosene on himself and lit a match. A guard intervened before Narkar could immolate himself, but the fumes from the kerosene left him unconscious. He had made his point. The government paid the fee, and the residents moved into their new 225 sq. ft homes in 2007.

When I toured Narkar's building again, I asked several residents about Narkar's story. All of them confirmed it and expressed gratitude. However, each of them also said they were certain that Narkar was skimming from the money they paid him for utilities and services. They also said they got less water per day than the agreement called for and that trash collection was inconsistent. They were fed up with him.

Shortly after he introduced me to Narkar, my guide Rajesh took me into Kumbharwada to meet Abbas, a thirty-year-old potter with a wife and daughter. Lean and handsome, with short hair and a slightly receding hairline, Abbas could pass for twenty-four. Unlike Narkar, he was willing to express his opinions immediately. He told me that the *kumbhars* (potters) were so adamantly opposed to redevelopment that they had thrown stones at representatives from an organization tasked with counting the structures in Kumbharwada and tallying up the residents. The MHADA needed the count before it could implement the redevelopment plan.

Abbas also wanted to talk about gas kilns. He had one at his home. He said they cooked the clay faster and more evenly than the outdoor kilns, which burned scraps of clothing and emitted plumes of smoke. The gas kilns did not pollute the environment. Nevertheless, most of the potters preferred the old kilns. Abbas thought they were stubborn and foolish.

However, he ultimately conceded that his fellow kumbhars' reluctance to switch over to gas kilns en masse may have been

warranted. According to Abbas, YUVA—an NGO dedicated
to 'collective learning' and 'deepening democracy' with offices in
several states in India—had sent representatives to
Kumbharwada to promote the use of gas kilns. YUVA offered a
free gas kiln to anyone interested. They also promised to train
the potters to use the kilns. Shortly after, YUVA representatives
showed up again and claimed that they needed to measure
everyone's home to fit it for a kiln. They also needed to know
how many people lived there. Abbas and many others are
convinced that YUVA either sold or gave this data to the
MHADA.

On 27 December 2009 I spoke with YUVA representative
Anil Ingale in their main office in Navi Mumbai. Ingale makes
documentary films for lobbying agencies. He was born and
raised in Dharavi.

Ingale confirmed that YUVA had encouraged the kumbhars
to switch to gas kilns to protect the environment and to keep
their kids from getting sick. Ingale also said that YUVA
conducted a survey in which they recorded the size of the
kumbhars' dwellings and the number of people living in each
home. YUVA then gave this information to the MHADA.
Ingale did not answer when I asked him if YUVA had informed
the kumbhars that they planned to give the housing data to the
MHADA.

These two examples illustrate what is wrong with most plans
to redevelop Dharavi: they interfere with the residents' efforts
to develop themselves, as they see fit. Outsiders who try to
redevelop the land do not consider the peoples' freedom—their
capacity to live the lives they want for themselves. To return to
Sen, true development extends one's freedom. It does not pursue
wealth for its own sake.

PROLOGUE

THE PERSPECTIVE OF FREEDOM

Amartya Sen

It is not uncommon for couples to discuss the possibility of earning more money, but a conversation on this subject from the eighth century BC is of some special interest. As that conversation is recounted in the Sanskrit text *Brihadaranyaka Upanishad*, a woman named Maitreyee and her husband, Yajnavalkya, proceed rapidly to a bigger issue than the ways and means of becoming wealthy: How far would wealth go to help them get what they want? Maitreyee wonders whether it could be the case that if 'the whole earth, full of wealth' were to belong just to her, she could achieve immortality through it. 'No,' responds Yajnavalkya, 'like the life of rich people will be your life. But there is no hope of immortality by wealth.' Maitreyee remarks, 'What should I do with that by which I do not become immortal?'

Maitreyee's rhetorical question has been cited again and again in Indian religious philosophy to illustrate both the nature of the human predicament and the limitations of the material

world. I have too much scepticism of otherworldly matters to
be led there by Maitreyee's worldly frustration, but there is
another aspect of this exchange that is of rather immediate
interest to economics and to understanding the nature of
development. This concerns the relation between incomes and
achievements, between commodities and capabilities, between
our economic wealth and our ability to live as we would like.
While there is a connection between opulence and achievements,
the linkage may or may not be very strong and may well be
extremely contingent on other circumstances. The issue is not
the ability to live forever on which Maitreyee—bless her soul—
happened to concentrate, but the capability to live really long
(without being cut off in one's prime) and to have a good life
while alive (rather than a life of misery and unfreedom)—
things that would be strongly valued and desired by nearly all of
us. The gap between the two perspectives (that is, between an
exclusive concentration on economic wealth and a broader focus
on the lives we lead) is a major issue in conceptualizing
development. As Aristotle noted at the very beginning of
Nicomachean Ethics (resonating well with the conversation
between Maitreyee and Yajnavalkya three thousand miles away),
'wealth is evidently not the good we are seeking; for it is merely
useful and for the sake of something else.'

If we have reasons to want more wealth, we have to ask: What
precisely are those reasons, how do they work, on what are they
contingent and what are the things we can 'do' with more wealth?
In fact, we generally have excellent reasons for wanting more
income or wealth. That is not because income and wealth are
desirable for their own sake, but because, typically, they are
admirable general-purpose means for having more freedom to
lead the kind of lives we have reason to value.

The usefulness of wealth lies in the things that it allows us to do—the substantive freedoms it helps us to achieve. But this relation is neither exclusive (since there are significant influences on our lives other than wealth), nor uniform (since the impact of wealth on our lives varies with other influences). It is as important to recognize the crucial role of wealth in determining living conditions and the quality of life as it is to understand the qualified and contingent nature of this relationship. An adequate conception of development must go much beyond the accumulation of wealth and the growth of gross national product and other variables. Without ignoring the importance of economic growth, we must look beyond it.

The ends and means of development require examination and scrutiny for a fuller understanding of the development process; it is simply not adequate to take as our basic objective just the maximization of income or wealth, which is, as Aristotle noted, 'merely useful and for the sake of something else'. For the same reason, economic growth cannot sensibly be treated as an end in itself. Development has to be more concerned with enhancing the lives we lead and the freedoms we enjoy. Expanding the freedoms that we have reason to value not only makes our lives richer and more unfettered, but also allows us to be fuller social persons, exercising our own volitions and interacting with—and influencing—the world in which we live.

SECTION ONE

ARRIVAL

This account of Dharavi begins in the home of Fareeda and Mohammed Rais Khan and goes from there to the home of Mehtab Khan, the widow of the late Waqar Khan, who was perhaps Dharavi's most famous social worker.

It is fair to say that Mohammed Rais Khan wanted to be in this book more than any single resident in Dharavi. It is also fair to say that no one is more surprised than I am that he made it in. Khan first introduced himself to me as a poet. My guide, Rajesh, had told me that he knew of three poets in Dharavi, and Jeet Thayil was interested in doing a story on them. Thayil was scheduled to meet each of them on a Tuesday evening in the December of 2009. That morning, Rajesh and I visited the school where *Slumdog Millionaire* was shot to schedule some interviews for another writer. On our way to the school Khan approached me, notebook in hand. He sat through several interviews with school teachers and administrators and looked through several collections of photographs. When I had to excuse myself to take a call from Thayil, Khan followed me out of the room.

The evening did not go well for Khan. While Thayil was interested in the work of the other two poets, he was considerably less receptive to Khan's material. Later, when Khan learned that Thayil would not be writing the story after all, he presented his work to Jerry Pinto with similar enthusiasm—and got similar results. From that point forward, Khan showed up nearly every time I brought a writer to Dharavi. He wanted to find an angle

into their stories. Then he wanted to be my fixer, but that was
Rajesh's job. Next he offered to write an article. I was beginning
to feel guilty that I could not include him.

Perhaps I should not have been caught off guard when Sonia
Faleiro's article arrived and featured an account of Khan and his
family. Faleiro, too, worked with Rajesh to get interviews for her
story, but I was not involved in arranging those meetings and
did not know who she planned to speak with. I only knew that
she would be writing about young women in Dharavi. As Faleiro
shows in her work, Khan may not be a poet but he is a storyteller
with a captive audience.

Waqar Khan is a very different man from Mohammed Rais
Khan, and no book on Dharavi is complete without an account
of the work he did to restore peace in the aftermath of the riots
of December 1992–January 1993. Khan died in the April of
2009, four months after I started this book, and I was unable to
meet him. The reader will meet him twice in the first section,
both times through his children. Faleiro writes about the
independent spirit Khan instilled in his daughters, and Suhani
Singh tells the story behind the famous 'We All Are One' poster,
which depicts four children, each of a different religion—a
Sikh, a Muslim, a Christian and a Hindu. Khan's son, Gulzar,
who had his head shaved against his mother's wishes in order to
pose as the Hindu child, has borne the mantle of his father's
legacy well: he runs the family garment business and is a social
activist in Dharavi.

Moving from the homes of Mohammad Rais Khan and Waqar
Khan, Section One attempts to cover Dharavi's history. In
Chapter 3, Jeb Brugmann traces the settlement patterns in
Dharavi and gives an account of how the business networks

there connect Dharavi to the rest of the city, the country and the world. Above all else, Brugmann dispels the notion that Dharavi is a slum—a term that should perhaps be struck off from what is considered acceptable language, as many ethnically and racially derogatory terms have. Brugmann calls Dharavi a *citysystem*—a word he coined to emphasize the intricacy and genius of its social organization—and argues that Dharavi is a model of progressive city building that, if it were properly understood, would demonstrate a viable way out of poverty.

Section One also includes chapters on Koliwada and Kumbharwada, Dharavi's fishing and pottery colonies—among the oldest communities there. Few people fish in Koliwada any more, but at one point the Kolis boasted that they did not even have to leave their homes to sell the day's catch. When that business dried up, they sold homemade liquor. In addition to noting the devastation that bootlegging had on the Kolis, Saumya Roy also writes about a man who almost made it big as a singer. Unlike Koliwada, Kumbharwada continues to thrive, as the pots made there are sold throughout the country. Even so, the teenagers coming of age in Kumbharwada seek a way out, some through the merchant marine, others by going to business school.

Such ambitions are consistent with Dharavi's history. It has always been a place where people dreamed of and worked for a better future. Jerry Pinto's chapter closes Section One with a history of movie watching in Dharavi. Once upon a time, Pinto notes, Bollywood played its films for the masses that lived in places like Dharavi. Not so any more in the age of the multiplex. Yet, even if the dream factory that is Indian movie production has abandoned the folks in Dharavi, these people still find a way to follow the stars, and they still aspire to be like them.

1

FATHERS AND DAUGHTERS

Sonia Faleiro

TWO GIRLS

Fareeda and Nargis Khan may wear rouge. They may wear kajal, foundation and powder, but no lipstick, never lipstick. 'Lipstick gives men the wrong ideas,' says Nargis.

They must inform the man of the house, Mohammed Rais Khan, when they leave the house and when they plan to return. He must know because he has to drop them off and pick them up.

'We never go anywhere alone,' says Fareeda. 'This is that sort of area,' she adds meaningfully. 'Gaana gana, seethhi bajana.'

Do you have a phone? I ask. That might help.

'We have three,' Nargis says. 'My brother carries two.'

What about you?

She shakes her head. 'Phones give men the wrong ideas. If a man sees a woman with a phone, he'll try to get her number no matter what. Then there are the sort of men whose whole purpose in life is to phone-chat women. Such a man will keep trying numbers, and if a woman answers that's it! He'll go mad and keep calling her for the rest of his life.'

Fareeda nods. 'Who needs such tension?'

What other things cause tension? I ask.

Fareeda answers in a roundabout way. 'Nargis goes to school. And she has a friend she sometimes visits; her family is like ours. But I never go anywhere. Why would I? Everything I have is here.'

We look around.

There is no TV, no landline phone, no apparent means of distraction. We are sitting on a bed bulky with bed sheets, and in a corner are pillows piled high. Above the bed are nails from which hang plastic shopping bags like overripe fruit, filled with everyday objects: 'home' clothes, books, papers and pens, a kerchief. Opposite the bed is a cupboard open wide, full of the better sort of clothes and shoes and photo albums and cardboard boxes spilling with the silver and gold costume jewellery from Mohammed Ali Road that Fareeda and Nargis are so partial to. To the left of the cupboard is a place to bathe with a tap and a plastic bucket. To the right is a gas stove. Next to the stove is a steep rank of metal stairs that leads to the narrow alley below where the light is at best intermittent.

To reach Fareeda and Nargis's door, light must fight its way past the distended roofs that nose into each other like gossips, slip through the low, swinging jumble of telephone, cable TV and electrical wires, or sneak in through the narrow entrance that connects the bustling main road and marketplace outside with the alley, which, because of its smallness and darkness, appears 'inside'.

Where the light does fall in the alley, it illuminates a blue wall, a sleeping cat, a watchful woman and a bicycle.

Fareeda says, 'If a woman goes out, people say, "What is she looking for? What does she seek that she cannot find at home?" So I stay at home. I cook food, wash the dishes, keep my house clean.'

You must go out sometimes, I say.

'On the weekend Rais Khan takes us to the park,' Fareeda lights up.

Nargis grins. 'We do a picnic and stay out till late. We gossip so much I can't tell you!'

About what?

She beams. 'You name it!'

Fareeda is twenty-one. She is the second wife of Mohammed Rais Khan. His first wife, Feimida, died of an electric shock. Nargis is Khan's daughter with Feimida. She is thirteen and studies in the eighth grade at the nearby Maria English High School.

Seated next to each other, Fareeda and Nargis appear less like stepmother and daughter and more like two girls, two friends.

They are beautiful girls with clear skin, full lips and big eyes lined with kohl. Each has tied her very black hair in a thick, ropey plait that falls all the way down to her waist. They sit hip to hip in their salwar kameezes and shawls and appear, in their innocence, completely, happily, out of step with the world outside.

'I walk with my eyes to the ground,' says Fareeda. 'Why should I look at anyone? If I look, they will look back.'

While Fareeda stays home and Nargis goes to school, Nargis' brother Qasim, who is eighteen, does as he pleases. Neither of the girls, not even the one who is his stepmother, ever knows where he is.

'He never comes on outings with us,' says Nargis.

'He is a boy,' she explains.

Khan, whose list of rules for the women in his house is considerably longer than may be enumerated here, is similarly free. He doesn't have a job, although he was once a tailor. He isn't clear about how he supports his family, but a friend of his confides that he's 'an organizer'. 'Anything you need organized,' says the friend, 'he organizes.' What exactly is organized is not explained.

Khan leaves home after breakfast, he returns for lunch. Post lunch he naps for an hour or so and in the evening, after drinking a cup of tea, he heads downstairs and through the alley into the world outside.

He returns for dinner and that is when, says Fareeda, their home comes alive with the sound of stories. 'Sometimes we go to sleep at twelve o'clock, sometimes at two. Rais Khan's stories are endless, and even when they do end Nargis and I beg for more.'

Khan's stories are often of a time before Nargis was born. They are of growing up in Lucknow, and of coming to Bombay. And they are stories of Dharavi, the neighbourhood across where they have lived in seven different homes before finally settling in the room at the top of the stairs.

'The one about how he came to Bombay is the best,' says Nargis enthusiastically.

Later, Khan, who is thirty-four, will tell me this story.

'We are Pathans,' he says. 'Warriors. My father sold eggs on the railway platform in Allahabad in Uttar Pradesh. My mother was a housewife. When I was eleven I fell in love. Reshma was twelve. She was a Pathan too. But our families had a long history of animosity. We solved the problem by running away to Bombay. You know, people who come to Bombay fall into two categories. Those who come for the glamour, and those who come to survive. We came for love. But the journey was so long that by the time we reached Bombay it wouldn't be untrue to say that we loved each other considerably less than we did when starting out. And so things fell apart. Never mind. I could sew and I hired a partner who could embroider and together we started a "ladies tailor" shop. But things between us fell apart as well—he was too bossy, you see—and I branched out on my own. Then I met Feimida. I followed her home, and home for her just happened to be Dharavi. At the time I was sixteen, she was fourteen. She loved me too, and even though her parents weren't thrilled, we married that same year. I renamed my tailor's shop after her.'

After Feimida died Khan says he brought up his children alone for several years before he fell in love with and proposed to Fareeda.

'Her family wasn't initially in favour of our marriage,' he says. 'Because I'd been married and had children, and she was pretty.'

'He liked how I walked on the road, with my eyes down, how I welcomed guests into my house, with such politeness,' says Fareeda, frankly. 'What more does a man want? These are the things we have that men want.'

'They thought she could do better,' says Khan.

'That's because we have our own house,' explains Fareeda. 'A poor family may want to give their child to any man. But a family like ours, with their own house and whatnot, we have our pride.'

'But when a man and a woman are determined to marry, who can stop them?' grins Khan.

'I robbed my family of their *izzat*,' says Fareeda.

Fareeda never completed her education and this explains, in part, why she doesn't leave the house. Her options, even if she wanted to work, are limited. And because she's so fixated on the idea of never looking up when she walks or going anywhere without her husband, she has no friends of her own.

But she also doesn't go out because, as she later reveals, her family never forgave her for marrying Khan.

'I robbed them of their *izzat*,' she says again with sadness. 'And for what reason is a girl born into this world if not to give her parents izzat? If she marries well, the izzat doubles and the world remembers her. But if she marries like I did, against the wishes of her family, who wants to know her, let alone remember her? The moment I decided to go against their wishes they disowned me.'

'There is no solution,' she says.

'If I happen to walk past they avert their eyes.'

'We live so close, but we may as well live oceans apart.'

To take her mind off the unhappiness in her life, Fareeda pours herself into Nargis's happiness.

'There's no question of sending her to school with a cold lunch,' she boasts. 'Madam will only eat hot food. So at 12.00 p.m. I start cooking lunch and at 2.00 p.m. Rais Khan sets off with her tiffin. I cook her rice and daal, and with that, it goes without saying, at least one vegetable. Now look at me, I'm pregnant. And the doctor says I have stones, one in each kidney. Sometimes it gets too much. But do I ever ask her to help? She has ambitions of becoming a doctor, she has to study. Let her. Now look at our girls in Lucknow, covered from head to foot. But Nargis? She's *bindaas*. Her father takes her everywhere—from the garden at

Sion to the waterfront at Haji Ali to the masjid at Mahim. And he never talks of religious matters with her.'

Can she visit friends? I ask.

'Once in a while,' says Fareeda.

'Can they visit her?'

'Yes.'

'But what's the point?' says Nargis without rancour. 'Our house is too small to play in.'

'I like what my father likes,' she says. 'I do what he allows me to do. He knows best.'

Fareeda continues. 'Her papa indulges her too much. If she wants clothes, he buys them for her. Jewellery, same thing. And if he doesn't have the money that day, he'll return when he does and get her whatever she wanted. And of course, he spoils her with stories.'

Khan's fabled stories are all skeins of the family mythology that Khan, the careful tailor that he is, unravels with delicate expertness for his girls each night. But they're also stories of the world outside their room—a world that Khan has convinced himself and the girls is fraught with dangers for them. But while Khan may claim that the world isn't kind to women, it seems that what he's really worried about is not how the world will react to Nargis and Fareeda, but how Nargis and Fareeda will react to the world.

And coming from him, this isn't a strange fear at all.

Khan eloped with one girl when she was twelve, married another when she was fourteen, and a third when she was twenty-one. All three young women came to him against their parents' wishes. If anyone knows how to beguile a woman away from her home, it is him. And perhaps because he did so, even if he did so with the best intentions, he is aware that a woman will leave her mother and father, perhaps even her husband, for love.

In a way then Khan is protecting Fareeda and Nargis not from the world, not even from men in general, but very specifically from men like him.

Perhaps the girls know this, perhaps they do not. But their open friendliness towards one another and easy camaraderie with Khan suggests that his rules have, so far, had no adverse impact on their happiness. If anything, it has brought them closer. Nargis spends all her time with Fareeda, and so Fareeda rarely feels alone. And Fareeda, who was disowned by her family, gets to be a mother and a friend to Nargis.

With both girls safely at home, Khan may come and go as he pleases, his fear of loss appeased at least temporarily.

'Who wants to be that girl who walks about on her own, chatting into a cell phone?' sniffs Fareeda.

'Not me,' says Nargis.

A SUITABLE EDUCATION

On the clench of street in Adarsh Nagar where Shagufta (eighteen) and Rukhsar (seventeen) Khan live, the women who work, work 'small-small jobs'. They string beads for necklaces, pack potato chips for sale on the local trains, hem kerchiefs, bedazzle dupattas and bake cakes. The more ambitious ones, the lucky recipients of encouragement from their husbands and parents-in-law, operate 'beauty parlours' out of their homes or work as daily-wage cooks in the houses of their better-off neighbours.

'The educated ones,' says Shagufta, brushing aside a strand of hair from her face, 'work as assistants in offices.'

'Low-paid jobs,' says Rukhsar, who has Shagufta's long hair, clear skin and petite frame and is sitting beside her on one of the two narrow beds in the room.

'To support their families,' cuts in Shagufta.

What is a low-paid job? I ask.

Shagufta thinks about this. 'Five thousand rupees monthly.'

'If you have five or six people in your family, what's five thousand?'

And a well-paid job?

'You get well-paid jobs only outside Dharavi,' explains Rukhsar. 'You get paid according to which company you work for. People outside have small families. They have just two in the family, and for two they earn thirty thousand rupees a month. That's a lot of money.'

'But for five or six that's also a good amount,' points out Shagufta. 'If a family of six earns an income of thirty thousand rupees a month, everyone's needs can be accommodated. No one is left out.'

'We have to go outside to make that kind of money,' says Rukhsar. 'Unless you want to do manual labour or work in a small industry, there's no future for us girls in Dharavi.'

The sisters live with seven family members above the family's fabric and shirt shop, in a pair of rooms no larger than 200 sq. ft. In one room are two beds and a few bits of furniture. The other room is the kitchen. Six other family members, including the girls' uncle, live down the alley. The families pool their resources, and decisions about the girls' futures are taken collectively. This happened after their father, Waqar Khan, died of cardiac arrest in Goa in 2009 at the age of forty-two.

Waqar Khan was considered one of Dharavi's most moderate

and respected voices. Like most people in the area, he was a migrant, born in Bareli, Uttar Pradesh. He was the oldest of five siblings and left school at age seven to help provide for his family. As a teenager he moved with his family to Bombay and began working on whatever jobs he could find. This included selling bananas on the street. By the 1980s, he'd earned enough to buy himself a sewing machine and start a tailoring business that recycled discarded garments from Chor Bazaar. Every week he'd take the newly resized clothes to the larger markets in Vadodara, Gujarat, to sell. After scrimping for years, he bought his own shop in Dharavi.

Recalls Shagufta, 'When we were growing up, Dharavi was still unclean and overcrowded. We didn't have regular water or electricity. We were embarrassed to tell our friends where we lived. They'd respond, "Oh, Dharavi . . ."'

In 1992–93, the tight-knit quality that had for long been associated with Dharavi's artisanal communities was revealed as fragile. Like so many parts of the city, Dharavi was marauded, looted and burnt by anti-Muslim rioters spurred on by the tearing down of Ayodhya's Babri Masjid. In Dharavi alone, two hundred people were killed. Although Khan and his family remained in hiding, Shagufta, who was then two, claims to recall the screams that rent the air.

'One evening we passed a dead body in the street, covered in blood,' she says. 'I asked my father, "Who is this? Why is he bleeding?"'

Some months before he died, father and daughter watched Mani Ratnam's *Bombay*, a film set during the riots. 'I turned to my father and asked, "Was this how it was?" He replied, "This is 10 per cent of how it was."'

'Hindus and Muslims were friends before the riots,' says Khan's wife Mehtab, who is sitting on the other bed slicing vegetables for lunch. 'But post-riots we couldn't stand to see each other's faces. We'd all seen too much of *jalana, marna, katna*.'

Although they would never want to live away from their family, it was from their father that they learnt the importance of going where the jobs are. And it is because of who he was that this possibility is even open to them.

'Over here in Adarsh Nagar, families don't mind sending their girls to school,' says Shagufta.

'But not college!' says Rukhsar.

'Not college,' Shagufta agrees. 'But maybe for courses. All the girls we know do courses. Starting from the age of eighteen they can do as many courses as they like in anything they choose— make-up, mehendi, cooking and so on.'

'Things that will help them after marriage,' says Rukhsar, looking fed up. 'The latest they marry is twenty-one. Courses fill their time. Otherwise time passes in gossip and in chatting about films and TV serials and reality shows. Or in deciding what clothes to buy next and on which festival to wear them.'

Don't you know any young woman who works? I ask.

They think about this.

'Nadira?' hesitates Rukhsar.

Shagufta tut-tuts. 'She works in her father's shop, behind the counter. No, wait, not even behind the counter, but in the house, doing accounts. But once she gets married as if she'll still keep accounts. She'll keep house.'

And you don't want to keep house, I say.

'We do housework,' says Shagufta. 'After we return from

college we do *jhadu-pocha*, dusting, help our mother in the kitchen. But that's called helping, not housework. If you do housework, that's all you do. And I don't want to do that.'

So what do you want to do? I ask.

Rukhsar grins sheepishly. 'I don't know.'

Shagufta knows. 'I want to be a social reporter,' she says with pride.

Shagufta earned 75 per cent in her most recent examinations, and has narrowed her search to two colleges. One of them is in Dharavi.

'I should get in,' she tells herself.

But if you don't?

'Then I'll study a language. Or, I'll do a course.'

In what? I ask.

'Journalism. Then I'll get a job. Who will stop me? Everyone encourages me.'

Shagufta traces this encouragement to her father. Although he'd barely studied, he understood the value of a good education. Strikingly, given how so many parents in their conservative community appear to think, he was particularly keen that his daughters receive an education.

'So many people used to come to meet him, and many of them would ask for his email address,' says Shagufta. 'But he didn't have one. So he asked me to arrange one for him. Even though he has a son, and I'm a girl, he asked me.'

'But she wanted to do it,' Rukhsar emphasizes. 'What's the difference between her and other girls? These girls,' she points towards the door, 'they have no interest. If a girl has no interest in working, then no one will be interested in allowing her to work.'

'These girls,' Shagufta takes off, 'one day if you say something to them, anything, the next day they'll sit at home. It's very easy for their parents to stop their education. They just have to say something, anything, and the girls get stressed and stay home. Next thing you know they're married. It's always an arranged marriage. Though sometimes, it's a love marriage that they pass off as arranged to save face.'

'No one in my family talks to me about marriage,' she says firmly.

I ask Mehtab if her daughter is right. Given that most people in Adarsh Nagar hold traditional values, will the young women really be allowed to make independent choices about their lives?

'Do I care that they're women?' says Mehtab. 'If they have brains let them use it. I won't stand in their way. Their father was determined they should have an education. Let them work he said. After all, it was their father who . . .'

Rukhsar starts to sob. Her sister reaches over to console her. 'Shh,' she says gently, stroking Rukhsar's hair. 'Shh. Don't cry, don't cry like this.'

Their mother stares at the ground.

'Their father . . .' she tries again before trailing off.

Rukhsar continues to sob. Shagufta, her own face now wet with tears, leans her head on her sister's shoulder.

'It was their father's idea,' says Mehtab quietly, still staring at the ground. 'And like all his ideas it was a good one.'

2

DHARAVI'S POSTER BOYS

Suhani Singh

Yasin Abdul Nadi Sheik, eighteen, a resident of Dharavi's Saibaba Nagar, worked as a tailor in Santa Cruz when the riots broke out between Hindus and Muslims in Dharavi in 1992. He was a curious onlooker from his house when an SRP (State Reserve Police) jawan on 90 Feet Road fired a shot that hit him in the head. 'He never got into trouble all his life,' his mother, Salimadi Sheikh, tells me when I visit her. 'He was never involved in brawls, or caught stealing. He was in fact scared of violence.' Mrs Sheikh still wonders why God chose her harmless son on that fateful day.

Yasin spent three weeks at Sion Hospital. Then he returned home, but the injury had left its mark. He was mentally disturbed. 'He wouldn't talk,' says his mother. 'He wouldn't eat. He'd cry at our feet or just lay motionless.' Admitted next to JJ Hospital, Yasin finally succumbed to his injuries exactly a month after he was struck. Just when another series of rioting struck the city.

Yasin was just one of the many innocent victims of indiscriminate police firing. Often it was sheer misfortune that one was caught in the storm. A resident of Kumbharwada, Geeta Goswami, also a tailor, was on her way to fetch milk, when she saw a mob in front of her on 90 Feet Road. She managed to hide in a corner. 'I thought I wouldn't make it alive,' she says. Hours later, recounting her narrow escape at her friend Kanta Solanki's place, a bullet hit Goswami in the left leg. The police had fired thinking that a troublemaker had made his way into the house next door. The sole breadwinner of a family of five, Goswami was bedridden for six months and limped her way to work for over a year. But she tries to be fair. 'They didn't do it on purpose,' she says. 'It was a mistake. But they should have been careful that there are people in the house.'

Ramachandra Korde, a Hindu affectionately known as Bhau throughout much of Dharavi, first encountered Waqar Khan, a Muslim businessman, through the Dharavi Mohalla Committee Movement Trust. The brainchild of activist Sushobha Barve, the mohalla committees were established in the aftermath of the riots to restore the public's trust in the police and also to maintain peace in sensitive areas. Barve and other social workers invited citizens from different social and religious backgrounds who had no political affiliations and who were well regarded by their neighbours. The police relied on these individuals to help spread community values and bring the Hindus and Muslims of Dharavi together.

It was at one of these meetings that Korde met Khan. While discussing the reasons for the sudden animosity between the two communities that had lived in harmony for almost half a century in Dharavi, Khan and Korde agreed that the immediate need was to work at the grassroots level and facilitate dialogue between Hindus and Muslims.

'We realized that we shared similar views,' Khan says. 'I'd been living next to a Hindu family for over a decade. In Dharavi, where there are so many people cramped into a tiny space, you're almost always neighbours with someone from another religion. We'd all lived together for so long, so what changed in 1992?'

Korde was impressed with Khan, who he learnt was well versed with many events in the Ramayana from attending Ramlila shows in his village. Khan began to visit Korde's house daily to discuss issues and initiatives that could promote the message of communal harmony. Along with members of Dharavi's mohalla committee, they organized programmes during religious festivals. During Ganesh Chaturthi, members from the Muslim community were not just invited to the pandal but were also asked to present awards to locals for their efforts at community development. Similarly, during Ramzan, Korde says, Hindus were encouraged to know more about Islam's teachings and invited to iftar parties. On one occasion, members of the mohalla committee presented Korans to Hindus who also observed fast during Ramzan.

Soon, Korde and Khan's alliance became renowned in Dharavi. Says Korde, 'Everyone said that Khan doesn't speak ill of Hindus and I don't speak against Muslims. We were known to speak only the truth.' Their endeavours won them the admiration and respect of the people. It wasn't uncommon for residents to alert Khan and Korde at the first signs of tension.

Khan wanted to launch a campaign that would spread the message of communal harmony beyond Dharavi. After considerable planning with Korde, the two decided on a poster with the message 'Hum Sab Ek Hain' (We Are All One) featuring people from four different faiths—Hindu, Muslim, Sikh and Christian. The tricolour in the background would emphasize the message of national unity.

Khan originally decided to ask four cricketers of different faiths, including Mohammad Azharuddin, the then captain of the Indian cricket team, to model for the poster. But his plans fell through when it was reported that Azharuddin would soon divorce his wife. Azharuddin had moved on to settle with actress and Salman Khan's former girlfriend Sangeeta Bijlani, and Khan felt that he'd no longer be the exemplary choice to headline the campaign. 'Khan called me and said, "Let's drop this idea of having cricketers,"' Korde recalls.

Khan then decided to invite local kids to pose for the poster. Having kids, the two men agreed, would work because they are innocent. Also, unlike adults, they wouldn't be judged and could instantly charm the watchers. 'We thought it was better because otherwise people would not see the message but only the stars,' Korde tells me.

Over 50–60 kids from the area auditioned. When the Muslim boy who was selected for the role of the Hindu priest was asked to shave his head, his family flatly refused to be part of the project. Khan soon realized he faced an uphill task in convincing members of his community to let their children's heads be shaved to play the part of a Hindu priest. He asked his son Gulzar, the oldest of his five kids, to go to the saloon and return only with his head shaved. And so it was decided: Gulzar, then just nine, would be the Hindu priest.

Gulzar Khan's mother, Mehtab Jahan Khan, remembers that

her son loved his hair. 'Since a very young age, he would first moisten and then comb his hair in front of the mirror,' she says. When his father asked him to get rid of his prized possession, 'he didn't say a thing, he didn't cry,' she recalls. Gulzar's Khan's cooperation didn't go unrewarded. He remembers being gifted a T-shirt and jeans for his sacrifice. Mrs Khan says that her son was nicknamed 'Pandit' by the kids in the area. Waqar Khan insisted that Gulzar turn a deaf ear to all their taunts.

For his part, Gulzar Khan has little memory of being called 'Pandit', but he remembers that his classmates were curious about his bald look. When his teachers asked him why he had got rid of his hair, Khan produced the poster as evidence. 'When they saw it, they were happy and pleased with the initiative,' says Gulzar, who now runs the family business.

When the original posters appeared in 1996–97, Waqar Khan faced criticism from some members of his community in Dharavi for letting his son wear the *rudraksha* necklace. 'People raised objections saying that it was against Islam,' says Korde. Khan's wife tells me that their neighbours thought Waqar Khan was 'mad' to spend his hard-earned money on the poster campaign and predicted that 'nothing would come of it'. 'But he wouldn't listen,' she says. 'He was occupied with the poster, the mohalla committee meetings and trying to solve the neighbourhood disputes.'

Until his death, Khan always opened his doors to listen to locals who came to him with many of their business and neighbourhood disputes. 'He couldn't see people suffering,' Mrs Khan tells me. 'He believed their troubles were his.' Even on his last day in Mumbai Khan was thinking about maintaining peace in Dharavi. He had attended a mohalla committee meeting in the morning at the local police station.

Despite the cynics, some from his own village, Khan was determined in his aim to have the 'Hum Sab Ek Hain' posters go beyond Dharavi. With the help of former Mumbai police commissioner Julio Ribeiro and his friends in the committee, Khan obtained permissions to have the posters put up not just at the police stations, but also at railway stations and on taxis, buses and shops. Khan's daughter Shagufta says that the idea was to 'spread the message' and 'get access to more people'. Gulzar Khan adds that many people who had reprimanded his father were won over when they realized how popular the poster had become. 'Few people are respected and remembered after they die,' muses Gulzar. 'I am proud that my dad is one of them.'

It was a mere coincidence that all the boys cast for the roles were Muslims, Korde points out. Dawood Khan played the Muslim cleric, Moiz Sayed was the turbaned Sikh, and Bilal Khan the Christian priest. Rehearsals were conducted at Khan's garment shop for over two months to determine how the children should face the camera and fine-tune their look. 'The aim was to come up with a pose that would attract people,' says Bilal Khan. 'Many would come to visit and give their suggestions.' Adds Gulzar Khan, 'At that time, we were not mature and didn't know the significance of what we were doing.' The sessions allowed the four boys, three of them students at Sadhna Vidhyalaya in Sion, to bond and forge friendships, some of which, like that between Gulzar and Bilal, continue till date.

Fifteen years later, when Bilal Khan sees the poster, he can't help but point out his younger self to his friends. They don't always take him seriously. 'They refuse to believe me,' says the twenty-three-year-old Bilal. 'I have to take them over to my place and show them the original photographs to convince them.'

Gulzar Khan, now twenty-four, continues his father's legacy with the Dharavi Mohalla Committee Movement Trust. He regularly attends the weekly meetings held at the local police station and the monthly gatherings at the Nehru Centre in Worli. 'Youngsters need to come forward and participate in the mohalla committee meetings,' he says. With the entry of the young, 'you get a different perspective. There is also a balance of views. The young and the old can work together.' Gulzar's mother isn't surprised by her son's activism. 'From a very young age I could see a bit of his father's personality in him,' she tells me. 'He talks and makes others understand his viewpoint. He is young but he is the man of the house now. He even lectures me.'

Gulzar Khan and Bilal Khan, who studies software engineering, still live in Dharavi. But Moiz Sayed, twenty-three, moved to Kurla seven years ago. He works as a travel consultant and hasn't been in touch with Gulzar or Bilal. Dawood Khan, twenty-one, shifted even farther away. He does embroidery in a store in the Delhi neighbourhood of Gandhi Nagar. Dawood Khan feels proud whenever he looks at the poster, which is still stuck on his bedroom wall. 'I feel I have managed to do something at a very young age,' he tells me. Whenever he visits Dharavi, he makes it a point to visit his childhood friends Gulzar and Bilal.

The poster wasn't only about modelling; Dawood Khan did it for a social cause. He also shot a three-minute film, *Ekta Sandesh*, after the devastating earthquake in Gujarat on 26 January 2001. Moved by an article, which reported the death of students in a school, Waqar Khan invested Rs 1,50,000 of his own money to make the movie. He also wrote the script and directed the film. Reprising his role as the Muslim kid, Dawood is shown stuck in the rubble and rescued by a man from another religion. In 2002,

Waqar Khan sent 2,000 copies of the movie to Gujarat after the state was struck by riots in which Muslims were targeted. Six years later, Waqar Khan's tireless work was recognized when he was given the Gandhi Peace Award.

The boys have turned men and Dharavi is no longer the place it was during the riots, Gulzar says. 'People have realized that there is no gain but only loss in fighting. They know it is wrong and that if someone benefits, it is only the big guys.'

Gulzar continues to produce the posters, renting them to people who want to use them at rallies. Many of the posters never come back to him, but that is little worry for Khan. 'The message should be spread,' he emphasizes. Adhering to his father's policy, Gulzar never gives the posters to political parties. As people continue to come and ask him for the poster, he says, 'Now I am understanding the value of what my father did and how important it was.'

3

The Making of Dharavi's 'Citysystem'

Jeb Brugmann

One evening in Dharavi my Mumbai colleagues and I visited a notable landlord at his charitable foundation. When we arrived, he was surrounded by accountants, working into the night on their laptops. He seated us around his desk and began a lengthy description of the many good deeds his foundation had financed, showing pictures and newspaper clippings of schools and temples he'd set up in Dharavi and in his home region in southern India. He complained repeatedly about the people of Dharavi. He would ask them for donations, but they were stingy, he said. So he had to carry on the good works with his own resources, collected here and there.

This earnest presentation went on for nearly an hour without the slightest grin or sideways glance. Our host, we all knew, was one of Dharavi's old-time underworld bhais, specializing in extortion. Throughout our meeting we had been speaking in a sort of Dharavi code. In addition to our host's story line, the code included the trappings of a legally registered charity and a foundation office adjacent to the slum area he controlled. It required framed newspaper stories of good deeds and a hardworking staff who sat around us, busily processing the day's collections and managing funds across who knows how large an extended territory.

Our local guide explained that this man had recently had his wings clipped by the police. This explained the bitter edge in his narrative. But then to demonstrate his kindness the bhai-cum-philanthropist invited us to his home, so that we could meet his family and celebrate his grandson's birthday. On the way, our interpreter, a long-time Dharavi resident, whispered that our host had recently had his men cook a local baker in his own oven, a demonstration of the consequences of a lack of generosity. Everyone in the family was extremely gracious to us, but the image lingered as he cut his little grandson's cake and served us each a piece.

A young settlement, Dharavi was born in a legal limbo, without any consistent government investment or planning support. In the early 1960s, during the Urban Revolution's peak migration years, Dharavi grew from distinct village-like settlements of indigenous Koli fishing families, tannery workers, textile-mill labourers, migrant artisans and slum dwellers pushed from the legal city to the south into a densely packed disease- and crime-ridden slum. Then, from 1985 to 2000, with occasional but minimal government investment, the mega-slum transformed itself again into a massive, globalized industrial economy in its own right. Now, on my visits to Dharavi, we meet with the executives of export-oriented companies funded by their destitute migrant fathers and grandfathers.

This process of 'upliftment', as it is called in Indian English, continues today. On one visit, my colleague, Prema Gopalan, took me to a workers' dormitory, or *pongal* house, where dozens of Tamil migrant men shared living space, a kitchen, meals and a washing area between work contracts in Mumbai or abroad and trips back to their distant villages. As one of the founders of a prominent Indian NGO called SPARC (Society for the Protection of the Rights of the Child), Prema co-managed the first real population census of Dharavi in the 1980s. To me, Dharavi seemed a crammed, horizonless hodgepodge. But with a kind of X-ray perspective and local knowledge, Prema could distinguish Dharavi's intermingled ethnic, caste and occupational settlements, and literally see the historical development pattern of the place.

We spoke with some established migrants in this heavily Tamil area. Two young men were tying up parcels to take on the days-long train trip south for Eid festivities at their village homes. They had purchased pressure cookers and gas lanterns with a down payment from Assadulah Rubena, who sat across from us. Rubena migrated to Dharavi in 1991, in his early twenties, encouraged by his elder brother who migrated before him. He now runs a business selling appliances and cookware on consignment. Each month, he sends half of his income back to his family in rural Tamil Nadu—an amount equal to what a Madurai brick-maker earns by producing sixty thousand bricks.

Sitting next to Rubena is Inayat Allah. He is from the same district that sent the original Tamil tannery workers to Dharavi. After moving to Mumbai, he found cash opportunities abroad via labour contracts in Saudi Arabia for agricultural and kitchen work. Then he came back and entered the labour-recruiting business himself. Now he goes to the villages of his home district a few times each year and recruits youth for positions in the Gulf. From the villagers' perspective, the migration of a resident on a foreign labour contract is an investment scheme. The young migrant has to borrow some $1,500 from family members and neighbours—more than a year's household income—to pay visa, travel and middleman costs. Then, by working twelve hours a day, seven days a week on a two-year contract, he earns $125–200 more per month than he could in the village. He lives expense-free abroad. His savings, sent home each month via the expanding global migrant remittance system, are his family's primary route to capital accumulation and investment. Inayat Allah earns $75 from a Mumbai travel agency for each worker he sends overseas. While the visas and contracts for these recruits are being settled, they stay at this Dharavi hostel and explore the other business opportunities available to them in this migrant city upon their return.

Dharavi is no longer a slum. It has a population equivalent to Nashville, Edmonton, Gdansk or Leeds. Its gross domestic product (GDP) is far lower, but its economy is every bit as diverse and vibrant as those of Western cities—if not more so. In a matter of decades it has matured into a global manufacturing and trading city built by hundredfold chains of migration from all over India. To use the jargon of Western development, Dharavi has a number of export-oriented industry clusters. It has strong secondary and tertiary economic sectors. Primary industries are supported by networks of secondary suppliers and service businesses, many of which are also located in Dharavi itself. On a walk through the area, one finds a full range of retail shops, warehousing, goods transport, lawyers, accountants, expediters, hotel and entertainment businesses, health clinics, religious institutions and local political organizations. Altogether, Dharavi has an estimated GDP of $1.5 billion a year. In spite of its remittances to villages across India, its continued economic growth, without significant external finance, suggests a very favourable balance of trade.

But in India, few consider Dharavi to be a city. Tradition, entrenched attitudes and colonial-era ideas about cities consign Dharavi, in the minds of the country's middle classes and elites, to the status of an urban blemish—a slum. For this reason, its success as a poverty-reduction strategy and its brilliant contribution to the theory and practice of city building is rarely appreciated.

Imram Khan was born into a family of poor agricultural labourers in a village in Uttar Pradesh. Now he sits under an aged tree in a one-lane roadway that also serves as the courtyard of his Dharavi leather-finishing business. Like all things here, the courtyard serves multiple purposes. It is a street, a lunchroom, a playground, a political meeting place, a pathway for religious processions, and a part of multiple supply chains and production lines. As we meet Imram, haulers pass with teetering carloads of crushed plastic from nearby recycling shops. We step aside as they navigate the steady stream of people who are looking intently at some task. There is no idleness here. It is typical Dharavi.

Imram takes us on a tour of his business. Each stage of the leather-finishing process is divided into a separate building, facing the others across the courtyard. The buildings are made of bare-bones concrete block with corrugated metal roofs, each measuring about 15-ft-by-20-ft. They are dim buildings, with few windows, but the floors are clean.

In one building you can see folded raw goat and sheep hides. This is where they are cleaned, salted and treated before tanning. In a nearby building twenty feet away, workmen mix dyes from plastic vats to match the exact colour of a customer's sample piece of finished leather, and they apply the dyes to the skins that they have received back from the tannery. Next door the dyed skins are buffed to a shine. The buffers look like equipment from an earlier industrial era, with big rubberized and clanking motors turning the buffing cylinders. A young workman holds up a shiny piece of finished leather, his head cocked back and a half-proud, half-jesting smile on his face. With his fashion-minded dress and cell phone, he is anything but the Westernized poster-image of the exploited young slum worker.

The final finishing and packing takes place in yet another building. The finished skins are then hauled to manufacturers, also located in Dharavi, to be turned into sandals and bags; or they are shipped from Mumbai to manufacturers around the world. One workman inquires about my background. When I tell him I'm from Toronto, he replies that he has taken loads to the Mumbai airport addressed to companies there.

Imram Khan's family was part of a chain migration from Uttar Pradesh forty years back, when Dharavi still had the character of village-like encampments. As each new family arrived, they joined the leather trade pioneered by those before them. Imram writes the names of his extended family's businesses in my notebook. Wahaz Khan and Sons. Irfun Khan Enterprises. Ilyas Khan Traders. Saba Khan Enterprises. Together they have twenty-eight buildings in Dharavi, not to mention their homes. As a family, he says, they generate about $500,000 each year.

Imram has touched upon a fundamental tenet of Dharavi's

economic system. Profitability and thereby 'upliftment'—in the form of hundreds of thousands of jobs and the rising income they create—flow from a chain of cost advantages that is unique to Dharavi's unplanned, yet inarguably *designed*, development by its migrant settlers from a slum into a full-fledged city.

The Dharavi story, like that of many cities, begins with land and location. Market demand for Dharavi's marshland was traditionally very low. Pioneer migrants had mettle not only to build on this land but to invest their sweat and hours into its filling and improvement without gaining any clear legal title to it. What they received in return, just like the tanners before them, was their own claim to unshaped urban advantage.

Even as they improved the land, the cost of a Dharavi location remained low because of the lack of legal titles. With cheap land available, many impoverished migrants could establish residence and begin to save, even on slim incomes. These savings were ploughed back into income-generating equipment like sewing machines, and into their own residential, commercial and industrial buildings. However, cost pressures forced them to merge these typically separated buildings into especially dense clusters that support a variety of functions in the same space. Dharavi produced a kind of mixed-use building that is not legally permitted in many parts of the world—there are residential retail buildings, retail warehouse buildings, even industrial–residential–warehouse buildings.

To put Dharavi's density in perspective, an estimated 187,000–300,000 people live here per square kilometre. This is 6–10 times the population density of greater Mumbai, which itself tops the list of the densest cities in the world. This is 16–25 times the population density of greater London, and an amazing

375–600 times the population density of metropolitan Miami. And all of this enterprising human density lives and works, recreates and romances in buildings that rarely exceed three storeys. Putting aside the question of whether such living conditions are desirable, healthy or even humane, it is this spatial condition that Dharavi's migrants have consciously used to create their own industrial revolution.

The first density-related economic advantage offered by the Dharavi model is low transportation cost. Most of Dharavi's workforce live here. Workers can work long hours because they don't have to waste time commuting through the city's heavy traffic from distant low-cost settlements. This creates cost savings and income benefits for both workers and employers.

The second density advantage is Dharavi's extremely high utilization rate of property. In more affluent suburbs, where different building uses are segregated, most property is used for little more than half of a twenty-four-hour day. Homes are empty during the day and businesses are empty at night. In Dharavi, the buildings and courtyards are in constant use. Dharavi, one might say, was the first place to invent 24/7.

Dharavi's residents operate some 15,000 small workshops. Many of these are also homes. An underutilized workshop building can be transformed into a hostel for someone else's workers. Or a storefront business can be appended onto a small manufacturing workshop. In addition to the manufacturing workshops, there are dozens of residences that double as retail outlets or service shops. On one stretch of street I passed shops for engine repair, hardware, phones and food, a barber, cobbler, butcher, tailor and a pharmacy, not to mention a video games room and an aquarium fish store, all of which appeared to be appendages of residences.

A third density advantage is the location of manufacturers next door to their suppliers and retailers. Many of Dharavi's industries have minimal logistics' complexity or cost. That is true of the local leather- and metalwork and soap-making. Whole value chains—from material inputs like scrap metal, skins or used food oil, to retailing of belts and soaps—are located within or adjacent to Dharavi.

With cheap land, low transportation costs, efficient utilization of property and reduced logistics, the resident–worker–entrepreneurs of Dharavi can support their families on low wages and long hours. But Dharavi's low wages and cost of living, which provide continuing waves of migrants with a chance to start accumulating wealth, is just one part of its competitive advantage.

Another advantage combines benefits of density and unique forms of association. Over decades, chain migrations have produced a micro-settlement pattern of eighty-plus distinct ethnic and caste-based residential–industrial areas. Many of Dharavi's neighbourhoods have evolved from their original village-like settlements into units of neighbourhood-based specialized production, based on the traditional occupations and business processes of their original settlers. These residential–manufacturing settlements, governed by trust-based relationships, permit the sharing of buildings and pooling of capital and costs. They further increase the high utilization rate of space and property.

Chain migrations have brought centuries of specialization to the city. Take again the example of the leather industry. The Syed family members are cousins of Imram Khan. They own and operate a fashion leather-garment company called INMA

Enterprises, which makes high-quality garments that are sold around the world for tens of thousands of dollars each. Syed Mushtaq Ali, one of the young executives of the Syed family business, explains how their business evolved from basic knowledge that came with them from Uttar Pradesh.

'Dharavi is the head office for raw skins in Maharashtra,' he asserts. 'Our first business here is to purchase the raw skin. Every Monday Dharavi has an organized raw skin market.' He explains how unique expertise in quality skin selection developed from the migrant family's long familiarity with goats and sheep. 'There is no technical study on how to buy raw skin,' he says. 'The grade varies widely between a male and female, the age of the animal, its history of diseases, the kind of food it eats, whether it has been pregnant. You need to know what kinds of field it has grazed in and the kinds of thornbushes that poke it when it goes there. You need a very trained eye to buy raw skin.'

Mushtaq Ali's grandfather came to Dharavi in 1947 when it was still largely marshland abutted by tanneries and leather-finishing shops. 'He started in raw-skin trading,' Mushtaq tells us, 'but by the third generation here, our family got into manufacturing because there was no future in raw skins alone.' Stage by stage, the Syeds leveraged their expertise in skins to the highest level of value-added leather manufacturing in the world—designer fashion garments.

Dharavi, in short, was designed to gain maximum advantage from density and association. But few Dharavi businesses, whether the traditional Kumbhar potters craft or the more modern, multinational enterprises like INMA, could have grown without also developing ways to use the combined benefits of the city's scale and extension.

From the start, manufacturers and migrant labourers were dependent upon access to scaled market opportunities in the official city to its immediate south. These opportunities were extended to markets throughout India and the world via Dharavi's location between three main railway lines and its proximity to the port. A basic example of how Dharavi's urban pioneers used the city's scale and extension can be seen along its bordering highways, where dozens of Dharavi-based retailers sell garments and leather wares manufactured only a few feet away. At the nearby railway station, hawkers sell Dharavi-made snacks and sweets. Thus, in this basic way, Dharavi's entrepreneurs use the city's public extension infrastructure to capture a part of the bigger metropolitan and world market.

Today, Dharavi's more cosmopolitan industrialists use extension to advance the migrant city's legal inclusion into the global city. Dharavi-based garment manufacturers are linking up with major national and multinational companies, and companies like INMA Enterprises are becoming little multinationals in their own right. As they become export oriented, they respond to commercial incentives to register their businesses and comply with legal requirements, altering their operations to satisfy the business standards of their buyers. This global legitimization of Dharavi enterprise—ironically, in advance of any local legalization of their property ownership and provision of government services—is an important step in the evolution of slums into cities. Extension of business relationships to other cities via the port, airport and the Internet—even as Dharavi is denied the status of a city in its own country—becomes a strategy for further 'upliftment', and an important way for multinational corporations to exert a progressive developmental impact through their urban-extension strategies.

But extension and legalization do not reduce the export company's dependence on Dharavi's unique local advantage. Mushtaq Ali of INMA Enterprises explained the synergy between the Dharavi development model and the global competitiveness of his legally registered companies. Even though regulations and the rising price of land on Dharavi's perimeter forced them to move tanning activities to distant Chennai, they have kept the raw skins, garment design, central management and cutting and sewing operations in Dharavi. This anchors all the INMA business units in Dharavi's competitive advantages. INMA still purchases most of its skins in Dharavi, where they are cleaned and sent to Chennai. The finished leather is sent back from Chennai to Dharavi, where brothers Irshad Ali and Mushtaq Ali oversee the design and production of coats, jackets and full outfits. Because Dharavi is so close to the international airport and four-star hotels, Mushtaq explains with a clear sense of pride, 'the designers come from Europe to our shop here in Dharavi to teach our tailors how to cut properly or to stitch a collar.' Finally, Irshad and his brother Anwar Ali oversee marketing of their products, which are shipped via Mumbai's port to retailers in Austria, Canada, Colombia, Denmark, Germany, Greece, Hungary, Portugal, South Africa, Spain, UAE, the UK and the United States. Anwar Ali himself has moved to the United States, where the Syeds have started a retail chain in several cities of Florida and Georgia.

'We need a place in Dharavi,' concludes Mushtaq. 'It would be very difficult to do this business anywhere else. The fashion apparel business is seasonal, and time is of the essence in delivery.

Leather requires skilled labour at the right time, and they need to have a cheap place to live and to save time by living close by. Here no time is wasted in travelling and labour is available at a cheap price. Other leather-manufacturing companies in Bombay have had a lot of problems with labour because of the time required to move around.' The migrant city itself, he knows, is a key part of his competitive strategy.

As garment making, metal smelting, pottery manufacture and waste recycling developed, the industrial–residential neighbourhoods of Dharavi built their savings. These disposable resources, rather than flowing to businesses outside of Dharavi in the form of consumer purchases, supported the cost-competitive tertiary services and retail. Dharavi has many jewellery shops, hotels, restaurants and food vendors. Restaurants are busy throughout the day and night because they are highly affordable. A breakfast staple in Dharavi is the popular steamed rice cake of south India called the idli. In Matunga, the suburb immediately to Dharavi's south, a pot of idlis costs 35–40 cents. But in Dharavi a restaurant serves a plate for less than seven cents. A woman selling idlis from a basket on her head will part with it for less than three cents. Similarly, a pair of jeans (which is probably manufactured in Dharavi) sells here for $8.75, compared with $12.50 in the nearby middle-class suburb of Bandra. A movie ticket costs twenty-five cents compared to a $2.50 ticket in a suburban movie house. Dharavi can host such an extensive hospitality and entertainment sector—unlike a typical slum—because the advantage designed into it allows the so-called poor people to partake of these urban luxuries.

Building on this foundation of low-cost convenience,

businesses diversified to serve Dharavi's growing internal markets. Local bakers are supported by local flower mills. Businesses that use machines are supported by neighbouring repair shops. Migrant labour contractors are supported by workers' hostels. 'Land owners', smugglers and money launderers are supported by trusted local lawyers and accountants. Jewellers are supported by local smelters. Statuary-makers are supplied by the local plastic recyclers. Garment-makers are supported by embroidery shops.

Dharavi's migrant city, in other words, is a specialized system, designed in a migrant zone of autonomy for overcoming the migrant's marginalization. The strategic priorities of the migrant city are reflected in its every aspect. It may fail to enfranchise residents or gain them legal status or public services, but it provides a powerful commercial platform for their interests. Its basic purpose is to allow very poor people from distant villages to incrementally create financial and business equity within the urban world in the shortest possible time. Dharavi residents suffer and complain of the system's shortcomings: of the migrant city's overcrowding, the intrusion of new arrivals, the stink of manufacturers next door, the lack of sanitation and the flooding, but they still stay to raise their children because this place is India's premier fast track to 'upliftment'. Dharavi, the city the migrants built, has achieved the most advanced practice of urbanism: the design, construction and evolution of what I call a *citysystem*.

4

HOME BY THE SEA

Saumya Roy

In Francis Kini's mind, Dharavi is the vast open space of his childhood. His was one of the first double-storeyed houses in the area. Kini loved looking out of the first-floor window at the trains passing by Bandra station on one side and Sion station on the other. In between was mostly marshland and a large pond filled with lotuses.

Every morning, he would walk a few minutes to the sea and go fishing with his father. In Kini's memory, the large nets they put out bulged with catches of prawns, crabs, clams and other species that don't seem to be available any more. The women would sell fish in the afternoons, and in the evenings the family would clean and sort through oysters in the lane outside.

It was a routine that many families in Koliwada followed for generations. Koliwada is said to be the oldest part of Dharavi. Its residents are Dharavi's original inhabitants. For more than 400 years, the Kolis have been living and fishing here.

By the time seventy-nine-year-old Kini became a teenager,

55

factories had started coming up along the coast and releasing effluents into the water. Then the flyover came up over the creek, connecting Mumbai to its western suburbs and narrowing the mouth of the creek. Together, the pollution and the flyover dealt a death blow to the area's catch and to Koli livelihoods. Kini's father tried several things to keep afloat. He farmed oysters in the now drying creek. He went further out in search of catch while Kini and his mother managed the oyster business.

The highways and factories that caused Koliwada's decay also led to Dharavi's explosive growth. Soon, the open spaces shrank and migrants from all over the country came here to create what is now seen as a migrant-filled mosaic of chaos and opportunity. In Kini's youth, Dharavi was populated by palm trees, a small settlement of potters, known as *kumbharwada*, and another settlement of leather workers. Where the lotus pond of Kini's youth once was, is now Mukundnagar, one of the most cosmopolitan and dizzyingly congested areas of Dharavi.

Koliwada is now a visual and cultural anachronism in this Dharavi. Compared to the hyperkinetic energy of the rest of Dharavi, its lanes have a worn and relatively calm air. There are stately old bungalows that now struggle to accommodate several generations, clashing gods and divergent aspirations. There is a sign at Kini's entrance door indicating that it was made in 1947 and, he says, the woodwork was done by a man who made their boats.

While the men tried in vain to continue fishing, Kini's mother and aunt got into the next sunrise industry in Koliwada— country liquor. Having spent generations learning only to fish, the Kolis did not know what else to do or how to fit into a new world when their fishing business declined. While the men slowly ossified, the women made alcohol in pits in the sand banks along the creek and sold it to keep their households running. Kini's mother and aunt bought country liquor at wholesale rates and sold it from their house.

Gradually the men took over making the alcohol and the women sold it. They earned Rs 100 per cask and often took in Rs 500 a night. Of course, alcohol can never be made properly without tasting it and, as it turned out, many Koli men had a talent for that as well. Many of them went to waste from the success of their new business.

A handful of residents, known reverentially as Seths, developed large-supply industries that kept the city in the drink during Prohibition. Koliwada's sand banks, once dotted with fishing boats, came to be used to bury casks of fermenting alcohol. Log fires lit up the night as the casks were dug out and brewed only at night to avoid the police. For fifteen days the alcohol would ferment in wooden casks. Sometimes it was infused with fruity flavours and at other times it was just the heady Dharavi concoction. The Seths would brew as many as 150 casks of liquor a night.

Kini and his son recall the dark glamour of Koliwada's liquor days. The business flourished in the 1970s and '80s and the Seths built flashy homes in the area, employing several Koliwada residents, and buying big cars. They devised elaborate mechanisms to carry on business while staying within the limits of the law. Their henchmen would stuff brewed alcohol into tyre tubes and load them in the boots of cabs, which they would then drive to Colaba, Kalina or other markets where the liquor was sold by the gallon. The cabs travelled in convoys with a sedan in front and behind, to conceal the stash and so that the cabs could veer away if there were cops ahead. Kini says cop chases were not unusual.

Now, the Seths and their Impalas are long gone. 'There were many police crackdowns in the early '90s that broke the back of the alcohol business here,' Kini says. 'It is hard to find Dharavi liquor even here. Foreign and branded liquor is sold at bars for those who can afford to drink it.' The children of the Seths are in cleaner businesses. Some run corner stores or transport businesses. 'They do not like to talk about their association with country liquor,' Kini says.

On a smaller scale, the liquor business allowed others to keep their homes going in the absence of fishing. Kini's mother and aunt also sold liquor from their home for many years, but he was lucky not to become part of Koliwada's lost generation of alcoholic men. When he was sixteen, Kini took a job with the railways, where he started writing and composing Koli folk and devotional songs at office competitions and events. He learned music from his father who had a *bhajan mandali* (a group that sings Hindu devotional songs).

As he got popular, Kini performed for a weekly radio programme that encouraged professionals to sing. This made him Dharavi's first rockstar. Many residents remember tuning in to his programmes at 6.30 p.m. on weekdays. He recorded albums and toured the country. That, along with his railways job and his wife's fish-selling, allowed him to stop his mother from selling alcohol. 'I did not want this black business and black money in my house,' he says.

Kini recalls his singing days with twinkling eyes. He pulls out yellowing certificates to show his participation in folk-singing competitions in Delhi, organized by the railways in the early

'60s. His sons grew up dancing at these shows. Many of his songs became iconic Koli songs. He still gets Rs 90 every month as royalty. Now, he pulls out carefully preserved books with his lyrics and LPs (long-playing records), which he cannot play because he does not have a gramophone.

As he talks of the slow death of the Koli traditions, dialect and folk music, his young grandson walks in with his hair carefully gelled into spikes. He is wearing a football club T-shirt with a curvy tattoo peeking out on his neck. He works as a choreographer and dancer and says he hears his grandfather's songs at functions sometimes, albeit in a remixed form with techno beats. He talks of how his grandfather should be paid a greater royalty for his songs, clearly something Kini doesn't quite get. In turn, Kini says, he tries to tell his English-educated grandchildren about the fishing life but they don't get that.

Koliwada is still a small and tight-knit community that lives in two worlds. The community is held together by the 'gaon patil', who acts as the village headman, and the Koli Jamaat Trust, which manages common property and has a committee of village representatives that resolves disputes and organizes community festivals. The trust runs a community hall and uses rent collected from it to give out scholarships to students.

The Koli Jamaat attempts to preserve Koli culture through an annual seafood festival, held every year in early February. The food festival is an occasion to live the Koli life that escaped young people here. Men wear triangular sheets with fish-patterned borders instead of pants. The women prepare vast arrays of seafood drawn from recipes passed down over generations. Gangly teenage girls make themselves up heavily in traditional ten-yard sarees. They dance with oars to songs asking

Koli goddesses for luck as they go out fishing. A huge crowd cheers on as they perform on a stage decorated with fishing nets filled with shimmery thermocol fish. One of the most popular songs seems to be Francis Kini's '*Amhi jatiche koli, daryavari aamchi dole hodi, gheun mashyache doli*' (We are kolis, our boats bob in the sea, loaded with fish). This is as close as many of Koliwada's youth will come to living the fishing life.

5

POTTERS, SAILORS AND FINANCIERS

Aditya Kundalkar

Crude kilns adjoin almost every home along the narrow lanes that crisscross through the twelve acres of Kumbharwada. The smell of burning rags, cotton and sawdust clings to the air and also to anyone walking through the neighbourhood. Inside each of these kilns a variety of terracotta objects is fired. Water pots and plates, decorative vases and diyas, to name just a few, are made here and sold to wholesalers, retail stores and boutique shops across the city.

Kumbharwada is home to about 1,500 families of potters, Nathalal Chauhan tells me when I visit him at his shop, which is one of the oldest pottery houses in the area. Nathalal, fifty-two, claims his family business is over a hundred years old. His family was among the group of migrants from Saurashtra that first settled in Kumbharwada. 'In those days, Kumbharwada wasn't in the heart of the city like it is today,' Nathalal says. The city limits ended at Dadar, and the area known today as Kumbharwada was an island surrounded by a creek, which Nathalal describes as 'khaadi'. Palm trees, which Nathalal calls 'taal', encircled the entire area. Getting on and off the island was difficult, so the *kumbhars* (potters) would spend eight months here working and go back home to Saurashtra for four months.

Their first homes in Kumbharwada were plain huts, made from the material available around them—palmyra tree leaves and mud—and provided basic shelter from the elements. They were also a fire hazard, and since the potters used kilns and dried palmyra tree leaves to ignite them, their homes were vulnerable. In fact, says Nathalal, the huts did catch fire in 1932 when a stray spark from a kiln ignited one of the huts. Following that incident, the British government decided to build *pucca* houses for the potters. At that time, about 385 homes were built, one for each family. Today, he says, there are nearly three times that many houses—some with an additional makeshift storey—crammed into the same twelve-acre area.

Before they moved to their current location in Dharavi, the only kumbharwada in the city was located near Null Bazaar in south Mumbai. Those families slowly moved away from pottery, shifting to iron and steel trading, and today that area is known for almost every other business except pottery. 'The only trace that remains of Kumbharwada's existence there is some streets named after it,' Nathalal tells me.

Like most other labourers from the towns and villages of Maharashtra and neighbouring states, the potters moved to the city in search of better employment opportunities. That promise of opportunity was so great that they thought nothing of working for as little as Rs 5 a day and living in cramped homes that were a fire hazard. Even today, Kumbharwada's potters use crude kilns, which look like 8-ft-by-8-ft square fireplaces made of bricks. Scraps of cloth and dirty rags discarded by factories and garment manufacturers serve as fuel. It is cheaper than installing gas kilns, which have been proposed to the kumbhars as an alternative to the outdated, polluting kilns they currently use. However, Nathalal says that gas kilns cost at least Rs 1 lakh per kiln. He will try one of Kumbharwada's first gas kilns on the next Diwali, and Dharavi's potters do the most brisk business.

Nathalal says that the early settlers in Kumbharwada would make about fifty pots a day, mostly the type used to store drinking water—about two bucketfuls per pot—for meagre amounts of money. Today, one of those pots sells for between Rs 250–300, and a large set-up like Nathalal's—spread over 700 sq. ft—can produce 300 pots a day. An average potter, whose 250 sq. ft home also accommodates a poky workshop on a mezzanine level, can make only as many pots as will fit in his work area: rarely more than twenty.

Nathalal has a small army of potters helping him meet his daily production targets. About fifty families assist him in the various tasks involved in producing the finished work, whether it's kneading the clay, shaping the semi-hard item, firing the finished work or decorating it. At any time, there are ten potters at work, putting in ten hours a day. 'A large portion of my earnings goes towards paying the labourers,' says Nathalal. Each worker in his shop gets paid daily wages, which range between Rs 400–1,000, depending on the skills the worker brings to the potter's wheel. 'Labourers don't only come from Saurashtra. These days there are people from Uttar Pradesh and Maharashtra too,' Nathalal tells me, adding that he pays them about Rs 200–300 a day. The cost of clay and fuel is very low because both are available in plenty. Even after the Rs 5,000 that Nathalal might pay his labourers, he still manages to earn a daily profit of about Rs 2,000. Only about a dozen other potters in Kumbharwada are as prosperous.

The generation of workers before Nathalal were 'mehnati' or hard-working too, but they had to do everything themselves. Right from collecting the clay, treating it, moulding it, firing it and selling it. Today, there is greater specialization and division of labour. It helps meet demand and keeps everyone busy. Whereas previously the potters would take two days off just for firing their work, today the kilns are burning every day of the week.

Since pottery in Kumbharwada is a family-run business, every member of the family has to chip in. Before education and family-planning became popular, spouses produced, on an average, eight to ten children. Since 1995, the average has dropped to 2–3. Before that, more children meant more workers, which meant more earnings. With smaller families, earnings are improved by diversifying into ceramic or porcelain work, which can be sold for a higher price. Using modern equipment, such as moulds rather than potter's wheels, allows potters to create a large identical batch without having to mould each piece carefully to ensure that it matches the others. Any family member, learned in the trade or not, can now pitch in, thus increasing the output of the family.

Expertise and creativity is the edge that potters use to compete for sales. Architects and designers who work with Nathalal help him to broaden the kind of work he produces. 'The idea is to offer something unique,' he says. The work has become less labour-intensive and more artist-intensive, with a focus on the detailing and prettiness of the finished pot and not just its utility. In Nathalal's shop, for instance, women carve intricate patterns into half-dry ornaments, press sequins onto the surface and paint the finished products with bright colours and glitter. Innovations like a terracotta gift box have become popular, says Nathalal. Ordered in bulk quantities of 10,000 or so, this corporate gift is a glittery, artistically carved-out deep dish, which is filled with sweets or chocolates. 'It becomes a multipurpose gift,' he explains, listing the dish's uses after the sweets have been consumed: as a bangle box, coffee table centrepiece, or a serving dish for special desserts.

Nathalal's customer base has grown mainly through word of mouth. Today, he has corporate orders for decorative vases that will sit in reception areas and lobbies of five-star hotels, like JW Marriott and Royal Palms, and multinational companies like Wockhardt, Cipla and the Reliance group of companies. Nathalal is quick to point out that some of his regular corporate clients also include charitable institutions like the Cancer Society, the National Association for the Blind and Child Relief and You.

Nathalal's popularity also helps him bargain for a good price. 'I tell customers, you wouldn't ask for a bargain price from other skilled professionals like doctors or lawyers. So don't ask us for it either,' he tells me.

Not all of his three children are carrying on the mantle. His daughter, Poonam, has done a bachelor's degree in mass media and works at the Grand Hyatt hotel. Both his sons, Mitul and Tushar, have joined the merchant navy, following a trend that started among the second and third generation of the potter families in Kumbharwada.

Among the various Gujarati castes that inhabit Saurashtra is a group of fisherfolk called kharwa. Being comfortable with the sea, kharwas soon got into the merchant navy business. To stay close to Mumbai, kharwa families began living with the potters as tenants. The potter families began to notice that the kharwas were earning more than they were. 'They had better education, were paid better, and got to see the world,' says Nathalal. 'It was enough to lure our boys to that trade.' He estimates that at least 2,000 boys from the potter community are currently in the merchant navy. Close to fifty of them have risen up the ranks to become officers. 'One of my sons will take the exam soon to become an officer,' he announces. 'It's better for him. There's more money in that line. Over here, after I'm gone, there's no one to make sure the business stays fresh.'

Although Nathalal's son is on his way up, many potter boys who are drawn to the merchant navy start out doing chores like chipping and painting the deck, checking oil levels in the engine room or chopping vegetables in the ship's saloon. One of these boys who recently returned from his maiden voyage is twenty-one-year-old Dharmesh Singadia. On his first trip outside the country, Dharmesh visited the ports of Egypt, Syria, Turkey, Romania, Ukraine and Lebanon, working on a cargo ship transporting iron, steel and raw materials for iron-ore refineries. The fine pottery skills he picked up as a child were useless there. 'I had to receive special training at a spot near the Nhava Sheva port, in a training institute called TS Rahaman,' says Dharmesh, who describes the eight-hour shifts as hard labour.

Although this seems like undignified work to his family, it at least pays him better. 'I might be able to make Rs 30,000 a year doing other jobs in Mumbai,' he says, talking about a job he took up at a sweet shop before deciding to become a sailor. 'But this way I can also see the world. It's like an adventure for me.' Dharmesh has sailor friends from Turkey who are on his Facebook friends list, and he claims he has learnt to speak Arabic fluently. He's learning on the job skills like steering, geography and using a gyroscope, and he hopes to become a merchant navy officer in the future. 'At least there is some chance of growth there,' says Dharmesh. 'If I become a potter, I'll always be a potter. Nothing more.'

The merchant navy isn't the only career option that's luring potters' sons away from the business. Devendra Tank decided early on that he didn't want to pursue pottery. This twenty-four-year-old son of a pot retailer took the Common Entrance Test to pursue an MBA degree. Prior to that, Devendra was working twelve-hour days as an analyst at JP Morgan, a financial services firm. 'I enjoy maths a lot,' he says, adding that derivatives are his favourite. He is the first in his family to have acquired a bachelor's degree in commerce—his parents didn't make it to the tenth standard, focusing instead on running the business and raising the family. Devendra's sisters are, like him, pursuing bachelor's degrees in commerce. 'Girls don't even make pots in this business,' says Devendra. Their jobs are restricted to sorting out the clay, placing wet pots out in the sun to dry, and ferrying the finished ones back—more like helpers' jobs.

Despite a 94 percentile score in the CET, Devendra is well aware that it will take him more than that to get into a good business school—he also needs an education loan, which the bank will provide only if he can prove that his father has the financial capacity to pay it off (which he doesn't). Even if Devendra doesn't get that loan, he is sure that he won't get into the pottery business. He has taken up employment with Mukesh Mehta, the man behind Dharavi's redevelopment scheme. Although he doesn't have an official designation, Devendra looks after Mehta's day-to-day business, be it explaining to Mehta's visitors what the development plans are or taking them for a tour of the area. Devendra is optimistic about what redevelopment will bring to Kumbharwada. 'Change always happens,' he says, adding that it's not always a bad thing. He expects to have a better-ventilated home so that the burning cotton doesn't make everything smell. There are also plans to install gas kilns, so the smells will be gone anyway. Speaking for the potter families who are against it, he says, 'They have a fixed mindset and it's hard to change that.' There is trepidation among potters that after the redevelopment, they won't get the space and facilities to continue making pottery ware the way they have been doing for so long. However, if more and more youth like Devendra and Dharmesh decide to leave the business, there may be fewer kilns burning in Kumbharwada in the future.

6

F FOR DHARAVI

Jerry Pinto

Dawood is twenty-eight years old. He drives my friend's car. When my friend is in the car with me, I sit in the back with her. When I am alone in the car with Dawood, I sit in the front with him. I think this is my way of saying to Dawood and to the many car-owning people who may see me in the car, 'I do not own a car. I just know someone who does.' But I also know that this is a false position. I belong somewhere between the front seat and the back seat. I grew up in Mahim, in west Bombay, where I still live. Dawood grew up in Dharavi, or Mahim east, as many residents there have taken to calling it.

'*Mera bachpan yahaan hi guzar gaya,*' says Dawood. It is as if someone were to say, in English, 'My childhood slipped by in this place.' There is a romantic resonance to this, a phrasing that sits uncomfortably on the busy intersection where we sit in an SUV waiting for a light to turn as we cross between Mahim west and east. Or, is it really uncomfortable? Bollywood once belonged to the masses. There are no masses so massed as those in this patch of land. Thus the surface refinements of Urdu probably belong here, spillovers from the many mini-theatres of Dharavi.

Dawood grew up in the 1980s, on the cusp of the great changeover in Indian entertainment, shifting the locus of Bollywood from the movie theatre to the home.

By that time, televisions had become accessible to all Indians. Colour had burst into the grimy monotones of our sets, and the first videocassette recorder arrived on our shores. Televisions crept into every shop and stall in the city.

But not everyone could afford a television set or a video cassette recorder. The middle class solved this by hiring the player by the day. You put down a deposit, you picked up your recorder and went to the local film library and got 10–12 films. The libraries were ubiquitous by then. My circulating library started hiring out films and books, and the chemist across the road slashed his shelf-space in half in order to cash in on the latest craze. Then everyone piled into their living room and watched movies until their eyes bulged. Sometimes the men went off for a nap when a tear-jerker played for the women. Then the women napped when an action thriller was playing for the men. Everyone was served but Bollywood was the staple.

Dharavi solved this problem in its own fashion. It set up the first of the mini-theatres, seating between 30–50 people. No one remembers when the first one came into existence. One day they were there and soon they were seen to be undermining the Bollywood economy. A single videocassette could be bought for about three hundred rupees. (Specials such as *Sholay* were sold in double cassettes and at roughly double the cost.) This could be played endlessly and yield no dividends to the producer or

anyone else because there was no accounting for the number of
eyeballs that squashed into these small shacks where you sat on
chairs and watched a film play on a television screen. '*TV-video
bahut hua, sab ke sar mein dard hua,*' sang Amitabh Bachchan in
Ketan Desai's *Toofan* (1989)—it was not so much of a statement
of the zeitgeist as it was a desperate plea. Don't let piracy take
away our Mercedes-Benzes.

Dawood does not remember going to one of these mini-
theatres until he was fairly old. When he was young, he simply
stood outside a tea stall, which he thinks was called the
Makhdoomiya Tea Centre. It played Hindi films on a television
set in a corner. You could either buy a cup of tea at the ordinary
rate and drink it and leave, or you could pay two rupees and stay
for the length of the film. As a youngster, Dawood would crawl
up to the shop and position himself under the counter to watch
a film. When he grew too big for that, he would simply stand
outside until the owner drove him away with a flick of the cloth
he used to clean the counter.

Dawood would wait a little while and come back again.

I decide to ask a stupid question, a class-inflected question.
Didn't he have the money to pay?

Dawood is unsurprised and not offended. Or at least, he does
not seem to be surprised or offended. His answer is pragmatic.

'If I had had two rupees, it would have gone into my stomach.
Or to buy marbles. Or kites. Why would I pay for what you can
see for free?'

Dawood soon learnt to time his movements so that he could
come and go between ad breaks.

'I developed a great sense of timing, a sound judgement about
when the film was about to begin again and I would come back
right in time,' he says.

This meant that he would see films in bits and pieces. Did this bother him?

'Films are for timepass,' he says.

In the city that produces the ultimate in timepass, one can never be sure what the word means. It is a Mumbai chameleon that changes its hue, depending on its position. If I say I am doing timepass, I mean that I am indulging in some harmless activity that has no useful purpose or end. If I say you are doing timepass, I may mean the same thing for you. But if I tell you not to do timepass, you must understand that I think you are wasting my time. If I say someone is a timepass, I mean I like him and I think he's fun but he's not to be taken too seriously.

The communal experience of movie watching still holds in Dharavi. In one of the miniature theatres on 40 Feet Road, I watch as Govinda begins one of his signature fast-talking sequences. There is much clapping and laughing and stamping of feet. At the end of the sequence, the audience calls for it to be played again. 'Once more,' they shout.

'Once more' is meant for live performances, but all over India cinema is a live performance. In Nagpur, where I watched my first 'adult' picture, *Dharmatma*, at the age of ten or thereabouts, the audience demanded replays of every song, and got them. In Kolhapur, I watched *Qurbani* on a rerun and understood that there may be subaltern ways to make money out of the fantasies spun out on screen. Every song or 'scene' (including the one that has Zeenat Aman running out of the sea in a bikini) was greeted by the patter of small change hitting the screen. If no money was forthcoming, the scene would not be played again. In Dharavi there was no charge but some scenes would be played on fast forward to make up for the lost time.

In the middle of a song that is being played on fast forward because it has no audience appeal, one of the young men in the audience shouts:

'*Ruk, ruk. Hilaaegi abhi.*'

(Stop, stop, she's going to shake her booty.)

The film is slowed down to the usual pace, and soon enough Karisma Kapoor obliges.

'*Abhi tu hilaa* (Now you shake yours),' says his friend to him, deliberately loud.

I did not see a single woman in the mini-theatres I attended in Dharavi. I asked the cashier in one of the theatres why there were no women.

'They come,' he said, 'Why won't they come?'

I had no answer to this and let it go. He was on the defensive.

Just as Dawood saw films in bits, often piecing them together, so the audience here seems to come and go. Phone calls summon them away and they rise and leave. Some mini-theatres allow you to reclaim your seat if it is available. Others say, '*Gaya to gaya.*' (If you're gone, it's gone.)

'It depends on how well they know you,' says Saleel, who describes himself as an office worker. On the day I first met him, he gave me a Muslim name. Then he told me that I should refer to him by a Hindu name if I were going to write down anything he said. He did not mind which Hindu name so long as it started with an S.

'What are you doing here?' he asks, when he feels he can, after two or three encounters. I try to explain what I am doing.

'*Paagalpan,*' he says briefly. Madness.

I wait for an explanation.

'How can watching a film here be different from watching a

film somewhere else? Even if you sit in an armchair with a soft drink at your elbow and a full screen and you pay three hundred rupees, it is the same film.'

It is.

'*Baat baat pe Dharavi. Baat baat pe Dharavi* (Again and again, it's Dharavi),' he says and he sounds angry. I ask him if he is.

'Everyone gets rich on Dharavi. Everyone wants to see Dharavi. Everyone wants to write about Dharavi. They even made a Hindi film with that name.'

Indeed they did. It was not a film marked by much, except for the glorious presence of Madhuri Dixit, then the reigning goddess of the silver screen, who made a guest appearance as the fantasy figure who haunted the dreams of Om Puri.

'*Tu kyon jal raha hai?* (Why are you getting jealous?),' asks Rinku Kumar, a friend of Saleel's who works at a club and says his age is '20–30'. '*Tu yahaan rehta bhi nahin abhi.* (You don't even live here now.)' Saleel does not look embarrassed at being outed as a non-resident of Dharavi. 'Does anyone ever leave?'

The influence of Bollywood is everywhere in Dharavi. It does not seem to have waned even if the film industry now no longer considers its residents as important. Manmohan Desai, one of the greatest of mainstream directors of the 1970s, often said that he had to make sure he delivered value for money because his audience often paid in blood for their tickets. This was literally true. In the time before AIDS, you could sell your blood at a city blood bank. And the price of a pint was about the price of a ticket in the stalls. Blood banks reported a spike in 'donations' whenever a Manmohan Desai picture was released. Raj Kapoor, who made his fortune playing an immigrant to the city (in the 1955 blockbuster *Shree 420*), also often spoke about how cinema was a medium for the masses.

An era is passing. Today, from the director to the stars to the technicians, everyone on the sets speaks English. The dialogues have more and more English words and phrases. *'Rahul, main tujhse mohabbat karti hoon'* has given way to 'I love you, Rahul'. The stories have always been aspirational—it could be argued that the nouveau riche aesthetic was fashioned by Yash Chopra in *Waqt* (1965)—but now more than ever they look above and beyond the immediate skyline. No one plays to the masses. Everyone is playing to the multiplex. Ram Gopal Varma put it explicitly to *Time* magazine: 'With my films, I'm targeting the urban multiplexes, the sophisticated media-savvy young crowd. Frankly, I couldn't give a f*** for the villages.'

He could as well have said that he couldn't give an F for Dharavi.

WORK AND MONEY

Section Two focuses on working and making money, with the first two chapters in the section highlighting illegal measures people take to get ahead. Chapter 7 features D.K. Rao, Dharavi's most notorious gangster, who is famous for having survived two encounters with the Mumbai police. It took over four months and countless postponements before we got the chance to meet him.

Like many gangsters, Rao is eager to have his story told in the movies. Unbeknown to S. Hussain Zaidi and me, that is how Rajesh secured the interview with him.

After his assistants had given each of us a thorough frisking, Rao stood up, walked around his coffee table, and greeted us warmly. He invited us to sit across from him on a couch and sat back comfortably to take Zaidi's questions. There must have been twenty handlers and aides in the room. For a moment Rao looked expectant, almost flattered. But very soon his eyes dropped, he frowned and asked us to leave. That was when we learned that Rao thought we were there to make a movie about him. As the aides came closer, gesturing towards the door, Zaidi convinced Rao that the book would be a bestseller. The interview reconvened and went smoothly from that point forward.

The evening ended with Rao posing for a picture. He sat proudly on a couch under a giant portrait of himself with Lord Ganesha in the background, aloft a throne hovering above a mountain. Subsequent to the interview, Rao was detained twice, once for extortion and once for murder. The apartment we were in was raided and four swords, a chopper and brass knuckles were recovered. In addition, Rao's brother, Sabba Reddy Bora, has run for office in Dharavi's Kala Killa ward.

By comparison, the gang activity in Priyanka Pathak-Narain's chapter seems benign. Here a group of citizens engage in a complex money lending scheme called a *bisi*, the explanation of which is best left to the author. The upshot is that those who participate in the bisis often use the money for community improvement projects or to launch small businesses. The rest of Narain's chapter details the legal means by which Dharavi residents share funds and procure loans. The hero of this account is Prema Salgaonkar, a collection officer who visits up to five hundred people a day, asking them if they want to put ten rupees for the day when trouble comes. She knows all her clients personally and logs their contributions in a notebook. In especially trying circumstances, residents can borrow funds if their bills exceed the balance in their accounts.

The three subsequent chapters give accounts of the long work hours Dharavi residents endure—some to break even, others to get ahead. Meena Menon goes inside Dharavi's brass factories where people work in close quarters and inhale noxious fumes for meagre wages. Annie Zaidi recounts the stories of several entrepreneurs who run prosperous businesses, and Leo Mirani writes about an ambitious young doctor who grew up in Dharavi and is torn between working there and going elsewhere to make more money. Invariably, the people who have risen above their circumstances feel a debt to the community. As the previous section did, Section Two also closes with Jerry Pinto writing about the movies, though here Pinto tells of two men who have made a living doubling as Bollywood stars and another man who writes scripts. So far, there have been no takers, but the writer's dream abides.

7

THE MAN WHO COULD NOT BE KILLED

S. Hussain Zaidi

T he building in St. Rohidas Marg may look inconspicuous, like most of Dharavi's slum redevelopment buildings. What makes it stand out from the other buildings is the motley bunch of men lurking outside it. At first sight they look like hangers-on. Some are sitting on the fence wall of the building; others have squatted on a *bakda*, a bench.

It is after you spend a few minutes waiting outside that you realize that the men are bodyguards in civilian clothes. They are primed to watch out for visitors, strangers. They eye you warily, coiled and ready to strike at the slightest provocation. You can sense that they even want to cover the sign you are likely reading—a description of Ravi Mallesh Bora, president of the Bhrashtachar Virodhi Manch (Anti-Corruption Forum) and the Mathadi Kamgar union, painted on the building's flank.

After a five-minute wait, you are ushered into the dark, dank, poorly ventilated and badly maintained building. On the second floor, the corridors are a zig-zag, until you come across a section on the far right that is cordoned off. There is a hound that is barking incessantly in a dark corner while a bulky man dressed in a safari frisks you. The frisking is thorough; they even ask you to remove your shoes before you step inside the metal detector and then the door that leads you to the waiting area.

It is after you step in that you feel the need to do a reality check. Is this Dharavi, you wonder. An interior decorator has taken a lot of pains to convert the place. With a coffee-coloured sofa in the narrow passage and striped coordinated curtains, an imported electronically operated water cooler and orchid floral arrangements at the entrance, the ambience is one of affluence. Two people who are waiting to meet the occupant of the house-cum-office are not really relaxed. They are tense and so are the man and woman coming out of the room. There is a closed-circuit camera watching you.

Once inside we are introduced to Ravi Mallesh Bora, alias D.K. Rao, the man who manages the affairs of mafia don Rajendra Sadashiv Nikhalje, alias Chhota Rajan, in India.

Chhota Rajan is the most wanted mafiosi head in India, next only to Dawood Ibrahim. In 2000, after he split up with his mentor Dawood, Chhota Rajan escaped an attempt on his life in Bangkok. Since then he has been holed up in some far eastern country, keeping both Dawood and India guessing regarding his whereabouts.

There were four of us: a photographer, my contact in the

D.K. Rao gang, my friend Joseph Campana, and I. The photographs of D.K. Rao over the years in newspapers had deceived us into believing we were to meet a fearsome, chubby, angry young man. But what is lying before us on the sofa is a five feet-something, gaunt and ill-looking shadow that does not befit a man with a reputation for being a notorious gangster. He is wearing a black shirt, has the trademark beard, but the eyes don't look deadly. His leg is in bandage. His left arm seems bonier than the right, and he wears lots of red threads on his wrists.

Eleven years of incarceration and two attempts on his life have probably reduced the man to half his size. There is no other explanation. And surprisingly, Rao is ill at ease with us, at least for the first few minutes. Later he lets his guard down a little, but remains wary throughout the interview.

The place where we meet him seems like an office. It is two 225 sq. ft slum-redevelopment rooms converted into a 450 sq. ft place with two partitions. His minders argue with us about taking notes and they want to know what the interview is all about. They are serenading us, standing too close for comfort. There is a lawyer who wants to be reassured about our intentions before we get the green signal to proceed with the interview, which is interrupted often by the lackeys who do not like us putting awkward questions to their boss.

Since his return from prison fifteen months ago, Rao seems to have done well for himself. We notice some nine phones strewn about him, some of them satellite ones. Most are state-of-the-art touch phones. All of them ring incessantly. On the tablet phone, the fanciest of the bunch, Rao simply rubs out the calls with his finger. He seems quite tech-savvy. There is an

English movie, *Speed 2*, running on the huge home theatre on his Samsung flat screen TV.

'I do property work. You should not ask such questions.' He bristles visibly when we ask him about his prosperity and the wads of money, approximately Rs 50,000, lying carelessly on the coffee table.

His team, breathing over our heads, quickly adds that it is their wages waiting to be disbursed. 'I give my opinion about the redevelopment of buildings in this area, especially Sector 4,' Rao says. 'I meet 200 people every day, everybody comes with an application. It is not as if I always take sides with the builder. Sometime back, I made the builder construct a temple which he had demolished for redevelopment. Basically I solve the problems of redevelopment in Antop Hill, Koliwada, Sion and Dharavi.'

Problem-solving in redevelopment is a euphemism for arm-twisting slum dwellers into agreeing to a particular builder for redevelopment of their slum colony.

Thirteen years ago, Chhota Rajan's first lieutenant in Mumbai, Matya, had told me during a court recess that the gang easily makes Rs 300 crore annually and that much of it is siphoned off to their boss through hawala channels. Around fifty crores were kept with Matya, who disbursed the money among the gang members, both in and out of jail. He also used it for procuring weapons. I wondered how many more zeroes had been added to the figure since D.K. Rao assumed the mantle.

And to think that once upon a time Rao started off as Ravi Mallesh Bora, a *chindi chor* or a riff-raff thief, with a poor standing in the criminal hierarchy. Bora hails from a denotified tribe called the Baria. Denotified tribes were branded as criminal tribes by the British for over seventy-five years, and all of them lived a life of indignity and hard labour for several generations. Originally from Gulbarga in Karnataka, his parents came to Mumbai to work in the mills, which were once the lifeline of the city. His father worked for the Prakash Cotton Mills in Lower Parel.

His first run-in with the police came early. He was involved in a murder case that, according to police records, 'happened at the spur of the moment'. It was a street brawl that went awry—an incident that was enough for his name to be etched in the police diary before the age of twenty. The Khalsa College in Matunga-Wadala was his hangout. This is where he cobbled his first group of robbers in the early 1990s. They might have been neophytes by experience but their loot was nothing less than 2.5 million rupees. Ravi Bora, the crime branch says, was the Ali Baba among his gang of forty thieves.

He planned meticulously, and they staked out their targets for days. Most of the time the targets were money vans leaving from bank vaults. In a short span Ravi Bora was turning out to be a big headache for the Mumbai police with warrants against him in all the police stations from Khar, Mulund, Vile Parle, Bhandup, to even Dahisar.

With this kind of record, it didn't take the law long to catch up with him. It was while he was incarcerated in the Thane jail in the early '90s that Sunil Madgaonkar, alias Matya bhai, decided to induct Bora into the Chhota Rajan fold. Soon Bora found himself in the company of other thieves like Babbu Pandey, alias Rohit Verma, Vinod Matkar, and Jaggu Shetty, alias Fakira. In 1995, Bora helped these heavy hitters loot a record sixty-six lakh from a bank in Thane.

Once out of prison, Bora took to carrying the identity card of

a person called D.K. Rao, who worked in a bank. It is not
known whether he stole the identity. The name remained with
him because of an encounter in Juhu with a policewoman at the
fag end of 1997. A lady police sub-inspector, Mridula Lad, had
been informed about a dacoity planned in the area by Ravi Bora
and another man named Aware. When the duo reached the
spot, they realized that the police were onto them. Aware fired a
round at Lad but she ducked. She then fired back. The bullet hit
Ravi Bora in the leg. He has a limp to this day. His accomplice,
Aware, escaped and is still at large. Ravi Bora tried to escape but
was nabbed. The identity card on him said he was D.K. Rao
and thus the born-again criminal was rechristened in the police
diary as D.K. Rao.

The name sat on him well. Ravi Mallesh Bora may have been
chindi chor, but as D.K. Rao he would grow larger than life,
eventually taking control of Chhota Rajan's vast crime syndicate
in India.

But the jaw-dropping story that both Mumbai's cops and the
mafia still talk about is D.K. Rao's miraculous rising-from-the-
dead story. It happened on 11 November 1998. It was a time
when Chhota Rajan and Dawood Ibrahim were into reprisal
killings. Chhota Rajan claimed that he wanted to eliminate
everybody who participated in the 1993 serial bomb blasts in
Mumbai to prove his 'patriotism', while Dawood's gang eliminated
Chhota Rajan-associated businessmen and rivals. Several
accused in the blasts were thus killed by Rajan. Rao was on one
such mission to kill Shaikh Mohammed Ehtesham and one
Baba Moosa Chauhan when he almost met with his maker.

Shaikh Mohammed Ehtesham and Baba Moosa Chauhan
were already sentenced by the special TADA (Terrorist and

Disruptive Activities (Prevention) Act) court in Mumbai. Shaikh Mohammed was charged with being part of the landing of arms and ammunition in Raigad in Maharashtra, while Baba Moosa was charged for being one of the persons going to film star Sanjay Dutt's residence to deliver AK-56 rifles. Both Ehtesham and Chauhan had got ten years' rigorous imprisonment and were in court for their hearing. 'We were going to target Ehtesham and Baba Chauhan that day,' Rao tells us without any flicker of emotion.

As it turned out, senior inspector of the Mumbai crime branch Ambadas Pote, a man known for his ferocious loyalty to his job and his derring-do, intercepted Ramesh Pujari, Raje Gore, Jairam Shetty, Vipin Khanderao and D.K. Rao at Dadar. The spot was Sayani Road, near Khed Gully, just below the Zandu Pharmaceuticals building. Recalls eyewitness Rajesh Vithal Kamble, who was eighteen years old then: 'The goons were in a Maruti Esteem and suddenly the cops came in a Maruti Gypsy van and intercepted them. They didn't give them any chance to open fire. They just riddled their bodies with bullets and piled them in a police van.'

In a matter-of-fact way, Rao recounts the day he came back from the dead: 'Raje and Vipin had died on the spot but Jairam, Ramesh and I were still alive when Jairam, unable to bear the pain, called out "Amma". That was it. The cops thought somebody was alive and fired more shots at us. Jairam slumped dead and so did Ramesh. I got the extra bullets on my feet. There were four bodies on top of me. I was conscious throughout. Once they took the police van to the morgue at the KEM hospital in Parel, I got up and screamed that I was alive. I got nineteen bullets that day and lived to tell the tale. I don't know how I survived. People say that I know yoga and could have held my breath. But I will not tell you that because I really think it was my destiny to live.'

The fact that he lived to tell the tale (or perhaps the fear of eternal damnation) has pushed Ravi Bora to religion. He says he believes in the Sant Nirankari movement and in Swami Samarth and also practises yoga as taught by Sri Sri Ravi Shankar. 'I once went to meet the yoga guru personally in Borivali. When I was in jail, their group regularly conducted art of living courses and that is how I ended up learning yoga. On my terrace, sometimes I take yoga sessions for youngsters,' he says with conviction.

For ten years after his recovery from the bullet wounds, D.K. Rao found himself shut away from the world in prison cells across Maharashtra. Along the way several developments in the Chhota Rajan gang helped. Rao rose up the ladder, even as he was serving time.

First, Chhota Rajan's key and trusted aide, Sunil Madgaonkar, alias Matya bhai, was killed in a police encounter in 2000. Matya bhai was a formidable gangster, a man Chhota Rajan could trust in Mumbai. The Mumbai police commissioner at the time, Subhash Malhotra, had given the term 'Director of India Operations' for Chhota Rajan. Matya bhai had executed three top hits for the gang: East West Airlines chief Thakiyudeen Wahid, businessman Mahesh Dholakia, and Arun Gawli's ace sharpshooter, Ashok Joshi. After that, scores of gangsters from the Chhota Rajan group were killed by policemen or locked up in jails under the dreaded Maharashtra Control of Organized Crime Act (MCOCA).

The day Matya died, Chhota Rajan was afraid he was done

for. He feared that his crime syndicate would collapse. It took more than a dozen of his trusted friends from the gang to fill Matya's huge shoes. He cobbled a small group to manage his affairs in India. These included O.P. Singh, Bharat Nepali, Ejaj Lakdawala, Rohit Verma, Balu Dokre, Fared Tanesha, Ravi Pujari, Santosh Shetty and Vicky Malhotra and, of course, D.K. Rao. At that point of time, Chhota Rajan would have laughed if anybody had told him that eventually Rao would be left holding fort.

Later, in September 2000, Chhota Rajan survived an attack in Bangkok by hitmen working for Chhota Shakeel, Dawood's head of Indian operations, but his friend Rohit Verma died that day. Then the rest of the wickets started falling one by one. Some of the men defected, some Chhota Rajan ordered to be killed when he feared they had defected, and others were assassinated by Chhota Shakeel. O.P. Singh was killed in 2002, allegedly by D.K. Rao himself, when both were incarcerated in Nasik jail; Ejaj Lakdawala had left the gang and got shot in Bangkok in 2003 (some say he is still alive); Ravi Pujari left to form his own gang; Santosh Shetty also left Chhota Rajan to form his own gang and declared war on his erstwhile boss; Balu Dokre was butchered in Malaysia in 2005; Farid Tanesha was killed in Mumbai in 2010; and Bharat Nepali, who left Chhota Rajan's syndicate to join Santosh Shetty, was shot in Bangkok in February 2011. And so by this process of elimination, D.K. Rao remained the sole survivor from among the inner circle of Rajan's men.

In the underworld, pedigree matters a lot. If you are a small-time robber, you can hardly expect to rise to the top. But it is to Rao's credit that he proved that he could outlast all the other men in the gang. Says Rakesh Maria, the chief of the Anti-Terrorism Squad (ATS), Maharashtra: 'In the Arthur Road jail, where Rao was lodged with the rival gang members, he stood his ground and got a lot of respect.' The way he is said to have killed his one-time colleague O.P. Singh in 2002 is testimony to his deadly skills. No wonder Rakesh Maria calls D.K. Rao 'the black mamba'. The long and venomous black mamba snake holds on to its smaller prey until there is no muscle movement and for larger preys it keeps striking repeatedly.

When Balu Dokre filled Chhota Rajan's ears about O.P. Singh leaving the gang to either defect or start his own gang, Chhota Rajan wanted Singh to be liquidated. Rajan squealed about his whereabouts to the Indian enforcement agencies, which then picked up Singh from the New Delhi airport in 2002.

O.P. Singh, who had gotten wind of Chhota Rajan's plans to finish him off, thought he was safe in the jails, but he didn't reckon with D.K. Rao. At the time, Rao was lodged at the Arthur Road prison for the attempted murders that had led to his infamous encounter with the Mumbai police. He used his tremendous pull and rapport with jail authorities to shift himself to Nasik jail where Singh was doing his time.

Rao, the story alleges, knew that he needed help killing O.P. Singh, as Singh was a huge and tall man. So he also got a few of his cronies shifted to Nasik jail where they lay in wait for the opportune moment.

Singh was the complete antithesis of Rao. While Rao had barely completed his tenth standard, O.P. Singh was a chemistry postgraduate from Mumbai University and didn't start off in crime. He was employed as a quality controller officer at the Mazgaon Docks in the early '90s when his elder brother Arun

Singh, a professor at the Jhunjhunwala College, was killed by the Amar and Ashwin Naik crime syndicate.

At the time, Rajan was desperately looking for a brainy and educated strategist and thought that Singh was a great find for the syndicate. He fitted the bill perfectly and was inducted into the gang. Though he started out with small robberies, he was 'fully absorbed' a short time later when he and his accomplices gunned down a security guard during an abduction attempt. Soon O.P. Singh's crime graph soared with a number of cases being registered against him in Goregaon, Pydhonie, Khar and Malabar Hill in Mumbai. His meticulous planning and research impressed Rajan immensely, and Singh graduated to becoming Rajan's Man Friday.

Why Singh decided to move out of the gang and set out on his own is not known, but there are at least two theories. On the one hand, there was a lot of resentment against him from the Rajan cadre because he was educated and smart. On the other hand, there seems to have been some financial dispute that prompted Chhota Rajan's decision to bump him off. To this day, the killing of O.P. Singh is a spine-chilling story because there were no guns used and it happened within the confines of a jail.

It was a Sunday and there was a cricket match between the inmates of Nasik jail. D.K. Rao was part of one team along with twelve of his henchmen. O.P. Singh was also on the team. While the match was on, Rao and a couple of his henchmen took Singh aside and slipped out. It was a matter of minutes before O.P. Singh found himself kicked, beaten and strangled to death. D.K. Rao reportedly strangled him with a jute rope. The then inspector general of police (prisons) U.D. Rajwade, while suspending the jail officials and instituting a probe, admitted to the possible connivance of the jail staff in the killing. The Nasik Road police registered a case of murder and conspiracy under section 304 IPC against Rajan aides D.K. Rao, Sarfira Nepali, Bala Parab and ten others for the killing.

There is a postscript to this: Most of the gang members involved in the killing were killed in encounters with the police including Sarfira Nepali and Bala Parab. The only man who managed to evade the long arm of the law and the rival gangs was D.K. Rao. Perhaps he had the protection of his political masters. Nine years after the killing, the trial for Singh's murder case had still not begun.

Six months later, after his release from jail, D.K. Rao was arrested by the Mumbai police in connection with the killing of a driver of Iqbal Kaskar, younger brother of mafia don Dawood Ibrahim. Rao was arrested after another co-accused in the case, Umed-ur-Rehman, squealed about Rao's role when he was arrested in Goa. Rao was also questioned in the killing of *Mid Day*'s investigative and crime journalist Jyotirmoy Dey, who was shot dead in June 2011. Dey had fallen afoul of Chhota Rajan at some point of time and somebody from the gang asked Rajan to eliminate him.

Rao apparently managed to climb to the top of Rajan's crime syndicate because he was not only loyal (he even planned to travel to Dubai to kill Dawood Ibrahim during his daughter's wedding) but was seen as somebody who shared a lot of the loot with his network of men. It is said that he is the first gangster who actually takes a smaller share of the loot for himself and disburses the larger share among his men. It is also said that Rao still recruits *chindis* or small-time robbers into the gang.

These robbers eventually end up as contract killers. But no matter who they are, Rao always takes care of his men. He arranges for their bail and provides for their families. Having been in jail for long, Rao is said to be well-versed with the law and can have an educated discussion with advocates.

Rakesh Maria puts Rao's success in perspective: 'He is no pushover. He is a survivor and he is a fox. He is a heavyweight in the mafia whom you have to watch out for. He is to Chhota Rajan what Chhota Shakeel is to Dawood Ibrahim.'

By the time the interview got over, it was evident that D.K. Rao wanted out. His minions were even more keen that we leave. We asked Rao about the lovely floral arrangements everywhere. He said he was celebrating his birthday the next day and there was going to be a big party.

8

OF MONEY AND
MONEYLENDERS

Priyanka Pathak-Narain

At 3.00 a.m., Lalita Sonavane's cellphone alarm rings, signalling the end of her night. Sonavane, a fish-seller who shares her home, scarcely larger than the guest bathroom in most middle-class homes, with her two sons, rises and begins her day. Under cover of darkness, she bathes in the public bathroom down her *gully* (alley) and returns to cook a lunch of chapattis and curry that her sons will carry with them to work. She bundles up her share in a little tin box and heads to the fish market of Mumbai, one train and bus ride away, to haggle over prices.

On a good day, Sonavane manages to buy and sell about 8,000 fishes, making about Rs 300 in the process. 'Some days are good. Some not so much. Today, for instance, the fish was too expensive,' she said. She returned without buying any because she knew she would not be able to sell such expensive fish to the poor residents of Dharavi. 'So today, I will not be able to give any money for repayment,' she said, referring to the Rs 5,000 loan that she has taken to expand her business. 'It makes my heart beat faster.'

Sonavane is familiar with debt and the fear of living on the edge. Twenty years ago, when her husband died in an accident, she pawned her home for Rs 10,000 to pay for his last rites. Thirteen years later, she finally repaid the loan and reclaimed her house. But by the time it was repaid, she had returned Rs 60,000 to the 'micro-lender'—almost a 100 per cent rate of interest.

She is not alone. Tens of thousands of Dharavi residents live some variation of her life, where loan sharks circle around debtors and getting by is a ceaseless race to repay small debts with long shadows. According to Kavita Kokare, a neighbour of Sonavane's, 'Almost everyone has a debt wrapped around their neck like a noose. One wrong move, one accident, one tragedy and you are finished.'

This is a story of all those men and women who save every day, who participate in risky chit-funds and take loans simply to stay afloat. This is also a story of those entrepreneurs who have used these rudimentary schemes to save, take loans and curry favours to establish small businesses that will help their families grow and thrive.

CHARACTER AS CURRENCY

A silver Toyota Qualis pulls up next to us. My guide and I scramble in and are face-to-face with one of the biggest loan sharks in Dharavi. D. Prakash (name changed) wears off-white trousers and a black silk shirt with pink and white polka dots.

Pushing up his Ray-Ban sunglasses, which he wears in the night for reasons best known to himself, he greets us in a cursory way before stepping on the gas and speeding us off to Kalina, a decrepit neighbourhood just off the Dharavi border, where men huddle in secret negotiations of the *bisi*.

Among his clients, D. Prakash is well known as a sort of godfather who can be kind in extreme circumstances. Dharavi legend has it that a debtor died and his wife came to Prakash, saying she could not repay the loan. In exchange, she offered him her house. He refused to take it and instead forgave the loan. 'Such things never happen in Dharavi,' said an aide, unwilling to be identified. 'That is why he is very deeply respected here.'

The heavy-set, soft-hearted Prakash has another side that he can summon up at will. In the late 1980s, when a Bollywood movie team that was shooting in Dharavi realized that the fake swords they had brought for the shoot would not work, they turned to Prakash to help them find real ones. Within the hour, a dozen real swords arrived. 'Everyone, including the police, was shocked at how easy it was for me to procure so many swords so quickly in the city!' he beamed.

On the way to our secret rendezvous, we learn the basic idea of the bisi: 'Supposing one person decides to organize a bisi of Rs 100,000. He will look for 19–20 trustworthy people to contribute to it,' explains Venkatesh Nadar, who is an expert on bisis of Dharavi. If the organizer is also a participant, then he needs nineteen others; if he is only a manager, he needs twenty others. Once the band is formed, there is an implicit understanding of secrecy. For the next twenty months, these men or women will not reveal the existence of each other or of the bisi to anyone outside the group, for what they are about to do is illegal and they could all be jailed if the authorities found out.

For each of the next twenty months, the twenty members will convene to bid for a pool of Rs 100,000. 'At every meeting each person contributes Rs 5,000 towards the common pool and a fund of Rs 100,000 is created between them. Then, the bidding for the fund starts,' Nadar explains.

The bidding for the money is a strange process where the one with the greatest need will endure the greatest loss to get the money. For instance, if one man has a medical emergency in his house that month, he will need the money instantly. So when the bidding starts, he might say, 'All right, I will pick up only Rs 90,000 from this fund. The remaining Rs 10,000, I redistribute back to the rest of the bisi members. Give me this money.'

Another woman whose daughter is about to get married might need the money even more desperately. So she might say, 'Well, I will pick up only Rs 80,000 and redistribute Rs 20,000 back among the members. You will benefit more if you give me the money. So give it to me.'

The man, for his part, might remember the pending doctor's bills and come back with a new offer and say, 'Well I will pick up just Rs 75,000 from this Rs 100,000 and redistribute Rs 25,000 back to the members. You will gain even more if I get the bisi.' The process goes on, until no one wants to underbid the others any more. Thus, one member picks up the money as he needs, redistributing the leftover for the members to split.

The catch is that the money can be withdrawn only once. So if you 'picked up' the bisi in the early months, you are forced to continue contributing Rs 5,000 each month until the end of twenty months without any further benefit. If anyone reneges on the promise and fails to return after he has successfully bid for the bisi, as is likely to happen—for what incentive can there be to continue investing when you have already claimed the returns—the bisi manager is held accountable. In other words, the manager would have to contribute Rs 5,000 for every no-show to ensure that the monthly pool is Rs 100,000. Thus, when he puts together the bisi, the manager only allows those he knows well.

D. Prakash explains that it is a win-win situation all around. 'Since no bank will lend us money, people in desperate need get it from this fund and tide over their crisis or use it to build their business. And due to this bidding, we do not actually end up contributing the entire amount. We get some portion back.' For instance, even though each member is supposed to contribute Rs 5,000 every month to the Rs 100,000 bisi, 'you usually effectively pay only about Rs 4,000. The benefit if you manage not to bid until the end of twenty months is that you take home the entire Rs 100,000 with you, without sharing any part of it with the others.'

When we arrive, thirteen men are huddled in a crimson room with white tiles and dark wood furniture waiting to bid for a fund of twenty lakh. Each member has contributed Rs 100,000. Seven others join them on cell phones and the auction begins. For tense minutes, numbers fly in the air, rapidly dropping from nineteen to sixteen lakhs. Eventually, it becomes a battle between two men, one on the phone, who Prakash says is a local politician, and the other on the chair opposite me.

The man on the phone wins and takes the bisi for Rs 15 lakh. The remaining Rs 5 lakh is redistributed among the other nineteen members, each one getting Rs 26,315. Of the evening's winner Prakash would only say, 'He wants to expand a business and needs the money for it.'

When asked what he uses the money for, Prakash is evasive. 'Oh . . . just business things, you know. . .' he says, shrugging his shoulders. Does he mean his loan sharking business? He just smiles.

All the while I am in the room, the fear is palpable. Never before had they allowed an absolute stranger to witness these secret proceedings. 'We don't involve people we don't know in our business,' says one man who wears a beige safari suit and two thick gold chains round his neck, as an excuse for not answering my question when I ask him his name.

Things do not always go smoothly. There have been instances when people have broken faith and fled with the money. Or instances where members refuse to give their share. 'My father often organized bisis. Two or three times, people ran off with the money when they won. My father was forced to sell his house once, sell the family gold another time,' Venkatesh Nadar informs me.

Which is why, in a bisi, a person's identity is everything. 'Character is the currency in our streets. No one will involve you in their bisi and give you money if they don't know your history, your life, your business or if you don't have old roots in the community,' says Prakash.

EVERY DROP MAKES AN OCEAN

For those who do not want to get involved in a high stakes' bisi but still want access to money to tide over life's sudden crises, there are legitimate alternatives in Dharavi's informal financial sector.

Prema Salgaonkar, a petite collections officer of the Mahila Milan (Women Together) bank in Dharavi, is a powerhouse of energy, who helps her bank create a crisis-time fund by encouraging every one she can to save for a 'rainy day'.

Every afternoon, starting from the railway tracks of Mahim Station on one side of Dharavi and making her way to the mosque on the other, she marches past 500 homes of depositors spread over almost a mile, knocking on every door, asking if they want to 'put something away for the future today'. Some give five rupees, some eight, some ten. She writes it down in her notebook and stows the money in a cloth pouch and knocks on the next door. All this money will go into a fund, from which depositors can borrow when times go ill.

Occasionally, a shopkeeper might even palm her Rs 50 in savings for the day. When one gave her a Rs100 note, she looked at it, impressed, and said encouragingly, 'This is what I am talking about! Keep putting money away like this. Then if something happens, you have a place to go and claim it back. You don't want to fall into the hands of moneylenders when problems come.' The shopkeeper looks at me and smiles. Evidently, he has heard this lecture before.

Over the years, Salgaonkar has come to know her clients intimately: their homes, their stories, their families and their problems. She knows whose husband is a drunkard, whose son gambles, which woman is giving away her husband's money to her mother, which one is a shopaholic, who is irresponsible, who is struggling under debt . . . She knows everything.

Salgaonkar's cellphone contains telephone numbers of over a thousand people. On these rounds 'I talk to hundreds of people every day,' she says. 'Fifteen years ago, when we started collections in Dharavi, we had barely ten homes to go to and savings were not more that Rs 60–70 a day. Now, we have almost 3,500 account holders and they have put together a fund of Rs 1 million.'

After collections, the money is brought into an office, accounted for and deposited in the Mahila Milan bank account to accrue some interest and provide for those who need it. Salgaonkar and several others share a sparse bank office on 60 Feet Road where they sit on the floor and write the tiny balances of account holders into hard-bound registers to ensure that when these residents come in to reclaim their money, they get every rupee that they are entitled to and a little credit more to see them through whatever they might be facing.

The idea of Mahila Milan began in 1987 as a way to create a crisis fund and set up survival strategies for women whose families live on the brink. 'Disaster comes to them very quickly. It can be medical emergency, death, a lost job. They have so little that the smallest tragedy can wipe them out,' says Jockin Arputham, who has spent four decades working for poverty alleviation by building organizations such as the National Slum Dwellers Federation. He works closely with Mahila Milan to provide the urban poor access to housing and sanitation.

Such a scheme, by nature, cannot meet larger capital needs like building a house or expanding a business, but the programme helps women cope with smaller, everyday troubles and inculcates a discipline of saving. For instance, for Asha, who gave only one name, it helps pay for medical bills for her three children. 'You know, children, they are always falling sick. And sometimes, when he [her husband] does not earn enough by tailoring, I pitch in with these savings to buy groceries for the month.'

Even children, who have seen their mothers save a few rupees every day, have learned the lesson. Wilson Naidu, eighteen, who lives on the edge of train tracks, has watched his mother thriftily put money away and then use it in times of need without turning to moneylenders for help. 'It makes such a difference. What is Rs10 every day? You don't even notice it's gone. And still, before you know it, you have so much of your own money safely put away for that day when you need it,' he says, as he puts a Rs 20 note, his savings for the day, in the hands of Prema Salgaonkar.

Prema is smiling proudly. Young Wilson has learned well.

There are some others, a clientele that is incapable of even these barethread savings. Amirunisa Abdul Madim, who stays under a bridge at the edge of an open drain clogged with plastic, leather, wood and cloth at the edge of Dharavi, is one of them. In a miniature room of simple furnishing, she lives with her husband, son, daughter and grandchild. Her son-in-law abandoned his wife and child for dowry. 'He kept demanding money from my daughter. I gave him as much as I could. I even paid rent for the room they lived in. Then, when my daughter was about to deliver her child at a government hospital, he got really upset with us for demanding money for medicines and left. My daughter has been staying with us ever since,' she tells me. Her eyes are empty shells, there is no emotion left for them to betray.

On a good day, Amirunisa's husband makes Rs 100 as a for-hire luggage helper to transport companies. Her own goli-biscuit business—she sells biscuits, a deep-fried snack wrapped in faded paper out of her home—brings in another Rs 100. 'We never have enough to make ends meet. We adjust. One of us is always working on less food, less sleep, less money . . .' She trails off, pushing the unkempt, greying hair off her face.

Like Lalita Sonavane, Amirunisa wants to expand her business but is reticent because she has had many harrowing experiences with usurious moneylenders. She was fortunate enough to find a better way to raise capital. Amirunisa discovered Vandana Foundation, which was set up last year to offer small loans to women who want to expand small businesses.

'We want to target our help to those who are really poor and help them deploy the money for income-generation,' says A.N. Roy, former director general of police, Maharashtra, who retired in May 2010 and now runs this foundation from his Sion office on the outskirts of Dharavi. During his thirty-eight years of service as a police officer, Roy says he has seen rural and urban poverty very closely. 'After being so connected with the poor for so long, there was a gradual resolve to do a little bit to alleviate a little poverty. I cannot make a difference to everyone, but I decided that when I hang up my boots and retire, I would try to make a difference to some,' he explained.

Even though borrowers are told they would have to pay 12 per cent interest on their loans, when the actual repayments are done, 'there is barely any interest charged at all. I tell them they have to pay interest, because I just don't want them to think that they are getting something for free,' Roy tells me.

The effort to make life a little bit easier for women such as Amirunisa has paid off, because, as she says, 'This loan is helping me make money. But for the first time, even though I pay back a little money every day, I don't feel the burden of it.'

AND FINALLY, THE BANKS HAVE BEGUN TO ARRIVE

Over the last few years, even as these various schemes and institutions have evolved to fill the vacuum left by banks in Dharavi, the banks themselves have begun to rethink their Dharavi strategy. Chennai-based Indian Bank set up its first pilot branch in there in 2005, when business began to boom, as a first step to ensure 'urban financial inclusion'. Two years later, it called Dharavi a 'showcase' of Indian entrepreneurship, 'bustling with economic activities such as tanneries, plastics, garments, confectionaries', and converted the pilot with 6,317 accounts into a full-fledged branch with an automatic teller machine. Within three years, the branch had 35,578 accounts and a total deposit of Rs 41.29 crore.

'Our bank has also helped set up 684 SHGs (Self-Help Groups), offering credit assistance of Rs 2.83 crore to some of them,' says T.M. Bhasin, the chief managing director of Indian Bank, in a telephone conversation. In an SHG, 10–20 women from a community come together to make small, regular savings deposits into a fund over a few months until there is enough capital to begin lending to each other and to others outside the group. Often, these groups are linked to banks for the delivery of microcredit to clients who have contributed to the group's bank account and need funds to carry out their business.

Rani Nadar grew her tailoring business from a Rs 9,000 enterprise into a Rs 50,000 business with nine sewing machines and hired help. She says she owes it all to hard work and the self-help groups that gave her interest-free loans every time she wanted to expand her business. Now a group leader to 200 women, Nadar says she encourages others to use loans wisely and invest in the future, such as on children's education and on tools to expand business.

Seeing the growth of the SHGs, the State Bank of India has set up a specialized microfinance branch in Dharavi. Dhruv Redkar, who is mobilizing women's groups across Dharavi to come under the SBI umbrella, says they have now expanded their cover to more than 200 SHGs. The bank has also partnered with the Tata Institute of Social Sciences (TISS), one of India's premier institutes of social work, to run training programmes in Dharavi to help group leaders such as Nadar understand the larger social implications of the small groups they run. 'We want them to know that it's not about saving a little here, a little there alone. We want them to understand that these are tools with which they can escape the clutches of poverty,' says Redkar, highlighting that these are essentially community-service programmes run by banks for altruistic motives.

And so, the picture within Dharavi begins to slowly change.

The sun still rises over open gutters, human faeces, squalour and deprivation, but the spirit of Dharavi has begun to change. As the Lalitas, Amirunisas and Ranis begin to understand the power of financial planning, and as banks begin to recognize the spirit of entrepreneurship, it is only a question of time before these women are able to transform their lives and the destinies of their children.

9

ALL SMOKE AND NO PLAY

Meena Menon

AT WORK

Four workers covered in soot huddle around melting brass in the corner of a 7 x 7 feet room and inhale dense black smoke. They work with bare hands, uncovered faces and sing along with the latest Bollywood hits, in tune with music coming from a battered set perched in the corner. The heat is tremendous. Your hair frizzes at close quarters. Temperatures in the brass moulds reach as high as 500° C. 'The heat is bearable in winter,' one of them says with a grin. 'In summer,' he adds, 'it can be intolerable.' In a corner lie bags of brass scrap waiting to be melted.

'I don't like wearing protective glasses or masks. It makes me nervous for some reason,' says Mohammed Phurkan, fifty-one, as he ladles melted brass to be poured into the dies for buckles. Phurkan wears reading glasses. He came to Dharavi three years ago. 'I have to earn to support my family. I have three children. I go home once a year to see them,' he says.

Brass is one of Dharavi's largest, most competitive industries, and this is a typical foundry, a rather grandiose term for the small smokey rooms that can be found in some of the snakelike passages here, mostly near Peela Bangla or the old leather tannery off the main road connecting to Sion station. There maybe 25–30 such buckle-manufacturing units in this area of Dharavi. There are also electroplating and buffing units, which the workers here consider as separate industries. Most of the rooms that house these factories are tiny, cramped and practically airless. Working hours are long—8.00 a.m. to 8.00 p.m., with about an hour's lunch break.

The unit I visit has four men, all from Uttar Pradesh, making brass buckles. A tiny window opening onto a dark passage admits a negligible breeze. The men kindly turn down the loud music so that they can hear me speak. Standing next to Phurkan is Mohammed Asif, aged twenty-four, from Moradabad, Uttar Pradesh. He has been working in this unit for four years and earns about Rs 5,000–7,000 a month. 'Our employer gives us a place to stay. Four of us live there,' he tells me.

Next is Mohammed Faruq Khan. With twenty-five years of experience, he is one of the oldest workers in all of the brass foundries. Khan started young. When he came to the city, his wage was Rs 15 a day. He sits behind a mound of tar and pours a mixture of mud and Mobil oil into moulds after the melted brass has been put into them. He explains the entire process— how they procure raw materials from among the brass objects discarded in Dharavi's markets and how they melt the brass down before pouring the liquid into small boxes with moulds in the desired shape of the buckle. The mud-and-oil mix keeps the melted brass from spreading around the box. He opens the mould and presto the buckles are ready to be cut, plated and polished according to the specifications of the order.

Finally there is Mohammed Salim, who at twenty-two is a relative novice. 'Even back in my village I did this only,' he says.

Dharavi's brass buckle industry is over fifty years old. Migrants from Uttar Pradesh, for whom brass work is a traditional art that evolved from their profession as locksmiths, originally established the industry here because there was no work at home. Even today, most brass workers hail from Uttar Pradesh. It is only recently that people from Bihar have come in as temporary workers.

The men's working quarters are a far cry from Naseemuddin Sheikh's air-conditioned and well-appointed office nearby. It, too, is small, but it is comfortable and cool. 'Since I was a child I have seen my father doing this business. Now I am in the business for twenty-five years. It is only through my traditional skill and knowledge that I have got here,' Sheikh, who is forty-one and a graduate of the tenth standard, tells me.

Sheikh's father is from Aligarh, famous for the Aligarh Muslim University and its once-flourishing brass industry. He came to Dharavi when the local market for traditional locks shrank due to competition from locks made from lighter materials. Like most of the early migrants to Dharavi, Sheikh's father shifted his production from locks to buckles, which are more profitable and easier to manufacture. As a whole, the brass industry in Dharavi has a turnover of nearly Rs 150 crore, which is second to only the garment sector here.

With a turnover of approximately Rs 10 lakh a year, Sheikh is among the frontrunners in Dharavi's buckle business. He attributes his success to perseverance. 'It's not an easy job to learn,' he says.'Mostly the buckles are sold in bulk to companies in other cities. Much of its goes for export, so the quality of work has to be excellent since the market is highly competitive.' It's a precision industry, and even a small change in design can make a big difference, he adds. In addition to belt buckles, Sheikh makes bolts, handbag clasps, door handles, and knockers and bolts. The brass used to make these finished products retails at Rs 255 per kg in the local market. The infrastructure is also affordable. A buffing machine, for instance, can cost Rs 3,000. All you need to do is rent a cheap place and find some workers, he tells me.

Ishrak Ali has run his electroplating unit for fifteen years. The company has an annual turnover of about Rs 3.5 lakh. Downstairs, workers clean the buckles and fittings in caustic soda. They wear rubber boots and raggedy masks over their mouths and noses. Some have long gloves. A narrow metal ladder leads to a 400 sq. ft room that houses large bubbling vats filled with copper and nickel. In an adjacent room with clean floors, several women sit at a table stringing clasps on wires so that they can be plated in the desired colours.

What frustrates Ishrak and several of the owners I interviewed is that the workers are erratic. Most of the workers are in their early twenties or in their late teens. They don't show up sometimes. Migrants from Bihar have come to Dharavi's brass industry, but they don't last long.

Ishrak claims that today the risks for workers are minimal, compared to what they once were.'There was no light then. We had gaslights. We had a place, which we rented for Rs 60 a month. Even the brass was filed by hand with sandpaper. It is only now that there are machines,' he says. One just has to be careful while working, he adds.

Naseemuddin Sheikh, however, admits that conditions remain less than ideal for the workers. It's an informal sector where people are paid by the number of finished pieces they produce. Because it is difficult, time-consuming work, buffing can fetch a worker Rs 300 a day. A skilled buffer can earn up to Rs 8,000 a month while a helper gets upwards of Rs 3,000. The catch is if there is no work there is no pay either.

Raju Korde, a resident of Dharavi and an activist in the Communist Party of India (Marxist), says that the entire sector, like most industries in the area, is unorganized. No labour laws govern the brass foundries, there are no service rules, and the Workmen's Compensation Act also does not apply. Most of the workers are brought as children from faraway places like Uttar Pradesh or Bihar. They learn the trade early and continue working in unsafe conditions for the rest of their lives.

They receive no benefits other than a place to stay while they are in the employ of their boss. I visited one such habitation, a terrace above a factory with a sweeping view of Dharavi, where thirteen workers lived. In one corner was a large black water tank. It was a Sunday. They were bathing, cooking and playing games. Here, outside of the foundry on an off day, a few discussed their working conditions more candidly. 'We just wrap a cloth around our faces, especially when we are colouring the buckles as the solution can splash around. Sometimes the chemicals can damage the skin,' one of the residents told me. 'We pay our own medical bills,' Mohammed Khalid from Bihar said, echoing a point that had been noted by several of the workers I spoke with.

Nevertheless, most of the workers I talked to either emphatically denied any health hazards or took a casual attitude toward the risks they assumed. No one complained of any serious ailments. 'We use a lot of chemicals and we have to be careful,' Sameer, a nineteen-year-old from Nepal, told me. Ghulam Mustafa from Katihar, Bihar, who has been working in the plating unit for ten years, told me, 'The employer gives us gloves and masks. It is a risky job we are doing since there are many chemicals, but we don't wear the masks. We don't have too many problems.' Mustafa also told me that in the last ten years he must have visited the doctor a few times but mostly for fever and minor ailments.

For Mohammad Faruq Khan, one of the four workers at the first buckle foundry I visited, safety precautions can be an annoyance and an inconvenience. 'I know it was very hot, but I can't wear rubber gloves since the mud I use is burning and it can melt the gloves,' he explained. He said that his mask suffocates him. 'I feel a choking sensation and then I can't spit out the *ghutka* (a readymade tobacco mix) I chew. There is no safe equipment supplied to us in any case,' he told me.

The owners were equally dismissive of the risks. 'We give them masks and gloves but they don't wear them,' one told me. 'If they fall ill I show them to the doctor. I don't give them any allowance,' he added.

HEALTH

While many workers are stoic about their conditions, doctors are certain that the dense smoke and pungent chemicals in the foundries gives rise to respiratory infections. Arshiya Haq, who works in a municipal hospital, says that workers from the brass industry regularly come to her with chest complaints. Dharavi's municipal hospitals report numerous cases of TB. According to

Mangala Surve, a social worker attached to the Urban Health Centre, each of the five major health posts in Dharavi has seventy to hundred cases registered. So far, there has been no occupational health study or intervention for the workers, not only in the brass industry but elsewhere as well.

Many of the sick are referred to the municipal Urban Health Centre on Dharavi's 60 Feet Road where the treatment is free and well supervised. Dr A.I. Khatri, who has worked in Dharavi for twenty years, says that workers often come to him with upper and lower respiratory tract infections that later develop into TB. Once the patients become asymptomatic, Khatri says, they tend to stop treatment. Slowly the disease becomes chronic and they start coughing blood. Since they toil in such close proximity, if one brass worker has the disease it transmits very quickly through the air.

Dr Khatri also refers to the brass workers' overall poor health, which he attributes to living in congested spaces and to the bad habits, like chewing tobacco, that they pick up. They have low immunity, he says, and often their diets are low in protein. Most of them work despite their ailments because it is a question of their survival, he points out. While they have a source of livelihood, they must work at something, and poverty and illiteracy bind them to this particularly dangerous work.

AT HOME

On a Sunday, it is easy to find Mohammed Faruq Khan. He is usually at home watching television in his tiny room at Sanjay Chawl, near Dambar Compound in Dharavi. He gets two plastic chairs but has to be coaxed to sit and talk. If the residents are surprised that he is being interviewed on the road adjoining the chawl, they don't show it. I had met Khan over a year before when I interviewed him at his workplace, in a room full of smoke and dust. It was refreshing to meet him in the open air. Unless there is some urgent work, Khan prefers to rest on Sunday.

Khan has three children. Salman, the eldest, is sixteen. Daughters Saleha and Gulnaz are ten and eight, respectively. Much to Khan's chagrin, Salman chose to drop out in the fifth standard and take up a job in his father's line. Above where we sit on the road is the electroplating unit where Salman has worked for the past two years. 'I thought I will teach him something else other than this, but he dropped out,' Khan says. Even so, Khan is still rather proud of his son. 'Salman earns Rs 4,000 a month and he is a skilled worker in electroplating,' he boasts. 'It was his wish. I wanted to send him abroad and teach him driving but he stayed here. I also thought he could learn *zari* (embroidery) work, which is highly paid, but he decided to choose electroplating. They like his work—not everyone can do it, and he is much sought after,' Khan grins proudly.

Khan's family comes from the Kasimpur village in the Raebareli district of Uttar Pradesh. His father eventually found reliable work in Calcutta and Khan was raised there. Khan made two forays into Mumbai, once in 1982 at the age of twenty-five, when he returned home, and then permanently in 1984. His elder brother had a job in one of Dharavi's buckle foundries. Khan joined him because there was no other job available to him. 'I learnt on the job,' he says matter-of-factly. If work is slow he earns Rs 1,000 or so a month. In a good month, he can make as much as Rs 2,000. He goes home to Uttar Pradesh once in a while, mainly for weddings.

'It's all fate. That will decide how long I can work,' Khan says. At forty-eight he is easily one of the oldest workers in the brass sector *bhatti* (furnace). He has no illnesses except for the occasional ailment. Reminiscing about his youth, Khan says, 'My father tried to encourage me to do something good. He used to work in the city electricity supply. Twice I thought I would try and do something in Calcutta, but I dropped out of school and after some years came here.' He regrets that he is not literate and quotes me a few lines: '*Bachpan khel mein khoya, jawani neend bhar soya, budhapa dekh ke roya*' (I lost my childhood in play, in my youth I slept and I wept in old age), from a song sung by Mukesh.

Khan especially loves the radio. 'They even tell us when the birthdays of the heroes and heroines are. Science has progressed so much. We can hear everything at home. I love to hear news now, earlier it was the movies,' he says. Now he has stopped going to the cinema. He enjoys cricket and is a big fan of former Pakistani fast bowler Wasim Akram. 'I usually take the day off for cricket matches. Even my employer does not mind. He knows how much I love the game.'

While his plans for his son may have gone awry, Khan has no doubt about his daughters' futures. 'I will get them married off soon. We don't let them work among our community,' he smiles.

10

BUSINESS TIME:
DHARAVI'S ENTREPRENEURS

Annie Zaidi

'Everything,' he says, 'is made here. Pots, pans, wafers, belts, shoes, clothes, needles, beedis, medicine, liquor. Legal, illegal, everything. Even money can, quite literally, be made here! There used to be a mint in Dharavi, but then one day the police found out.'

Ghulam Waris, proprietor and editor of *Sapna Times*, laughs as he recounts how the police had driven away lorries full of coins after the local money-minting 'industry' was busted about a decade ago. We are talking about entrepreneurial spirit and Waris, who co-founded *Aapka Dharavi Times* before this current venture, describes Dharavi as a mini-industrial estate that has made millionaires out of hundreds of people.

The stories are often similar—stories of desperation and grit, initiative and very, very hard work. Then, one fine day, lady luck smiles.

So goes Haji Sayeed Khan Bucklewala's story. He came to
Mumbai in 1979, a teenager from Jamshedpur who had just
cleared his high-school exams. Khan hadn't intended to stay in
the city. He'd applied for a passport so he could go to find work
in Iraq. But then the Iran–Iraq war began, and Sayeed found
himself stuck on the streets of Santa Cruz.

At first he worked in a slipper store, sleeping on the footpath
at night and bathing with water taken from a tank that supplied
to toilets nearby. Then someone told him to come to Dharavi
instead. Here, he was hired to polish buckles. Over the next few
years, Sayeed learnt everything he could and in October 1984,
he was ready to break out on his own.

He began by 'plating' independently—the process of covering
a buckle with nickel and gold plating. It was a rented space, and
he was paying Rs 30 a month. He'd also hired the machinery by
taking on a loan of Rs 16,000. The machines were old and
needed fixing, Sayeed says, 'So I told the owner that I would use
his machines and work off his loan slowly. At first, I worked all
alone. Some women would do the wiring work on the buckles in
their own houses. I paid them four annas (twenty-five paise) for
a dozen buckles. I worked day and night, and within three
months of the Diwali season, I had paid off the loan.'

Then Sayeed began to make his own buckles, visiting big
companies and asking for orders. He chuckles and blushes
slightly when I ask him how he succeeded in winning those big
orders.

'I had a beautiful personality,' he says. 'People used to joke that
I should go join films instead of plating buckles. They called me
"Sayeed Chikna" in those days.'

But it wasn't just his looks he was counting on. He visited

stores to scout for ideas that he could adapt. For instance, he'd look at a hair clip and decide to apply the design on a belt. Slowly he built a reputation as Sayeed Bucklewala. He still remembers a three-piece buckle he created that became very popular. Soon retailers began to ask for 'Sayeed Chikna's *maal*'.

His first big break came between 1987 and '89. 'An aunty from Nairobi had asked me to create a mango-shaped stud in metal. She liked my work and placed a big order. I made cashews, almonds, all sorts of metallic studs that went onto caps, hair clips, etc. She took everything I could make and I couldn't make them fast enough.' Those 'fruit' studs earned him up to Rs 4 lakh that year.

Sayeed expanded to include belts in his product line instead of just buckles and kept plowing his profits back into business. He now owns Heena Imitation, which specializes in polishing metal buckles and jewel studs; United Metal, which makes buckles; and Adeeba Export, which supplies buckles to places like Walmart. 'GAS, Lee, CK Jeans—many of the big brands get their belts and buckles made here,' says Sayeed. The turnover for each firm is about a crore.

The last few years haven't been easy, with cheap garments and accessories flooding the market. Chinese-made goods are particularly cheap and this has hammered local sales for Sayeed, who refuses to make his goods any cheaper. 'I cannot compete against China,' he sighs. 'Material and labour costs are higher in India. Anyway, Chinese maal is [to be sold] on the footpath. I don't make stuff for the footpath.'

His competition, he insists, are the Italians, not the Chinese. His goods are mainly for export and must adhere to international standards of quality. So he would rather spend a year 'sampling'—

sending goods abroad and waiting for export orders—than take up local orders for a few hundred buckles.

In this respect, he is very similar to Mohammad Mustaqeem Siddiqui. The fifty-four-year-old owner of CM Crafts and CM Exports, better known as just Mustaqeem, has a garments manufacturing and export business with a turnover of at least Rs 10 crore. Before the international markets crashed, his businesses were doing even better.

Mustaqeem's clients include firms like MKK and Burlington, which sell garments in the US. Like Sayeed, he doesn't want to supply to the domestic market, and yet, he must conduct his research in Mumbai. He must find the kind of ready-to-wear garments that might be popular with American or European retailers. For this he routinely goes about town, sifting through heaps of clothes at roadside stalls selling 'export reject maal'. Then he sends out samples with his own labels and waits until a sufficiently large order comes his way.

I ask him the secret of his success and Mustaqeem says trends have to be watched. 'If you want success, especially while exporting garments, styling is the most important factor. You also have to look at quality and service and price. On these counts, I score higher than most others. This might be because I was doing the actual work myself. I knew how to cut and sew. I knew what worked and what didn't.'

I ask him what happens if an export shipment gets rejected. He smiles patiently at me. 'It doesn't,' he says. 'It has never happened.'

Mustaqeem owns 3,200 sq. ft of work space in Dharavi and rents another 8,000. In total he runs twelve manufacturing units there, each with its own quality controller. Where we sit is a cordoned-off, heavily air-conditioned cabin in a corner of a vast work floor. Just outside his employees work, doing the same tasks that occupied Mustaqeem for most of his life. Of the thirty-nine years he has spent working with garments, twenty-two were spent as a 'job worker' in the garments sector, which means that he was a tailor who did all the work himself. And even the tailoring job did not come easy.

When he came to the city from Raebareli (82 km south-east of Lucknow) as a thirteen-year-old without any work skills, he went to his relatives, who lived in Kamathipura and ran a tailoring unit. But he was not taught tailoring work. 'I used to clean and fetch tea for the tailors. I wasn't paid anything at all. All I got was food. There wasn't even a place to sleep. The owners slept inside the shop. I slept with the other workers on the footpath outside. There were just three shops; nobody had houses.'

But money or no money, house or no house, Mustaqeem stuck on. A few years later, he had learnt how to sew. And on 1 April 1974, he came to Dharavi.

He remembers the exact date for it was in this slum that he began to build his fortune. He hired two sewing machines for Rs 25 a month and was paid just one rupee for every piece of clothing that he sewed. For one year, he worked day and night, all alone.

It wasn't until 1976 that he began to hire other workers. 'There was a "half-trainer" with me initially. I taught the rest of them.' Today, he pays an average per garment rate of between Rs 15 and Rs 25 (though skilled workers get up to Rs 40, depending on the complexity of the garment) to about 900 employees.

Business has suffered over the last few years, partly because of the economic downturn in the West, partly because the dollar has weakened against the rupee, and partly because cotton fabric is 20–30 per cent more expensive. Yet, Mustaqeem has few fears about the future. 'Those who work honestly have no need of fear,' he says.

Whether it is his wealth, his attitude or his habit of making time to address people's worries, Mustaqeem is an influential man now. His phone rings incessantly and it is hard to finish an interview without some important matter calling for his attention. There are boxes of sweets in his office, brought by visitors whom he has helped in some way and who have come to thank him. Now that his sons help him run his businesses, Mustaqeem devotes a lot of time and attention to social work, and also helps maintain law and order in Dharavi by mediating disputes. For his efforts, he has been awarded a Shantata Puraskar by the Mumbai police.

There seems a distinct trend in Dharavi of successful businessmen gathering social cred by helping other people individually, or through welfare groups, and many of them go on to lead a particular trade association. The leaders gain influence since the welfare associations are not just a trade promotion forum. They also help resolve disputes and function as a support group in times of distress. Not surprisingly, some of those who head the associations end up joining politics.

One such man is P.N. Natarajan, one of the biggest cable operators in the area and president of the Nadar Merchant Association. Natarajan came to Dharavi from Tamil Nadu in 1969. Though he had been in school up until standard VIII, he had no employable skills and so ended up trying his hand at several different businesses.

When he first moved to Mumbai, he went to Chembur, where

he worked as a helper in a general store. Next, he sold vegetables for two years. He didn't move to Dharavi until 1971, where he set himself up as an egg wholesaler. It made him a bit of money for a couple of years. Then he started his own general store and worked there for ten years, later converting it into a *chikki* and biscuit shop.

It was only in 2000, just a few years after the television boom had happened in India, that Natarajan entered the cable business. 'JPR was one of the biggest cable operators in Dharavi. When I started out, I took a [cable] line from them. That used to cost me Rs 500 per household/member,' he recalls.

Profit margins were slim. But television was the one thing a lot of families did invest in. Even those who did not have adequate housing wanted access to cable television. For Natarajan, it was all about timing. He says he made the right move at the right time. Today, it is almost impossible to get into the cable TV business without stepping on someone else's toes.

'There are about 150 cable operators in Dharavi now. We don't have new operators coming into the business. Actually, we don't allow new members [in our association] because then turf wars will be waged. There is not much growth in Dharavi as far as cable TV connections are concerned. People aren't building many new houses, and business is not growing. Growth is possible for my business only if redevelopment happens. When the number of Dharavi's homes grows, we will also grow.'

At any rate, Natarajan has built a small fortune over the last decade. He has a joint partnership in JPR now and about 2,500 'members' (households with cable connections). He has to pay his workers, of course, and taxes, but he says he makes about Rs 20–25 lakh a year.

He still keeps the biscuit shop too—it earns him about Rs 1 lakh each month—but Natarajan is becoming more and more active on the political front. He has been a member of the Congress party since 1971 and is currently serving as Block Congress president within Dharavi.

Oddly enough, his own political leanings have not interfered with that of the group he represents. The Nadar Merchant Association (Nadars are a community, most of whom have migrated from Tamil Nadu) used to be affiliated with the Shiv Sena, and is now affiliated with the nationalist Maharashtra Navnirman Sena, while Natarajan himself works for the Congress (I).

There are currently several challenges for those who run manufacturing units in Dharavi. The lack of skilled workers is a major problem. Sayeed says he cannot find people to do 'buffing' for him. 'The process of buffing is messy work. Makes your hands all *kala-peela* (black and yellow). Nobody wants to do it.' He complains too of having to keep an eye on his workers through CCTV cameras. 'They don't want to work even eight hours a day. They have mobile phones now and they tend to slack off if you don't watch them.'

Work ethic is important to Sayeed because he works as hard as his employees. He still shows up at work at 9.00 a.m. and sometimes goes on until 10.00 p.m. He doesn't hire a chemist, he tells me with some pride, because he does the work himself. And he is also responsible for the designs and 'finish' of the product.

Sayeed also tries to be a good employer. In 1981, Sayeed had bought a tiny house and an office for Rs 47,000. As his profits grew, he began to buy adjoining space. That continues to be his work area and the workers who live there don't have to pay any rent. In a city like Mumbai, this is one of the biggest perks an employer can offer a migrant labourer. Still, Sayeed cannot easily find willing workers. 'There is so much construction work going on all around,' he says. 'Builders pay labourers up to Rs 250 a day, just for lifting bricks. Why will they make buckles for me?'

Another source of worry is the rising cost of labour and metal. Profit margins are more slender than ever. His buckles cost between Rs 16 to Rs 45 per piece, depending on heft and size. But shoe buckles can sell for as little as Rs 2; his profit is only 25 paise per buckle. He must sell hundreds of thousands of buckles to make a living for himself as well as his employees. Sayeed regrets the global slowdown on account of his workers rather than himself. 'My workers are paid Rs 6,000–7,000 a month. How will they survive? Right now I have forty-five workers living here. But there was a time when I had seventy. I couldn't afford to keep them all.'

Business, he concludes, is a stressful way to make a living. He would rather see his sons find salaried jobs—he calls it 'getting into service'—than get into business. One of his sons is in London, doing his MBA. His daughter is doing an MBBS, studying to be a doctor. He has two other girls who study in high school. An older, adopted son helps with the business.

Natarajan too has educated his children so that they are in 'service' of some sort. Of his three daughters, one studied hotel management and became an air hostess, another is learning physiotherapy in Mangalore, and the third is studying for a master of arts degree at Bombay University. His son is studying for a B. Com degree, and might inherit the cable business or a new venture.

L. Kannan is very certain that he doesn't want his sons to
inherit his business. The fifty-seven-year-old runs Murugan
Laundry, a branch of the oldest laundry in Dharavi, which was
started by his own father. 'My father came from Madras to join
the military. But he didn't clear the physical examination. So he
stayed on in Mumbai and ironed clothes. He used to work from
home and deliver clothes to other people's houses. When I was a
boy, he set up the shop. I wasn't a good student, so my father put
me to work. There was no electricity then. We used coal to press
clothes and worked in the dark. I used to iron one garment for
twenty paise. After accounting for coal, we used to make Rs 150
a day. At that time, it seemed like a lot. Now I make Rs 400–
500 a day and have hired a helper.'

He isn't rich but he isn't poor either, not in Dharavi. And
though Kannan says he wants to go on ironing clothes as long as
his arms have the strength to lift an iron, there was a time when
all he wanted was to get away—from his school, from the
laundry. But his options were limited. His parents had sixteen
children to feed, of which only eight survived to adulthood. He
jokes, 'My dad didn't build as much property or business as he
built up the population of this country.'

Yet, he remembers his father with a pang and now wants his
younger son to join the armed forces. 'If that happens, it will
fulfil my dad's dream,' Kannan says.

At any rate, he is determined that his sons should find salaried
jobs. His younger son is still in high school and the older one is
in the third year of engineering (mechanical) at VJTI, one of
the better-known engineering colleges in Mumbai. He tells me
with pride that his son scored 94 per cent in the senior secondary
exam, and he took on a bank loan to support his higher education.

Kannan is willing to let him study further—get an MBA degree for instance—but his son wants a job so he can start supporting the family and, perhaps, move to a place where it's easier to get around. 'The lanes here,' says Kannan, 'are so narrow that if somebody dies, it is difficult to carry the corpse out.'

Sayeed is one of the few who moved their families out. When he was younger, he used to look at the tall apartment complexes in Sion and wonder at the rich people who must live there. His dream was to be able to live in one of those apartments. 'Maybe God wanted to grant me my dream. I bought an apartment in Sion in 2000 and moved my family out of Dharavi,' he says.

When I ask why he didn't just buy a better house within Dharavi, Sayeed tells me that what I see of the place, squalid and slum-like though it might seem, is a vast improvement on what it was like. 'When I came here, families were squashed into rooms 10 ft-by-15 ft, and there would be 10–15 people sleeping in each room. Liquor was made in open vats—molasses, water from pipes, distilled into bottles like blood dripping into bottles in the hospitals. There were open toilets, stench, maggots! If municipal commissioners came to visit, they would be stamping their feet all the time they stood here, to shake off maggots and other insects.'

Water and electricity were one of the biggest sources of conflict. 'There was a time when there were fights every single day. The first thought in my head used to be: who is going to fight today? We used to get five minutes of water for each household. A table clock was kept nearby and everyone was timed to prevent violent fights from breaking out at the tap. Now we don't have problems of water or electricity. A single light meter [connection] serves several homes,' he says with a mischievous twinkle in his eye.

Sayeed's love for the place is evident and, whether or not he lives there, he believes that Dharavi is the heart of Mumbai. It is a large heart and all hearts' desires are fulfilled here. Or at least, there was a good chance they would be fulfilled if only the city was more inclusive.

Certain businesses have never flourished in Dharavi. For instance, despite its central location and readily available space, nobody has made a fortune through hotels or restaurants. Even well-known chain stores selling sweets and snacks do not set up an outlet in Dharavi, although a lot of their goods are actually produced there. Perhaps Mumbai doesn't want to know that the chikki, *farsan*, *halwa* it eats is cooked or packaged by slum-dwellers.

Waris says the government and administration have been discriminatory too. 'They don't give licences easily. Chai shops don't have a health licence. Small businesses don't get trade licences. You need all kinds of licences and documents [to prove identity, bank statements, etc.] before you can apply for a trade licence. That just forces some businesses to function illegally.'

Nevertheless, Waris is quite keen on exposing illegalities in Dharavi, particularly if it involves politicians. Currently, he is focusing on the way contracts were awarded for the maintenance of public toilets, each of which is worth a significant income of up to Rs 2 lakh a month. Asking questions about infrastructure and the rule of law brings him nothing but trouble and *Sapna Times* is a loss-making venture.

As a matter of principle, Waris has decided not to take money from commercial advertisers. He runs a digital services shop, which he uses for designing the four-page newspaper. Information and funds come from a network of about twenty-five supporters that includes a lawyer, a taxi driver, a government employee and a leather goods worker. He also gets quiet contributions from businessmen who don't want to be seen as supportive of his newspaper. But he is willing to pump in Rs 2,000 from his own pocket each time he publishes an issue. He also distributes 90 per cent of the copies free of cost. The total independence of *Sapna Times* means that the monthly only appears when it can—printing can be stalled by a lack of funds, an illness or a crime that consumes all of Waris's time and energy as he tries to get the police to intervene instead of just reporting it.

I ask him why he does it and Waris says simply, 'Dharavi needed its own paper.' And whenever Dharavi has seen a vacuum, whether of goods or service, someone has always stepped in, rolled up his (or her) sleeves and gotten down to business.

11

A Pampered Slum

Leo Mirani

Santosh Narayankar cringes in embarrassment every time his mother visits him at college. Having your carefully cultivated university persona suddenly shattered by the arrival of a parent is traumatic enough for anyone. For Santosh, a final year MBBS student at Sion's Lokmanya Tilak Municipal General Hospital and Medical College, it's worse. Born in the same hospital at which he now studies, he must put up with being repeatedly told of the ward to which his mother was admitted, the bed on which she gave birth to him, the various complications over ten days of hospitalization and how, at the end of it, he came into the world through a caesarean section.

In 1985, when Santosh was born, his mother had little choice but to go to what is popularly referred to as Sion Hospital. Dharavi, where the family lived, had a scattering of private general practitioners and public dispensaries, and Sion Hospital on its south-eastern edge. There was nothing in between. 'We had to go out of Dharavi for everything,' said Santosh. 'When I was two, I broke my arm and there was nowhere here to get an x-ray.' With no other diagnostic centres, pathology labs, nursing homes or maternity homes, the hospital was the only port of call for major illnesses.

Today, says Dr Kailas B. Goud, who set up his practice on 60 Feet Road in 1983, there are numerous private hospitals—or, more accurately, nursing homes—with 10–15 beds each. Evidence of this is visible all along the road; I counted three pharmacies and two nursing homes within a 50-feet radius of Dr Goud's clinic. One reason for the recent proliferation of clinics could be the much-maligned SRA developments; it's a lot easier to set up a nursing home in a legal, brick-and-mortar building than in flimsy slums held up with sheets of tin and planks of wood. Path labs, x-ray facilities and specialists have mushroomed and the number of private general practitioners (GPs) in Dharavi has more than doubled since Dr Goud arrived, going from 100 to 250 in his estimate. The GPs charge anywhere from Rs 12 to Rs 300 for a day's treatment, catering to every economic level of Dharavi's residents. NGOs too are all over Dharavi; it's easy to access, well-known and somewhat glamorous, and a pretty good environment compared with the desperate slums of Deonar or Ghatkopar.

Still, Sion Hospital was where Santosh returned two decades later. The son of illiterate parents from Dharavi, Santosh wanted to become a doctor for three reasons. He wanted to make money, he wanted respect and he didn't want to work particularly hard. 'I was eight when I decided I wanted to be a doctor,' he said. 'I was a sickly child and often needed to get injections. Our GP would charge Rs 20 a shot. At a hundred patients a day that's Rs 2,000. I wanted to make that sort of money for doing nothing more than poking people. Of course, now I realize that being a doctor is a lot of hard work.'

The youngest of seven children, Santosh was a strictly average student until the eighth standard, when he was assigned a seat next to three of the brightest students in his class. From them he learnt how to take notes, memorize chapters and study effectively. In junior college, he took the science stream but spent his free time playing chess and reading English grammar and vocabulary books. At medical school, he discovered spirituality as a way to help him concentrate on his studies and keep him from the path of temptation.

Santosh offers any number of excuses for his dedication. 'I am actually very lazy. I didn't want to help set the table or clean up, so I would keep my nose in my study books' is one. 'We had no TV or radio or mobile phones when I was a child, so I had nothing to do but study' is another, as is 'I took up the science stream in junior college because everybody was doing it'. While these remarks may contain within them kernels of truth, perhaps the most significant reason for Santosh's hard work is plain old ambition: 'My parents were happy with my marks when I was getting 50 per cent,' he said. 'But I was jealous of other students who got more.'

Dharavi is often cited as proof of that tired old trope: India's progress, goes the conventional wisdom, is despite rather than because of the government. The figure of $665 million is bandied about for the 2.2 sq. km area's local economy. In the absence of governance, we are told, the people of Dharavi have set up quite the life for themselves. With no affordable housing, they built their own homes. With no jobs, they created industry from waste. And with scarce public health services, hardworking self-starters like Santosh and those who spotted a gap in the market like Dr Goud rushed in to fill the void. While it isn't within the ambit of this chapter to comment on the economy or housing situation in Dharavi, it is painfully obvious that the conventional wisdom has it all wrong when it comes to health care.

Dharavi was described by the *Sydney Morning Herald* as recently as February 2011 as a slum where 'disease is rife and there are no government-run health facilities'. This is the popular perception not only in other countries on far-off continents but in India, in Mumbai.

However, the opposite is true. If anything, Dharavi is an exceptionally pampered slum, says Dr Armida Fernandez, former dean of Sion Hospital and co-founder and trustee of the Society for Nutrition, Education and Health Action (SNEHA), an NGO that addresses health issues for women and children in slums across the city. SNEHA started in Dharavi as a natural extension of Dr Fernandez's connection to Sion Hospital, which caters primarily to slum dwellers.

G/North ward, the administrative district that covers the area west of the Central Railway tracks from Parel station to the Mithi River, covers 9.07 sq. km. It is home to nine public dispensaries and eight health posts run by the municipality. Of these, five of each are in Dharavi, which covers less than a fourth of the ward's area. In addition, the Urban Health Centre sits in the middle of Dharavi, making it exceptionally well-served by public health care facilities.

The only problem is that residents of Dharavi, like residents of every other corner of Mumbai and of India, prefer local private health care. Walking through the corridors of Sion Hospital, which appear to be in a permanently semi-finished state, it is not hard to see why. The oppressive atmosphere common to government buildings all over the city pervades the complex. Large, dimly-lit corridors, malodorous toilets, bored-looking staff, patients resigned to interminable waiting; it could be a ward office or a development authority building or the Brihanmumbai Municipal Corporation (BMC) headquarters. Santosh Narayankar says the toilets in the hospital are in such bad shape students avoid them unless absolutely necessary. Instead, they either use the relatively cleaner facilities in the library or make the short walk to their hostel over the road.

According to the National Sample Survey Organization's Morbidity and Treatment of Ailments report in 1998, only 19 per cent of Indians in rural areas and 20 per cent in urban areas used public health services for outpatient care. Three other surveys conducted in 2000 and 2001 found that less than 20 per cent of Indians use public health services. Studies done by Dr Fernandez's organization found that 70–80 per cent of slum dwellers in Mumbai prefer private health care. When Santosh Narayankar's father was dying of cancer, the family admitted him to D.Y. Patil Hospital in Navi Mumbai. The day I spoke to Dr Fernandez, she was seeing a malnourished child who had been diagnosed at Sion but whose father refused to admit him there. 'Nothing doing,' Fernandez quoted him as saying, 'We're going to a private hospital.'

The reasons are many and they extend far beyond notions of ambience. The biggest one is a lack of faith. According to Dr Goud, people are suspicious of things that are free. Dr Fernandez concurs: 'The perception is that where we pay there is better quality. And where people talk to us nicely there is better quality.' Public health's image is not helped by the fact that private hospitals transfer patients to Sion when it's clear they won't survive, says Dr Fernandez. A second reason is personal attention. Public sector doctors aren't interested in mollycoddling their patients or satisfying their (entirely natural) need for personal attention. For them, it's about dealing with numbers. Private doctors, on the other hand, listen to their patients, counsel them, greet them by their names. Service, in hospitals as in the hospitality industry, plays a big part in repeat business. The third reason has to do with price. While private doctors may charge more than public health clinics, whose fees are nominal, a day's medicine is included in the charges. Public health care facilities often lack basic supplies and write prescriptions that the patients must then procure at market rates, somewhat diluting the point of free health care. For comparison, England (not Wales or Scotland) also charges for prescriptions on the free National Health Service but everything from flu medicine to cancer drugs costs the same—£7.40.

Awareness too can be raised. According to Dr Fernandez, not enough Dharavi residents know about the existence of the Urban Health Centre. 'It is empty,' she says. 'They could access it but they are not coming.' A 1995 study by the Department of Health Studies at the Tata Institute of Social Sciences found the same thing, attributing it to inconvenient opening hours, in addition to the other reasons listed.

But perhaps the most important reason of all is the treatment. When public doctors see a patient with diarrhoea, they prescribe a simple (but effective) salt-sugar solution and send them on their way. Private GPs are far more likely to prescribe drugs or refer them for tests, both of which are unnecessary but appreciated by credulous patients.

Private health care isn't merely exploitative of unsuspecting patients but often dangerous. According to a health official at G/North ward, who declined to be named because he isn't authorized to make public statements, the problems with private doctors in Dharavi extend far beyond corruption. 'A number of them do not have the required degrees needed to practise,' he said. 'We have attempted to crack down on them but sometimes they are using other people's certificates. Sometimes the degree is fake. Sometimes they make up degrees with random letters: DB, DHHS, IC.' Another big problem, not just in Dharavi but in many poor parts of India, is that doctors with qualifications in homeopathy, unani or ayurveda practise conventional medicine.

Santosh Narayankar could have been one of those doctors. On his first attempt at the Common Entrance Test for admission to medical school, Santosh scored 151 out of 200. Despite the quota for members of the scheduled castes, to which he belongs, Santosh could only gain admission to the Bachelor of Ayurvedic Medicine and Surgery course. He soon realized it wasn't what he wanted.

With the support of his parents, Santosh dropped out of the programme and studied all day, every day, for the months until the next entrance exam. 'I didn't listen to one song or watch one movie in those months,' he said. 'But I was also very lucky because my parents never tried to make me work. They always told me to concentrate on my studies.' The next year, Santosh ranked 27th in his category and easily secured a place at Sion Hospital. 'I was very happy. If you have an MBBS from Mumbai, it's easy to get a job.'

Santosh is one of Dharavi's remarkable success stories,

especially considering the circumstances into which he was born. In 1985, much of Dharavi still lacked running water and adequate sanitation, both essential to good health. In 1971, when Dr Fernandez joined Sion Hospital, some 60 per cent of newborns were underweight. Today, the figure is lower than 30 per cent.

Dharavi's improvements in health care over the last three decades has as much to do with the provision of basic civic amenities as with health care itself. The things that residents of Bandra and Colaba take for granted—water, toilets, cleanliness—are what make the biggest difference to the well-being of Dharavi's residents. A 2002 research paper by S. Kumar Karn and H. Harada of Japan's Nagaoka University of Technology concluded that the 'provision of safe and adequate water and sanitary facilities in the slums and effective wastewater management seem among major issues of immediate concern for reducing the burden of such diseases and consequent impairments.'

To that end, the Municipal Corporation of Greater Mumbai monitors the water quality in the area on a regular basis and has been providing taps to clusters of houses if not individual homes. According to Dr Goud, sanitation has improved since local groups converted fetid municipal toilets into pay-and-use facilities following the Sulabh model. The toilets are still owned by the BMC but are now better maintained and more usable. However, a lot of work remains to be done in this area.

The BMC's health posts, which work more in preventive care than the dispensaries, which are for treatment, conduct routine immunizations and give polio drops and inoculations. Sion Hospital's Preventive and Social Medicine department sends doctors and students into the slum every week. 'We get people's medical histories, advise them on health and investigate local conditions for health hazards like mosquitoes,' says Santosh, who regularly goes into Dharavi for his PSM module. Numerous NGOs also work to educate residents about seeking early treatment and preventing disease. But the long-term solution lies in educating people about preventive care through a sustained mass-media campaign, says Dr Fernandez, citing the example of the polio drops campaign.

The health problems in Dharavi are scarcely different from those in the rest of the city. The most commonly reported ailments are cold and cough, influenza, diarrhoea and malaria. Malnutrition continues to be a problem, says Dr Fernandez, but this has more to do with incorrect diet than with no diet at all. Citing a study from 1983, *The Economist* reported in March 2011 that 'even when the poor do spend more on food, they do not buy the stuff that is most nutritious or best value'. Violence against women is a major issue but this is a pan-Indian affliction that cuts across demographic and geographic lines.

Diseases specific to the sprawling slum have more to do with occupation than location. The potters of Kumbharwada, for example, make their wares on open-fire kilns. Every evening, a thick plume of smoke hovers over Dharavi, contributing to pulmonary and respiratory diseases.

Perceptions play a big part in the development of a place like Dharavi. Just as locals perceive public health care to be inferior to private doctors, for many Mumbaikars the word Dharavi itself is associated with squalour and poverty. While this works in Dharavi's favour to the extent that it is a magnet for social workers and NGOs, it also drives out some of the wealthier, better-educated residents. As they move up the social ladder, 'Dharavi' carries with it a social stigma they would rather leave behind. In their place come new immigrants, and the cycle starts afresh.

Santosh Naranyankar sits at the cusp of this cycle. He moved out from Dharavi to his college hostel in Sion after the death of his father and the subsequent wrangling between real- and step-siblings over his property. Sitting in his hostel room, which is furnished with old patient beds from the hospital, Santosh tells me it is his parents' wish that he practise in Dharavi when he is done with his internship and compulsory two-year government service. Santosh is unconvinced—not to distance himself from the area but because, having seen the struggles of his family and the sacrifices they've made for the sake of his education, he would rather have a secure government job where 'you start earning from the beginning and don't have to make any investments'.

Santosh isn't thinking too far into the future. His plan is to finish his compulsory service, get a job and then maybe get married. Perhaps one day in the future he will open his own practice. But whether he eventually does so in the sprawling slum where he was born or in a more prestigious neighbourhood, Santosh is adamant he will never try to disassociate himself from his roots. 'If I forget about Dharavi,' he said, 'I will never succeed in life.'

12

DREAMING THE MOVIES

Jerry Pinto

Rajesh Prabhakar tells me of the duplicates.

'There were many of them. Now only two are left. Do you want to meet them?'

There are two kinds of duplicates in the film industry. There are the stuntmen who do the body double work, and there are the duplicates who are supposed to resemble the heroes and villains and comedians. Some of them do not look very much like the originals but they serve as mnemonics; they simply do what the stars do and they get paid to do it in stage shows and in variety programmes.

The best way for the latter type of duplicate to operate is to find a star with recognizable mannerisms: Rajnikanth's way of lighting a cigarette, Dev Anand's effete shambling walk, Rajesh Khanna's coy smile and way of turning his head. This goes down well in B-towns where the audiences know they are unlikely to get a real live movie star. In a place like that, a double is as good as it gets, and even though you can find the star you love on a television channel sometime in the next twenty-four hours, the magic of having someone perform live still obtains. The duplicates strut their stuff to whistles and hoots on small proscenium stages.

It takes years of work to turn yourself into yourself; it takes a moment to be recognized as someone else. That is precisely what happened to Dharavi resident Ashok Chhavan, who doubles up for the star of the late 1960s and early 1970s, Rajesh Khanna.

'I remember the exact date on which it happened,' he says. 'It was 28.6.1988. It was the naming ceremony of my daughter. I was shaving and when I had finished I turned my head. My brother-in-law was watching me and who knows what he saw but he said, 'You can do Rajesh Khanna's duplicate'.'

And so it began, the careful study of the star, the memorizing of his dialogues, the familiarization with his best-known movies.

'We have to do what [the audiences] remember. So we ask, what do they remember? They remember how he danced in [the song] 'Jai jai Shiv Shankar'; they remember how he spoke to Sharmila Tagore in *Amar Prem*. That is what they have come for. They have come for their memories.'

Chhavan came to Mumbai in 1974. He lived for a while in Byculla, close to the railway station, but when the slum there was demolished, he moved to Dharavi. He remembers that in the beginning the entertainment was in the form of the *mela* (a fair). And at its heart was the man on the bicycle, the man who would cycle for seven days and nights, without ever stopping.

'Like *Shor*,' I say. Manoj Kumar, the hero, undertakes to cycle for a similar period of time to earn the money for the operation that he hopes will help his son regain his hearing.

'Like *Shor*,' he agrees.

I am intrigued. 'Did the man do everything on the bicycle?'

'Everything. Potty *se le ke* shave *tak*. (From potty to shaving.) Everything.' Coconut water would keep him going in the last dark days, says Chhavan.

'There was not much money. Sometimes, the organizers would give you ten rupees, sometimes hundred rupees, but we took what we could get. It was a chance to show our talents.' People came backstage. Fans came and took photographs. That was enough. The magic of cinema had rubbed off a little.

Chavan shows me an album of photographs with various other duplicates. 'One of us will get a call from someone who wants us to appear, and then he will call the others. No one wants a single duplicate. Because an audience will always have different-different favourites. So you have someone who wants to see Salman Khan dance and someone wants to hear Amjad Khan's dialogue. This is what we do.'

For Chhavan, the duplicates' moment truly came when comic actor Javed Jaffrey's *Boogie Woogie*, one of the first talent shows, brought them into the living rooms of middle-class India. 'That gave us real respect. It gave us a showcase for our talents.'

Now Chhavan commands Rs 1,500 per performance. He has been on various shows including *Boogie Woogie* and on *Zoom*, *Kaboom* and *Channel [V]*, all popular entertainment channels. He shows me a programme printed for the Hungama Charitable 2010 hosted by the Narayanpur Evam Bastar Sangeet Mahavidyalaya. It promises 'Junior Rajesh Khanna ka rangaram karyakram evam orchestra'.

If Chhavan is a man who is contented with his lot, Sheikh Mansoor Ali, alias Lucky, is a man with dreams, a man with plans. He exudes this from his shiny black shirt, his elegantly gelled hair, his state-of-the-art mobile phone. Lucky lays out his biodata: he has participated in *Boogie Woogie* and has twice won an award on the show. He has starred in a documentary called *Emotionally Yours*. He has worked on lots of other shows with the best choreographers.

That's because he likes to dance.

'When I was in school, my parents would force me to study but *mera man nahin lagta thha*. Finally, they said, let it go, let him dance. But now it is up to me. I must make something of my life.' Like so many other young men in the city, he is a struggler. He's waiting for his big break.

'But I know my limits. I have my family to think of. I must not worry them. They must not think *ki* where is the next meal coming from. So I do my business and I wait.'

The business is event management. Right now Lucky specializes in children's parties. 'I do everything except the catering. That side you get too many complaints, so I don't do that. Otherwise everything else, decoration, lighting, set-up, entertainment, DJ and child name cutout, everything I do.'

At one of these parties, he did his Hrithik turn under the eyes of the star himself.

'It was the party of a child of a customs officer. Nearly forty celebrities had come. He was also there.'

'Did he say anything?'

'Who are we in front of them? Why they'll talk to us?'

But if Lucky doesn't make it to Bollywood, he doesn't mind. He has a Dream B, as it were. 'I want to be the best at what I do. I want to be the best in my profession. I would like to do some big events like the Filmfare Awards night. This is my dream. This is my *lakshya*.'

Thakurbhai Bahadur Singh dreams of a life in cinema, too. He has written eighty stories that he knows could be made into significant films. The only thing he lacks is a *'tagda* financier'— a financier with money muscle.

'Ek zamaana tha jab writer *aur* director *milke kaam karte the,'* he says. (At one point in time, the writer and director worked together.) Singh does not explain how he knows this. It is knowledge that may be plucked out of the air, so rich in the city's lore. It is what we all know together: that once upon a time, the set was like a picnic; that in those days Raakhee cooked her famous fish curry for the entire unit; or that Amitabh Bachchan arrived before everybody else and began watering the ground on which he was to sing in order to settle the dust. *'Aaj milna mushqil ho gaya hai. Wahaan tak pahunch nahin paata aam aadmi,'* Singh says. (Today, it is difficult to meet them. Ordinary people just can't get to them.)

Singh does not look defeated or angry about the inability of the industry to take even a single one of his ideas to the audiences. He did come close once. A friend who owns a medical store in Dharavi wanted to turn one of his screenplays into a film. Singh persuaded him to abandon the idea.

'It is too big a risk,' he said. 'I did not want him to go under.'

He's philosophical about that missed opportunity. 'It's a game,' he says. 'A game of luck.'

Singh was no maddened gambler. Instead he focused on his business and his family. His three children were born and brought up in Dharavi; the eldest is an engineer. And yet, as a monument to hope, his visiting card says, simply and poignantly: writter.

Acting and screenwriting aren't the only careers available in film. And Bollywood isn't the only game in town, either. No one knows this better than Rajesh Prabhakar. The articulate and intelligent forty-one-year-old has made a living out of the world's fascination for Dharavi. The son of a chemical engineer and a housewife, Rajesh began his career with a local news channel that beamed content out of what was then known as the world's largest slum. Word of mouth brought him to the attention of children's book illustrator and film production coordinator and location manager Amit Vachhrajani, and soon he was being asked to scout for locations, permissions and everything else that television crews would need when negotiating a space that was at once enticing, exotic and completely unfamiliar to anyone.

'The first programme I worked on was called *Slumming It* with Kevin McCloud,' Rajesh says. 'It was basically about architecture in Mumbai. I was editing for a news channel and Amit met me around that time. He asked me where I had learnt my skills and I said I sat down at the machine and I learnt recording, editing, that kind of thing.'

Over the years, Rajesh has assisted television and film crews from all over the world. The queries now come in thick and fast.

'Sometimes when they call up and say, "Rajesh, we want this-and-this", I think, "Do these things happen? *Aisa hota hai kya?*" But my next thought is: "If they happen anywhere in the world, then they happen in Dharavi." I don't have to look far. Last month someone called up and said they needed people who had been involved in medical trials. I had heard of one fellow who had done something like that only, so I went and met him and I asked, "It's like this. They're coming. You'll appear?" and he said, "Yes".'

But it isn't always like that.

'Other times I have to look. Then I go around asking.'

'Who does he ask?' He does not answer the question directly.

'I do not take holidays. From the time I get up I am on duty, direct. Whoever I meet, I ask them questions. What is this guy's story? Why is he here? What is he doing? Most people tell. Then it goes in my file. I know. If I don't know, then I should know someone who would know. If I don't know that also, then I must go and find. I tell you I have such faith in Dharavi, anything is here, everything is here. I am standing at the corner shop, I am looking.'

Rajesh has ten telephones, he says, and different SIM cards for each one. 'For the crews,' he says.

'See every story that comes here, it goes and gets lost in one area only. Where do people go? They go to the same people. They go to Joachim Arputham. They go to Raju Korde, to Sheela Patel. To SPARC (the Society for the Promotion of Area Resource Centres). Now Raju has become very busy. He knows that there are still many people who want to see Dharavi. They have come from France. They have forty minutes time. Who does Raju call? "*Chalo* Rajesh Prabhakar will take them. He will show them Dharavi in forty minutes." Now I am not getting paid for all this. Why should I do it? I do it because I want to understand what it is that they want to see. If I know what they want to see, I know what I have to show their reporters when they come here. I keep a relation with them. I exchange cards. I write some lines to them on email.'

Rajesh is ready to help. If the job is dangerous, it adds to his enjoyment of it. He has set up a spy camera in a brothel in order that a foreign film set may show the ugly face of child prostitution in India.

If this sounds difficult—and it is not merely difficult but life-threatening as well—it is just one of the many demands that are made on Rajesh's ingenuity.

'Amit got a shoot. They wanted two taxi drivers and two construction workers. The taxi drivers and construction workers must speak English and they must have passports. And they have to be willing to go to Germany and the construction worker must work on a site there and the taxi driver must drive a taxi there. And from Germany two will come here, and work, like that. Amit took it on. Because he knew I would make some *jugaad* (improvise something). He knows. So I said to myself, "This is a challenge. There is a construction worker who speaks English here. Somewhere." So I went and asked everyone. I figured he would be south Indian because they speak English more. And I found one chap. *Bahut tragedy ka* story *hai.* (It's a tragic story.) He was hurt in an accident, could not study because no money, but had done some college. Now he was working on a construction site. He spoke English. Passport he did not have but I told Amit, "You can do a *tatkal* (instant) passport. That is your part of the jugaad." This is the challenge.'

But the taxi driver was an even bigger problem and finally, there was only one solution.

'I have appeared on television sometimes. They have taken my shots. So one day, the producer there was looking and he said, "Why not Rajesh?" I said, "Why not?" So I will go to Germany and learn to drive a taxi. I have decided not to learn to drive a car here. I will go there only and learn it. I have a licence but it is for a two-wheeler. That is the challenge I have set myself for there.'

Rajesh did not end up going to Germany but he did manage their shoot in Mumbai and has lived to tell the tale. However, it was not an easy shoot. It never is. After it was done, he slept for an entire day.

THE DAILY GRIND AND TIMEPASS

The stories that follow discuss ambition and work, as the others before them have done, but the emphasis in Section Three is on the basics of daily life: making a marriage work, raising children, getting water, going to school and passing time. Most of the stories here focus on women. The section opens with an interview between Kasturi Kadam and Anna Erlandson and Stina Ekman. Erlandson and Ekman were part of a group of artists and architects from the Royal University College of Fine Arts in Stockholm who collaborated on *Dharavi: Documenting Informalities*, originally published in 2009. Kadam explains how she kept her family together after her husband lost his business and took to drink. She managed for a time by sorting waste in Dharavi's recycling district and takes pride in having found good husbands for her daughters.

The following chapter, Sharmila Joshi's 'The Women of Wasteland', is another tale of mothers and daughters and is also set in Dharavi's recycling district, known by locals as the 13th Compound. Like Kasturi, Hanumanti Kamble raised her children without a husband, except Hanumanti was not able to lift any of them beyond their circumstances. She dreamed that her daughter Laxmi would grow up to be a nurse, but Laxmi also sorts waste in the 13th Compound. She, too, hopes her daughter will go into medicine, as a doctor.

Freny Manecksha explains how the women and children procure water each morning. With each passing year, more and more Dharavi homes have running water, but to this day many have to lug it home every morning. They live at the mercy of the men who control the tap. Manecksha gives an in-depth account of how the members of Dharavi's water mafia siphon off water from the main line into Dharavi and sell it away.

In her chapter on Dharavi's schools, Sameera Khan notes the efforts many women make to give their children a chance to succeed. Zubeida Khatoon stitches buttons and rents out space in her house to put her kids through one of Dharavi's private high schools. It is the only way she can guarantee that they will learn English, which for Zubeida is the surest path to a better life. Khan also profiles Thayapa H. Santi, principal of Dharavi's Ambedkar school, and documents the way Santi changed the institution's curriculum and lengthened school hours to make sure the students learned English. Santi keeps the building open on nights and on weekends for kids who cannot study at home. Former students regularly prep for college exams there, as Santi has provided for many the quiet place they cannot find elsewhere. He's also created a culture of academic success, a room where it's hip to talk about a career in math or dentistry and okay to be nervous about an upcoming test.

From school the section returns to the theme of fame and glory. Mansi Choksi writes about Jameel Shah, who failed to impress choreographer Sandip Soparrkar with his dancing skills, but did the next best thing: teach himself how to make dancing shoes. From his small shop in Dharavi, Shah has made shoes worn by stars in some of Bollywood's biggest numbers, his ascent made possible by an aunt from Bangalore who took him when he was penniless and found him a job. Choksi follows with the story of Lalu Ashok Khaura (aka Ajay) and his group of break dancers, known as the B-Boys. Ajay and company are

An overhead view of Dharavi's hutments in Saibaba Nagar, with Slum Redevelopment Authority buildings in the distance. Taken from 90 Feet Road.

A view of Dharavi's recycling district, also known as 13th Compound.

Mohammad Rais Khan
and family (from left:
wife Fareeda holding
daughter Iram, daughter
Nargis, niece Aysha, son
Qasim and mother
Runnisha).

Nargis Khan, daughter of Mohammad Rais Khan.

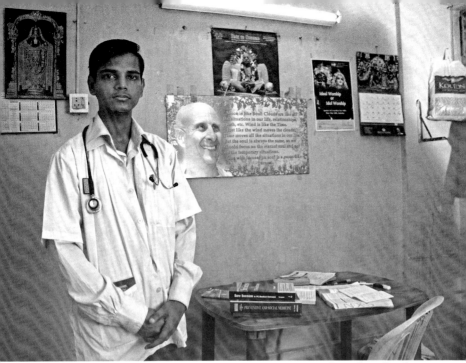

Dr Santosh Narayankar at his study table.

Gulzar Khan, son of activist Waqar Khan, poses before the 'We All Are One' poster, made in the aftermath of the 1992–93 riots to promote communal harmony. Gulzar, who is posing as the Hindu boy, had to shave his head to make the poster.

Harish Shamji Siangadia takes some pots from his mother, Kuvar Shamji Siangadia, and sets them to dry in the sun.

Courtesy RAJESH PRABHAKAR

Courtesy RAJESH PRABHAKAR

Harish's grandmother gets ready to polish a set of dried clay fixtures.

Courtesy Shriya Patil Shinde

A waste sorter in Dharavi's 13th Compound examines his goods while three young boys look on.

Courtesy Rajesh Prabhakar

Going through discarded plastic spoons, knives and forks.

Retired school administrator and social activist Bhau Korde reads the newspaper.

Ghulam Waris, proprietor and editor of *Sapna Times*, stands before his computer, the day's headline displayed on the screen.

D.K. Rao, survivor extraordinaire, at home, seated before a portrait of himself.

Two workers in Madhukar Khandare's leather tanning factory, in the Kala Killa section of Dharavi.

Former Shiv Sena MLA Baburao Mane watches as students at Raje Shivaji Vidyalaya, a primary school in Dharavi that he oversees, file past.

Qasim Khan, son of Mohammad Rais, prepares to go out.

regular entertainers at weddings in Dharavi and the surrounding neighbourhoods, and give impromptu performances on the streets of Mumbai's wealthier neighbourhoods to great popular acclaim.

Jerry Pinto ends this section as well, this time with the account of two poets, Nisar Ahmed Khan, who writes in Urdu, and Vadivel Thambi, a milkman who texts poems to adoring fans in Tamil Nadu. For Thambi, a man of disarming innocence, it is his many female fans who sustain him and carry him through his day job.

13

THE KADAM FAMILY

Anna Erlandson and Stina Ekman

On our first trip to Dharavi we often met the Kadam family on our walks on Poonawala. Coming back a year later, our friendship grew deeper and we were invited to spend time with the family. With great generosity the Kadam family shared stories about their life, gains and drawbacks, their struggles and hopes for the future. We laughed, cried, made food and rested together in the blue interior of their apartment on Poonawala.

KASTURI KADAM: My father and mother lived in Sion, and I was brought up in this area, the Dharavi–Sion area.

I was educated up to the seventh standard. My father died when I was studying in the fifth standard, and my older sister had to look after me and my family. My family arranged my marriage, and when I was sixteen years old I married Devidas. By the age of eighteen I had my first child, a daughter.

ANNA ERLANDSON/STINA EKMAN: Can you explain how your marriage was arranged?

KK: Earlier my father had a business and his business partner said, 'I have a son, will you give me one of your daughters?' I was looking nice then, so I was chosen from among my two sisters; they offered me and we got married. But then there was a life turn. After I had my first child, the story is very sad—crying and crying. At the beginning my husband was a good man, a businessman in leather work. The first five or six years he was very nice. We had a decent life, but after six years he lost his business.

AE/SE: Why?

KK: There was a quarrel between the business partners and because of the partner he lost the leather factory. After that he became a very heavy drunkard. The following years were very difficult for me. My husband was always drunk, and he used to go early in the morning, at four o'clock, to drink. When I was at work he came home, taking all the food from me and the children. He beat me often, so I always said to the children, 'I am earning and my husband is sitting here drinking up all the money so there is no use.'

We were living together with Bhimsen's family [Devidadas's brother and his family of five], but because of Devidas's drinking problems, and of all the quarrels and all the beatings, our families separated. Bhimsen said, 'Move out', so our family moved out with the children to a place for rent. And at that time, I was the only one working, not my husband. My youngest daughter, Sarika, was two years old at that time. So it's fifteen years ago. You see, out of submission, I was doing work in a plastic industry, separating the plastic from all the garbage. That work I had to do. All day, from ten in the morning to ten at night. I was standing in water, sorting and washing out the plastic, garbage and all. I was doing full work.

At that time my husband was always drunk and ate lots of food. There was hardly any food but he was eating all the food in the house. I earned sixteen rupees per day. Sixteen. One, six. Every day I was working hard for my family, allowing my husband to drink and daily I gave him five rupees to drink. I was doing very hard work at that time.

AE/SE: But how could you manage the family with just sixteen rupees and a drunk husband?

KK: During this period, my father-in-law supported us. After 10.00 p.m. he gave me 10–20 rupees per day saying, 'Give this to your children, buy something for your children.' My father-in-law was very supportive.

AE/SE: And you have five children?

KK: Yes, I had five children to manage, four daughters and one boy. So I was always looking here and there for more money. And when the first daughter was 15–16 years old, my husband's brothers helped us with the marriage of our first daughter. After the first daughter's marriage, I looked after the three daughters and the boy. I will always remember my great father-in-law. My mother-in-law was very aggressive and she did not want to help us, but my father-in-law always helped us.

My son, Atish, believed that his mother was suffering with all these problems, and that his father was not supporting us. Atish didn't want to stay with us. He went to stay somewhere else. My husband's brother took him and gave him an education. And whenever my son came to me and asked for money, I took him to the plastic industry and the boss gave him some. My boss also helped with the education of my son, Atish's education. He was very good. Because of my boss and my father-in-law I could manage, otherwise I would have collapsed.

My first daughter, Sandhya, at the time when she was in tenth standard, when she was trying to study, my husband did not allow her to, saying, 'Don't study, turn off the light, I want to sleep, don't study now.' Although this happened, my daughter passed her tenth standard and studied until graduation and now, since two years back, she is married. Sandhya is very talented and she wanted to become a doctor. I said, 'I don't have enough money to make you a doctor.' I feel very bad now, to me my daughter is very talented but still we did not have the money to support her.

I suffered very much because of my husband being a drunkard. I always cried and cried and cried and my husband's brother said, 'Don't cry, I will do something.' So, my husband's brother took Devidas to a center in Pune where they try to stop men from drinking, and after that my husband has never been drunk again.

AE/SE: And that was how many years ago?

KK: This was ten years ago.

AE/SE: But how is it to come back to someone you have to get to know again and build a new confidence with? How is it to come back to the person who had done so much damage and . . .?

KK: At that time when my husband was at the hospital, the doctor called me and said, 'If you want to keep your husband sober, you have to do one thing: don't allow him to eat meat and fish, because when he eats fish or meat, he will always remember the taste of alcohol.' So we slowly stopped eating meat and fish. And I am feeling very good because now my husband is okay, though we are still suffering lots of things but one good thing is that my husband lives with me now and is in very good condition.

AE/SE: Seeing you and Devidas together, it seems like you have something good in common, humour or something.

KK: Now, when my husband is in front of others, he always says that he is a very good man because of his wife—because of her help. Nowadays he appreciates me.

And he says, 'Until your daughters get married, until then you are working. But after that you are staying home and only I will work.'

AE/SE: And Atish has come back home too? He's staying with the family now?

KK: Yes, Atish, yes.

AE/SE: Poonawala Chawl seems to be an enclosed neighbourhood. If something happens, like a husband is falling out of the system, do other women around or other families support? How is it treated in the neighbourhood?

KK: Nobody was supporting us, no, nobody was supporting . . . Only my father-in-law helped us, no one else.

AE/SE: So even though everyone can see that he is coming home drunk and falling around in the street, no one is doing anything?

KK: He was not falling here and there, he was always drunk and came directly to me. If he had not eaten well, because of the alcohol he would have died . . .

AE/SE: The house that you're living in, at Poonawala Chawl, I understand that it belonged to Devidas's father. You moved out of here and moved back in again, is that so?

KK: This room, now we are living in this room, it is now transferred to my husband. Before, it was in my father-in-law's name.

AE/SE: But last year when we were here, Bhimsen, Soni (his daughter) and her mother were also living in the house?

KK: Last year we were all living together here, but now, there is a former workshop of my father-in-law that the Bhimsen family is reconstructing. It has one room and Bhimsen and his family are living there right now.

AE/SE: You will be giving away your daughter, Anjali, in marriage. How do you foresee your daughter's and your coming grandchildren's future? Do you think Anjali will be happy?

KK: Her husband is very good and wealthy, he lives in Kolapur. Anjali will get a good husband.

I was always wondering if there would be any peace in my life—and I think this is the time of peace now, because all of my daughters are getting married, our son Atish has a good job and he is staying in our house. My husband is not drunk now. It is very good, no? This condition is very good.

14

THE WOMEN OF WASTELAND

Sharmila Joshi

ACROSS THE STREET

The fire started late at night. At four in the morning, when the women woke up to fill water, they saw the flames. Hanumanti was at home. 'There is a fire, a fire has started, they began to shout,' she recalls. Hanumanti went running barefoot across the bridge over the big drain and saw that her shed was on fire. The entire row of sheds was ablaze, their stock of discarded plastic and paper rising up in stinging smoke against the Dharavi skyline. Hanumanti stood and looked. 'We could not do anything,' she says.

On that Tuesday in February 2007, Hanumanti lost the business she had worked for decades to build. It happened to be a time when she had an unusually high stock of plastic, bought when rates were low in the market. She was waiting for the prices to rise before sorting and re-selling the material. The next morning, only a few charred storage drums remained, the shed and everything inside it were flattened, embers smouldered on the ground. Even the four street dogs Hanumanti kept in her shed were incinerated.

The police came, television crews arrived, but no one knew how the fire started. Hanumanti believes it was an act of arson. The recycling sector in Dharavi is competitive and territorial, and fights over land and material are common. Perhaps someone wanted her and the other tenants to vacate their sheds on the centrally located plot of land parallel to the arterial 60 Feet Road, or maybe it was an act of revenge. It is impossible to tell.

Hanumanti never fully recovered from the loss, either financially or emotionally. 'To this day, the distress and the memory of watching it all burn have not left me,' she says. After the fire, she and her daughter Laxmi stayed at the shed through days and nights, dousing the embers, clearing the debris. Work came to a standstill for three months while Hanumanti tried to recover from stress-induced high blood pressure. 'I struggled for months, but nobody helped me—the landlord, other businessmen, local politicians—nobody helped.' She pawned her gold jewellery and started again. 'Somehow, topsy-turvy, I have brought things back to this point,' she says.

We are sitting in Hanumanti Kamble's workshed, built with tin, plywood, some bricks and concrete on the same patch of land where the shed that burned stood four years ago. Sacks upon bulky sacks full of plastic are piled from floor to ceiling, the ground is thick with years of waste fragments. As before, an upturned plastic bin is offered to me to sit, a young boy brings tea in plastic pouches and it is poured into little plastic cups while we talk. A lone and scrawny dog now stays in Hanumanti's shed.

Like many others in recycling, Hanumanti started work as a sorter in a godown a quarter century ago. The owners had a contract with a pharmaceutical factory to use its waste. Hanumanti and other workers would sort through paper, plastic, medicine cartons, syringes. She worked at this godown for seven years for Rs 2.25 a day.

Hanumanti had grown up amid recycling. Her mother and uncles worked with glass waste, sorting bottles and other items by colour and quality. Her father intermittently worked in a textile mill and also brewed illicit liquor for sale. When he died, Hanumanti was seven. She had to start working to add to the family income. She would stand in the food rations line for others and get twenty-five or fifty paise, she carried bags and sacks for a tiny fee, she filled water during limited supply hours for neighbours for a monthly payment. 'We struggled a lot,' she says. 'We would earn whatever we could. At times, we would not get to eat properly for a week. It was a lot of poverty, hard work and effort.'

Despite her family's destitution, Hanumanti managed to go to school and studied till class ten. She has a sharp memory and can do complex calculations in her head. 'My children comment on how well I know numbers and accounts,' she laughs. 'I was good at studies, but who would educate me?' When she was thirteen, Hanumanti's mother and uncles arranged for her marriage to a farm worker. The young Hanumanti lived with her husband's family in a village in Karnataka, working on the farm land. 'My husband drank, he had other women. His family gave me no respect,' she recalls. 'If I worked, I would get to eat. If I could not work, there was no food for me.'

When Hanumanti was visiting her ailing mother in Mumbai, her husband, who had tuberculosis, died. Hanumanti went back to the village only for a day and returned to Dharavi. 'Laxmi was with me, she was three and a half years old,' she says. 'We had no money. I begged at the railway quarters in Sangli and got two idlis and fed Laxmi. I was three months pregnant with my second daughter. I returned to Mumbai for good.'

This return, at the age of eighteen, marked Hanumanti's entry into the recycling sector. After seven years in the godown sorting medical waste, Hanumanti started working on her own at the Mithi Creek. With Rs 200 as capital, she bought unused plastic from a godown, sorted and washed it according to a multi-stage process of recycling, and re-sold it for a tiny profit. Hanumanti did this every day for more than a decade, eventually earning Rs 100–200 a day, sometimes more, sometimes dealing at a loss.

At the time, the recycling business in Dharavi was less crowded and space was not so scarce. 'My place in the nullah was fixed,' Hanumanti, now in her mid-40s, says. 'But when the sale of huts and land began to escalate, the police started harassing me. They would not allow me to use the creek for work.' Hanumanti put together her savings, took a loan from local lenders, and rented a shed close to where she now works. It took her seven years to repay the high-interest loan. Just as she reached this milestone, the fire destroyed her business

The most important quality for any woman who wants to work in the recycling business in Dharavi is courage, Hanumanti says. 'The courage to work hard as well as the courage to confront people, both are required. Without that, a woman will not survive here.' We are sitting at the back door of her shed, facing a wasteland between buildings. Spools of ripped-out tape are glinting in the evening sun; yogurt containers, biscuit boxes, rubber soles, all kinds of garbage cover the ground. Children small and big, with or without sandals, with or without clothes, are playing on the waste.

Like other work sectors, the recycling world in Dharavi is hostile to women. People would not sell waste to Hanumanti when she first started, or they would quote exorbitant rates. 'When I went to the market, they would try to harass me or abuse me, the men would mock me,' she recalls. 'I learned to talk nicely to everyone, calling the men "brother", "baba", and kept working. I learned not to wear nice clothes or jewellery because that would attract unwanted attention. In a new business you learn as you go along, with a rhythm of loss and profit. But as women, we face additional hurdles and sexual harassment. Of a hundred men in this business, eighty are scoundrels. We have to constantly face such men.'

Years after her first husband died, Hanumanti married again. She did this, in part, as protection against being a single woman. She is entirely capable of looking after herself, she says, but having a husband around can reduce unwanted attention from other men. Her husband drinks a lot. When he is sober, he sporadically helps her. 'He does a bit of the work, but the real labour is mine. He is a husband in name only,' she says with a disdainful smile. 'I have to look after the house as well as the business. My entire family depends on me. I have no option but to keep working. Even after all these years, I cannot rest,' she says, her eyes always exhausted, her half-grey hair dishevelled.

Recently, two fans and a rusting bicycle were stolen from Hanumanti's shed. All godowns here, even those that are locked, are frequently burgled. 'Even if I ask a male worker to sleep in the godown, one man is no guarantee against a group of men who easily break the lock,' she says. 'Sometimes, the men who sleep there overnight are in partnership with the people who steal. Nobody can do anything about this problem.'

Complaining to the police does not help; the police don't take any action. Instead, they are a source of harassment. 'Every week, they come here,' Hanumanti says, pointing to the silver-grey tin door of her shed. 'All of them have to be paid *hafta* (weekly sum).' Extortion eats into the hard-earned incomes of people at the low end of the recycling business.

Rents for godowns can range from Rs 8,000 to Rs 20,000 or more, in addition to deposit amounts. Numerous other costs and overheads are due every month. The dealers who bring plastic to the godowns have to be paid a commission, the handcarts or tempos in which the sacks are brought have to be hired. The unsorted plastic, once available for free, has to be paid for by the kilo. Hanumanti employs four sorters at daily wages. After expenses, the godown operators are left with a modest profit, though when selling rates are high, the margins can be good.

When Hanumanti saves some money, she tries to help neighbours: for marriages, hospitalization, food, anything that is required. 'There is a lot of poverty here in Dharavi, a lot of people in need,' she says. She also purchases gold. She gave gold to her daughters when they got married. She now plans to give gold to her granddaughters and future daughters-in-law. 'If they look after me in my old age, that will be my good fortune,' she says. 'If they don't look after me, I will beg and live. Whatever happens, my children should never be penniless like I was. When my mother died, I had to borrow for her rites. I don't want my children to have to do that.'

Hanumanti has four children. Her eldest daughter Laxmi works in the recycling business; her younger daughter is at home, expecting a second child. Hanumanti's two sons, from her second husband, are fourteen and eleven. Both are in school. The younger boy, she says, is smart and will look after himself, but she worries about the older boy. 'I am at work all day,' she says. 'After school, the boys wander about and it is easy for them to get into the wrong company here and pick up bad habits.' For a while, Hanumanti tried to find a suitable school with a hostel outside Mumbai, to move her son away from this environment. 'Whatever the cost, I will put the money together somehow,' she had said. That didn't work, and now Hanumanti hopes her son will study and join the army as a *jawan* (private soldier).

At dusk every day, Hanumanti's son or a helper places the hens running around in the shed in an empty drum, which he covers with a sack. Sometimes, in the morning, an egg or two emerges along with the hens. The tin door to the shed is locked, and Hanumanti walks, barefoot, silver anklets shining against dark roughened skin, down the lane, towards 60 Feet Road and the bridge across the open drain, which will take her to her house. She stood at this bridge four years ago, watching her shed go up in flames. Now, the fear of fire is accompanied by the fear of Dharavi being demolished.

AT THE CREEK

Hanumanti is one of only four or five women who run their own plastic recycling business in Dharavi. Her shed is located to the east of 60 Feet Road. Spillovers of the sprawling recycling sector are located intermittently in other parts of Dharavi. The bulk of the recycling work in this part of Mumbai operates from a plot of land to the west of the arterial 60 Feet Road.

If you walk along this straight road, where a crumbling grey parapet separates the road from the slow-moving sludge of the broad open drain, you will reach one of the busiest hubs of the recycling business in Mumbai. The northern boundary of this sector is the open tract of land beyond which the swamp-like Mithi River merges into Mahim Creek. Two or three women run smaller plastic recycling businesses from makeshift sheds at the edge of this tract. This is where Laxmi, Hanumanti's daughter, works under a canopy made from poles of bamboo covered with tattered plastic and jute sheets, and pieces of cardboard. Here too there are sacks full of plastic items, though fewer than in Hanumanti's shed.

This is the edge of the so-called Tera Compound or 13th Compound. The area apparently consists of thirteen sub-divisions, or some say thirteen lanes intertwine here from one end to the other. It is difficult to count, with sub-lanes and micro-lanes branching off and multiplying in different directions, all brimming with godowns and an occasional bakery and hair-cutting salon.

Official records of licenced godowns—as the sheds or warehouses are called—are likely to be available (though not of the various sub-letting arrangements), but no one here knows precisely how many godowns or workers operate in 13th Compound.

Informal estimates range from 10,000 people working here to
200,000 including itinerants in the network of recycling.

In this crammed and compact patchwork of big and small
sheds, some of them three-tiered, a multi-layered process of
recycling unfolds every day, involving human beings who make a
living from the detritus of the consumption of others. Each
item is put through an assembly line of recycling, passing from
hand to hand, person to person, process to process, before it is
transformed into another raw or complete product.

An endless chain of items arrives here from all parts of
Mumbai, on handcarts and by hand; tempos and trucks load
and unload material along the impossibly narrow lanes, machines
clang and clack, metal is burned and melted to make reusable
sheets for factories outside Dharavi. Rags, sludge, congealed
paper, decades of fragments carpet the streets. At the creek
bordering 13th Compound, plastic items are burned in the
evenings to extract high-value metal parts. The acrid smoke
hovers over the area.

The ecosystem of recycling in Tera Compound has a finely
tuned internal logic: a matrix of buying and selling arrangements
is in place, people use work-specific terminology, successive
steps of the recycling process are well-established, and each
person specializes in one or more tasks. *Raddiwalas* or scrap
dealers, waste-pickers and *pheriwalas* or itinerant dealers deposit
daily collections at the sheds. Vehicle drivers and helpers unload
material at *kaantawalas* (dealers with a weighing scale). The
khaadiwalas work only along the creek. Then there are the *seths*
who own the godowns, the supervisors to whom they sub-let,
and the workers engaged in a million tasks—both men and the
bai log, the women who work in this sector. A few are shed-

owners, but most of the women work as sorters in the godowns or at home.

The workers are busy in numerous godowns, sorting plastic items, remaking cardboard boxes by cutting out the good portions from used boxes, putting the rubber soles of old footwear into a churner that breaks them into pellets, cleaning jerry cans and stacking them in gigantic piles on the roofs. Old washing machines are dissected in 13th Compound, their innards interchanged to make a workable 'new' machine, and the remaining metal and plastic parts are moved along for recycling. Computer keyboards are dismantled for their plastic and metal, old furniture is broken down or repaired, empty barrels of oil and paint are cleaned and prepared for a second life, while their virulent residues flow fluorescent in the open drains. Above all, there is plastic.

People who have smaller businesses, such as Laxmi Kamble, either buy the plastic items that are discarded or not used by the bigger warehouses, or a second lot of lower-quality from the kaantawalas or from waste-pickers. All the buying and selling arrangements are more or less fixed along the long chain; people know each other in the business. 'What the godown owners buy and keep is number one, that plastic is strong, not mixed,' Laxmi says. 'What we get is mixed, number two items, for which the purchase price as well as the selling price is low. Then we start our work, separating metal parts like wires and bolts, sorting them and then immersing the plastic in saltwater in drums to further separate heavy and light pieces. I deal with 15–20 types of plastic.'

Everyone who works here knows an entire typology of plastic, terms that are a mix of the colloquial and technical: rough, soft,

PVC, colour LD, ball-cage LD, *kadak, phuga, dubban.* 'I've heard that there are more than 135 types of plastic here from all over the world,' Laxmi says. 'Anyone who wants to work here has to understand plastic. If a woman has worked with plastic, she can survive here, as a sorter, a dealer, or in her own business. But to be able to do that we need minute knowledge of plastic. Even after years in the business, I don't know a-to-z but only a-to-f of plastic. I don't know all the types. This is intricate knowledge acquired over years of labour.'

This land where the boundary between waste and self is blurred, where people work and live on and off waste, looks different to those on the inside. The waste that merges with their lives is invaluable, it is the raw material they work with, it is the thing that sustains them and their families. 'Have you seen any other *gaav* (homeland) like this?' Laxmi asks, standing by her windswept canopy near the creek, vehicles rumbling by on the bridge above. 'This place can give you everything. Anyone who comes here can find some work. At the end of the day, no one goes hungry here.'

Official identity paraphernalia—ration cards, voter cards, house survey slips, rent receipts—is prized here as an uncertain buffer against possible eviction in the future. The papers are not a guarantee of space in the new buildings if Dharavi is restructured. Even if all the godowns in 13th Compound can provide all the required proofs of occupancy, the various tenants who sub-let will be at a loss, Laxmi says.

'Perhaps the big godown owners will benefit if they are given work spaces in the new building. But the others will die a slow death. Where will people like us do our plastic sorting and washing? There are many people living in Dharavi on rent for three generations. They don't have the income or capital to buy their own room. What will happen to them?' Everyone here talks about a secure and safe space for their recycling work. 'What we need,' Laxmi emphasizes, 'is a sliver of space in this city.'

We are at Laxmi's makeshift shed, next to half-a-dozen other sheds, close to an incline leading to the Sion–Mahim link road. When it pours during the Mumbai monsoon, water streams down the hillock of mud and waste, and rainwater also drips through the flimsy roofs of the work sheds. On days of incessant rain, work has to be halted and the small businesses lose their daily earnings. If the rain is light, Laxmi fortifies the roof of her shed and tries to keep working.

Unlike Hanumanti's shed, which can be locked, Laxmi's canopy remains open. She ties and covers the sacks for the night, but there is no way to guard the material. A few hundred rupees paid to local heavyweights as 'rent' does not ensure any protection. 'Thefts are common,' Laxmi says. 'And usually done by people in the same business, because only they will know the value of waste material or what is worth stealing. They simply pick up our plastic and keep it in their godowns. Because all the material is the same and in similar sacks, it is impossible to distinguish what belongs to whom, or to "prove" that it has been stolen. We cannot do anything about this, we live with it. If we catch someone stealing, we fight and try to recover our material.'

An upturned computer monitor has been dusted for me to sit on. Laxmi, who is close to thirty, recalls a fight some years ago with a man who abused her mother Hanumanti and stole from her godown. 'I used a hammer to hit him on the head,' she says. 'He needed eight stitches in hospital. I went to the police station myself, a case of half-murder [assault] was registered against me, and my mother got me out on bail.'

If a woman is unable to face the harassment, 'she will be torn apart here,' Laxmi says. 'If you cannot fight back, if you remain quiet, you cannot function. If you talk to them nicely, they think you are simple and can be taken advantage of. Talking roughly is a way of ensuring that they stay away, that they don't try to molest women. I was shy and scared at one time, but after being in the plastic line I have learned how to deal with men. If I am hit four times, I will hit back at least once. If I am abused, I abuse back. I am not like that at home or with my neighbours of course. At work, it is a different environment. I decided whatever happens, I will fight. I dug my heels in and stayed.'

If the gaze of the men at work is lustful or hostile, the people outside the recycling sector view the workers as dirty. 'People think that we work in dirt, that our children are dirty, that our nature and character is not good, we get multiple diseases,' Laxmi says. 'They feel a sense of revulsion about us.'

Once, two boys in Laxmi's daughter's school started teasing her that her mother was a 'garbage woman'. 'My daughter, who is nine, came home crying, saying she will not go to school,' she says. Laxmi went to the school and talked to the boys. 'I asked them what their fathers do. One said his father is a tailor, the other said his father does zari work. I explained my work to them, told them that just as your fathers work, this girl's mother works to run the house. Then the teacher asked me, don't you feel bad about this work? I asked her: why should I feel bad? You may think it is "dirty" work, I don't.'

The nature of the work, however, causes recurrent health problems. 'From morning to evening workers handle waste and we get dirty, and at the end of the day there may not even be enough water for a wash,' Laxmi says. The toxic smoke from the burning of waste results in acute respiratory problems; Laxmi has asthma. Tuberculosis is common, especially amongst workers who drink heavily. Carbon and other residues cause severe skin rashes. Workers handle toxic chemicals from used oil and paint drums. The women working in the godowns as sorters talk of constant backaches and stomach aches from sitting on the floor all day or lifting heavy sacks.

Before she came to recycling, Laxmi worked as a domestic helper in Mahim. Domestic work tied her down to a fixed schedule, she says. 'I had little time left for my daughter. All day, it was running and rushing, and still I did not make enough money. Recycling work gives me some control over my time; I can drop off and bring my daughter from school in between working at the shed. And if I invest one rupee and work really hard, I can make at least 1.50.'

As a young girl, Laxmi's mother Hanumanti wanted to become a nurse. Then she had the same dream for her daughters. But Laxmi got engaged to be married after studying till class seven; Laxmi's younger sister did a course in nursing but has not worked as a nurse. Now Laxmi has the same dream for her young daughter. 'If not a doctor,' she says, 'I want her to be educated and become a nurse.'

We are sitting at the bridge near Laxmi's shed, along Dharavi's northern border. The glass-fronted buildings of Bandra-Kurla Complex gleam in the sunlight in the distance. From the bridge you get a panoramic view of 13th Compound, its roofs miraculously balancing mountains of jerry cans waiting to be recycled. Someone has set on fire another heap of plastic at the creek. Its flames are reflected in Laxmi's exhausted, watchful eyes. Dark, stinging smoke rises across the evening sky.

Beyond 13th Compound, off 60 Feet Road, Hanumanti is in her tiny windowless one-room home abutting the large open drain. She is preparing for another day, praying she will not wake up to see her godown going up in flames.

15

WATER WARS

Freny Manecksha

Huge pipelines supplying water to Mumbai from the lakes of Maharashtra pass through the very bowels of Dharavi. For the families in the Sunaullah Compound, who live alongside the pipelines, and the many thousands who live nearby, these giant tubes serve as walkways, an easy alternative to the labyrinthine lanes that run through most Dharavi settlements. Ironically, though, the water that flows beneath the pedestrians' feet is difficult for them to access. As Rafiq bhai, a dealer in scrap and recycled waste, ruefully said, 'I work and walk along this huge pipeline but pay a heavy price to get anything out of it. The only happy time I can recall was when the pipeline sprang a leak two years ago and we could revel in the gushing waters.'

The challenge of procuring water has shaped the lives of countless Dharavi residents over the years. For some, water has proved to be a lucrative business, as with the local dons who have established themselves as part of a water mafia. But for most, getting water has been a back-breaking, time-consuming domestic chore that colours all aspects of daily life—health and hygiene, of course, but even a more fundamental matter like physical safety. Fetching water and rationing it have been the cause of domestic squabbles and quarrels with neighbouring families. Water is a hot-button issue in local elections. Entire communities have fought furiously over disputes related to it. In some grim incidents water has been the flashpoint for terrible violence and brutal assault—even murder.

Until the 1970s, when authorities finally sanctioned water and electric connections, Dharavi was denied all civic amenities. Neighbourhoods created their own irregular network of systems for basic necessities and services like water, drainage and electricity. Today, whilst some neighbourhoods with high-rise buildings can boast of proper toilets with taps and some standard of sanitation, the poorer sections of Dharavi, like Sunaullah Compound where Rafiq bhai works, continue with an informal system of water procurement. The standard line goes that the topography of this neighbourhood—it's swampy under the pipelines and there is a large dumping ground of recyclable waste near the row of homes—makes it difficult for the BMC to set up a network of pipelines and taps with water meters. Some residents, however, believe that local dons and water thieves are determined to keep the government away.

On a torrid day in May, with the city reeling under water cuts, I visit the Sunaullah Compound in the north-western corner of Dharavi. Stepping off the Mahim Bridge I descend below street level on a crooked flight of stairs. This leads me into a narrow alley that twists and turns before bringing me to the two pipelines alongside which some hundred families reside in parallel rows of shanty tin-sheds or cubicles.

Outside one of them sits Fatima, meticulously unwinding copper wires from a circuit as part of her work in the recycling business. In her mid-forties, Fatima, who has lived here for the past five years, exudes a brisk and robust spirit. A goat tethered to the tin door makes a desperate bid to chew up my kurta as Fatima explains the features of their rudimentary water supply and sanitation systems. I learn that although these families possess television sets, chairs, and a 'kapbard' (cupboard) as one child proudly tells me, there is no question of having a toilet or washbasin or even one's own tap.

Fatima has a *mori*, or wet area, where the water is stored in a small tank, some drums, buckets and barrels or *hundis* (special utensils traditionally meant to store up to ten litres of water). Family members, particularly the women, can bathe here and wash in some degree of privacy.

Clothes are generally washed outside the house near the deep trenches that function as drains carrying water, bits of garbage and human waste. People use the trenches as toilets. Else men and women must defecate in the open, often near the railway tracks.

Like many others, Fatima is dependent on one of the private networks operated by Dharavi's water mafia. She takes me to the communal water tap that she shares with the others. The ten-minute walk entails balancing atop the pipeline, clambering over a mound of garbage, and then walking along a small strip. Water is provided in the early mornings and again in the evenings. Although it is only mid-afternoon, little girls are already crowding around the tap, talking and playing games. However, an array of containers—jerry cans, plastic bottles, drums, hundis and so on—neatly set out in rows points to the existence of a queue system.

'If we don't line up early we may not get our turn till 7.00 p.m. and then the supply may dry up,' says Fatima, who averages two hours in a day collecting water. Filling the household's water is woman's work in rural India, but in Dharavi the gender barrier is being breached. Most of the women in Dharavi contribute to the family's income through various home-based industries and have a busy work schedule. Fatima's husband, Aslam Ansari, who works for an NGO, and her fourteen-year-old son both pitch in to help as they know how arduous it can be.

Mangal Kashinath Jadhav also works in the scrap recycling business. She keeps a 200-litre drum in her home that she uses for washing and bathing and has to refill every four or five days. Umesh, her son, who has been entrusted with this domestic chore, is a hearty youth in his twenties, but he grimaces and points to his shoulders as he describes his day. 'My body is so sore,' he says. 'I have to lug a ten-litre drum up and down for at least eight trips on the days I have to fill water. And for that I have to get up at the unearthly hour of 4.00 a.m. That is because the morning supply is only from 6.00 a.m. to 8.00 a.m. It takes me at least two hours to fill up the water and by six o'clock the lines are already huge,' he complains.

For those who live in the hutments that fringe Dharavi, the task of fetching water assumes herculean proportions. Rafiq bhai remembers the ordeal he faced for the two years he spent in the Nai Bustee. 'We had to cross the main road, go down a steep flight of stairs to the Narang Compound and then make the one-kilometre trek back to our hutment. Sometimes the pressure was so low it would take half an hour just to fill up four water bottles.' Today Rafiq bhai lives in the M.K. Lala Chawl with his mother, two sisters and a niece. He pays a neighbour Rs 100 a month to fill his drum and twelve hundis each day from the neighbour's taps.

For Daulat Bi, fetching water is especially harrowing because she is pregnant and finds it difficult to carry her *dabbas* or tins of water up and down. She is apprehensive about the monsoon when the ground will turn slippery. 'I'm willing to pay someone to help me out but everyone is just too busy,' she says. 'This is no place for pregnant women.'

Lakshmi Garaware or Maami (aunty), one of the oldest residents in the Sunaullah Compound, refuses to even engage in a lengthy conversation. Dispirited and tired, she says, 'Nothing has changed since I came here as a young girl. My feet are swollen and I am exhausted in this heat but that daughter-in-law of mine refuses to help me. I don't really have the time to discuss this with you.'

Factory work intensifies the water problems, as leather tanners, potters and recyclers use large amounts to run their businesses. 'When you have to recycle plastic bags you literally grind them down which needs huge quantities of water to wash the plastic at least three times. We have no alternative but to shell out at least Rs 300–400 a month to private suppliers for the provision of pipes and taps in our godowns,' Rafiq bhai explains. This means that Rafiq has to think twice before he can quench his thirst. 'On a hot, humid day one longs for a cool glass of water but eateries and tea shops will not give you that for free. You have to pay for a cup of tea if you want to drink water as well.'

Adjoining the Sunaullah Compound is S.K. Nagar, the industrial unit where home-based small-scale businesses are carried out. Work here includes making tarpaulin sheets for protection during monsoon, stitching gunny bags, recycling old oil tins and producing *chuna*, or quicklime, which is Jahanbanu's primary source of income. A single mother of six children, Jahanbanu works out of her multi-spaced cubicle that functions both as a work and living area. Her two young daughters are helping her out, as it is vacation time.

Using a moulding machine, she fills up hundreds of ampoules with chunam. Bits of chunam are everywhere—stuck on her glasses, staining her clothes, all over the floor before her. The white powder floats thick and heavy in the air. For Jahanbanu a bath and shampoo are luxuries she cannot indulge in too often. Her work is labour intensive and there is simply no time or energy to fill up more than the two drums of water she currently uses. Even that demands considerable effort because, as is the case for so many others, her day begins at 4.00 a.m.

As Laxmi Kamble, who once lived in Sunaullah Compound, says, 'We try to get by using the bare minimum for bathing and we change our clothes only every 3–4 days.'

Besides being extremely frugal in their use of water, Dharavi women also resort to various forms of water recycling. Mehnaz, one of the women with small children, tells me, 'I don't throw away the water I use to wash my rice and vegetables. I just use it again to wash the vessels.'

Dharavi residents pay disproportionately large sums for the amounts they consume. The average rate for getting access to a communal water tap at Sunaullah Compound and other neighbouring areas is Rs 100 per family per month with profits flowing into the pockets of slumlords and the water mafia. No concessions are made even if the family is going out of town or has been unable to fill up water.

On another day I meet with a don who is an old hand in

Dharavi's water business. He exudes the confidence of a man who has not only learnt to survive in these slums but has mastered the socio-economic dynamics of it. In his small room he holds forth on the art of water *chorigiri* (pilferage).

'I came here thirty years ago. At that time we used to have to go to the *shamshaan bhoomi* (cremation grounds) to fetch water. It was in the late 1970s after the BMC's twenty-four-inch pipeline was laid that we began our network.'

Hacking into these main pipelines and siphoning water off to the slums are highly specialized jobs but there is no shortage of technical expertise in Dharavi, which is home to hundreds of plumbers. At least fifty or sixty of them make a living solely by siphoning water and redistributing it to Dharavi residents. However, there are only three or four men who possess the expertise to actually hack into the pipeline.

The don rattles off their names and then describes the nature of the work. 'One needs to pierce these huge pipes with a specially designed punch which is made by the *lohar* (ironsmith). The punch is placed on the pipeline and then deftly hammered in. Carried out in the dead of the night, the operation is dangerous and requires skill because the flying shards can permanently damage the eyes. Each piercing with the punch costs at least Rs 1,500,' he says.

Once the pipeline has been hacked with the punch, another pipe is fitted in. The depth and width of this pipe will determine the flow of water and according to this 'setting' the charges are levied. A network of smaller pipes siphons the water from the pipe that has been installed into the main pipeline and carries it to taps in the neighbourhoods or even directly into people's homes. In addition to the setting of the pipe in the hacked pipeline, the water prices are also determined by the distance and length of the new pipeline used. For a distance of ninety feet some seven pipes are required and the cost works out to Rs 20,000. Typically five households share the expenses.

In comparison, the cost for acquiring a legal BMC water supply is around Rs 40,000, which includes an initial deposit, a water meter and the laying of the pipelines. I ask if the sanctioning of water meters and pipes by the civic body has impacted the chorigiri. With a contemptuous look he dismisses any suggestion of competition. 'Those who opt for the regular connections don't get an uninterrupted water supply but we can guarantee them that. If the pressure is low in the pipe we just use the booster pump to pull it up. The BMC is all about making gestures. Once it grandly distributed hand pumps because they said they would provide water from the boring wells. What happened? The groundwater levels fell. There was no water in the pump and people sold them off. And you have to wait for months before you get a connection. *Chori* (stolen) connections are instant,' he declares.

Significantly, the use of motor pumps to snatch the meagre supply can lead to acrimonious quarrels in the various communities. Those whose connections are at the tail end of the pipeline are naturally incensed to find that the water has petered out. Laxmi Kamble, who now lives in Kamla Nagar, says the frustrations of trying to fill water coupled with the enervating heat of summer can explode into physical fights as residents try desperately to fill up the water and object to those who have the pumps running.

The don himself shares a poignant example of how water became the flashpoint for a particularly violent incident. 'Do any of you know how Gopinath Colony got its name?' he asks hitching up his lungi. 'It is named after Gopinath, the CPI [Communist Party of India] leader, who was killed some thirty-five years ago. It was Gopi who enabled people to draw water from a tap outside the party office. One day a man abused and lashed out at his own sister for not filling the utensils quickly enough. Gopi stepped in and reprimanded the man and a fracas broke out. A little while later the enraged man came back and killed Gopi in anger.' Today the small signboards in the colony carry the moniker Shaheed (Martyr) Gopinath to commemorate the man who died helping the urban marginalized.

Rais Khan, a social activist who is now recording Dharavi's chequered history, remembers vividly the problems his family used to face in his youth. 'We were terrorized by a local *dada*—toughie—called Villondon. We would stand for hours in the line to collect water and every so often our buckets remained empty because he threatened us and wouldn't allow us near the tap. Then one day Villondon and a barber who played loud music got into a scrap over the noise and the police were called in. We mustered the courage to complain about him and after that things got a little better. His men actually started urging us to go forward with our buckets.'

Not just the police but even local-level politicians and leaders recognize the obligation to at least pay lip service to the people's pressing need for water. Recalls Rafiq bhai, 'In the Nai Bustee we once told an aspiring political leader it was a question of no water, no votes. He promised us a pipeline and we got it when he won. We were very happy for a month and then the pipeline went dry . . . as dry as his promises.'

Seediya (name changed), a plumber whom I met in the narrow

alleys of Shastri Nagar, tells a similar story of broken promises. Born and raised in Dharavi, Seediya studied only up to class four, but like many other residents here he has picked up the skills he needs to make a decent living. Juggling work for the BMC with moonlighting for the chori water business, Seediya has seen both sides of the water business and is sceptical about the BMC's will to deliver. 'See these pipelines laid down by the BMC,' he says pointing them out. 'It's very good of the local leader to get the work done. But it's been three weeks and still not a drop.'

'Here, look at my hands,' he says thrusting out worn, calloused palms, 'I've been working as a plumber ever since I was eleven years old. My father was physically disabled. My mother went blind. But I learnt my trade under Billa Papa. He taught me everything. He was my guru, my ustaad.'

Displaying the pride of a true professional, he proceeds to give a graphic description along with some miming of the mechanics of his trade—how the punch is laid on a pipe, the tonk tonk tonk of the hammer, and the placing of the pipe. He explains that setting the new pipe into the hacked pipeline requires some calculation. 'Take Sunaullah Compound. Because it lies below the huge pipelines we have to rig up a special extension. Then we have to do a very thorough estimate of the requirements of the people. If there are twenty members, how do we distribute the water equally?'

From his conversation, replete with technical terms and details, it becomes evident that the chori business flourishes because it is carried out with an expertise and zeal that is perhaps lacking in those carrying out the official civic works. Seediya is also representative of the Dharavi spirit which can adapt to changing circumstances and situations with amazing ease.

'The chorigiri provides us plumbers with enough work. There's a constant need to keep replacing pipelines which get corroded because many of them lie in the drains. Am I scared of getting caught whilst doing the illegal works? No. I know some BMC officials [he names one of them] and all I have to do is make one phone call. I continue doing jobs for them as well, so they know me,' he adds.

16

SCHOOLING DHARAVI: *ANGREZI KA REVOLUTION, PRIVATE KA SAPNA*

Sameera Khan

If Zubeida Khatoon has her way, all her four children will graduate from English-medium schools. '*Inshallah!*,' murmurs the thirty-year old widow who lives in Dharavi Transit Camp, one of the many slum neighbourhoods in the vicinity of Sion railway station that make up the larger settlement of Dharavi.

Zubeida earns a meagre Rs 250 a week by doing home-based piecemeal work such as stitching buttons on export clothing. She supplements that income by renting out a room above her house. Her everyday life revolves around housework, child care, and completing as many pieces of stitched clothing as she possibly can. Yet Zubeida, who herself was educated only till class seven in the Urdu language, has a keen understanding of the world around her. '*Jo achhi Angrezi jaanta hai, wahi zindagi mein aage badhenge* (Only those who know good English will move ahead in life),' she says, her eyes suddenly afire and her voice a tad sharper.

English, she and many others in Dharavi believe, is the language of agency, the language that will open doors to higher education, specialized professional and technical courses and, of course, to better, higher paying jobs. Several young people in her slum community have studied in Hindi and Urdu languages and now work in retail outlets selling TV sets and posh cars. Zubeida is hopeful that fluency in English will ensure superior jobs for her brood.

But the journey ahead is not going to be easy or cheap. When her twelve-year-old son, Sharique Shaikh, graduates from class seven in April 2012, he will have to leave the Dharavi Transit Camp English School No. 1, the free municipal corporation-run school that he currently attends, and be forced to scramble for a fairly expensive class eight seat—costing anything between Rs 250 to Rs 600 per month—at a local private English-medium school.[1] That is because, though the Brihanmumbai Municipal Corporation (BMC) runs more than forty tuition-free schools in Dharavi, in no less than seven language mediums, almost all of them are primary schools that go only till class seven. The one secondary school (till class ten) run by the corporation at Dharavi Transit Camp is a fairly new Urdu-medium school that is only open to girls. For a population of almost a million people, obviously this is woefully inadequate.

---

[1]Several parents also mentioned that in addition to the regular fees, some private schools also demand 'donations' at the time of admission—anything upwards of Rs 30,000–50,000 for a seat. Other private schools adjust that initial donation against the monthly fees.

So students like Sharique (and later his twin brothers Armaan and Rehman, now in class three), who wish to study further, have to look for private secondary schools, of which there are more than a dozen in Dharavi. A few are partially government-aided but most of them are wholly private with varying fee structures.

'For my older son Shafique, who is now in class ten at a private English-medium school in Dharavi, I somehow put together the funds with great difficulty. I now pay Rs 300 per month for his school fees. But how will I afford a similar private-school education for my other three children?' asks Zubeida, a note of despair now entering her voice. Even the extra money her father-in-law, an ageing barber, gives her will not be enough. 'This worry keeps me awake at night,' she says.

Zubeida is attending school today. So are the other parents of Dharavi Transit Camp (DTC) municipal school. Inside the bursting-to-the-seams school hall, parents are being instructed about the importance of participating in the new, enlarged and allegedly more powerful parent–teacher school management committee which is being set up as per the recent Right to Education Act.

If there seem to be a lot of parents, it's because this municipal school has a lot of children. More than 1,200 children study in two shifts at DTC English School No. 1. Another 800-plus students study in DTC English School No. 2, which is housed in the same building. The building also has the DTC Urdu School with over 1,400 children, and another two Urdu Shramik

schools with over 1,600 students. The venue also runs two
shifts of DTC Marathi School (almost 450 children) and one
shift each of DTC Telugu and Tamil schools (with more than
200 students). Between 7.00 a.m. and 6.30 p.m., the building
holding these multi-level, multi-shift and multi-lingual schools
is humming with the activity and noise of nearly 6,000 students.
To teach them, there are about 120 teachers on the rolls and not
all of them show up every day.

Unlike many other municipal schools which have a run-down,
aged appearance, the Transit Camp school looks fairly spruced
up thanks to its recent repair and renovation at the cost of
almost Rs 4 crore under the aegis of the Sarva Shiksha Abhiyan.[2]
The entire facility consists of a modest three-storeyed building
and, across from that, a set of low-rise buildings that resemble
trailers. There is a small open ground between the main building
and the trailers.

The shrill sound of the bell at half past noon announces the
end of one school shift and the start of another. Books are
closed, blackboards are erased and children rush up and down
the staircase. Outside the hall, Sunama Bi, who has two children
in the school, echoes the same concerns as Zubeida Khatoon.
Her biggest worry is what to do with the children once they
finish class seven at the municipal school. 'You don't want them
to stop studying, you don't want to send girls too far away from
home to study, you want an English-medium education locally,

---

[2]Sarva Shiksha Abhiyan is the Government of India's flagship programme
for achievement of universalization of elementary education. It seeks to
open new schools where no schooling exists and strengthen existing school
infrastructure through provision of additional grants, classrooms, toilets,
strengthening teacher capacity, etc.

you want to save money by not sending to private schools, but what do you do if there is no government secondary school nearby?' she asks. 'Why just renovate the school building? Why not also scale the school up to SSC level?' [3]

Another parent, Aas Mohammed Sheikh, who runs a *zari karkhana* (embroidery unit) on 90 Feet Road, also wants to discuss the quality of English education in a government school. Currently his son, Asif, is in class one of the English-medium section and his daughter, Shifa Parveen, studies in class three of the Urdu-medium section of the DTC school. He wants both to be fluent in English, so he has enrolled them both in what he calls 'double tuition'—which is morning and evening supplementary classes in English-language skills. 'The English taught in government schools is not of the same level as in private schools, so I have to ensure that my children are not left behind and acquire more than adequate proficiency in the language,' says the thirty-two-year-old father, who feels the additional expense of a few hundred rupees every month is worth it. As he walks away, he turns around to ask me, '*Madam, private mein daloon kya?* (Should I put them in a private school?) I feel they will study better there.'

In fact, a study has shown that slum children in private English-medium schools did 246 per cent better on standardized English tests than children in government schools.[4]

---

[3]SSC or Secondary School Certificate is the Maharashtra State Board school examinations at the level of class ten.

[4]This study by James Tooley and Pauline Dixon, 'Private Schools Serving the Poor: A Case Study from India', CfBT Report, Reading, 2003, is quoted on p. 96 of Nandan Nilekani, *Imagining India: Ideas for the New Century*, Penguin Allen Lane, 2008.

However, most of the children of the Indian poor go to government schools—that is if they make it to school. Marred by an image of poor quality teaching, truant teachers, bureaucratic systems and high dropout rates, government school education is often the only option, a grim choice for the children of the poor. 'When poor parents are forced to send their child to a municipal school, that is when a child experiences discrimination at the first level,' says Bhau Korde, a seventy-three-year-old Dharavi-based social activist and retired school administrator. 'The child knows "I am poor, so I go to municipal school"'.

'The government spends crores but the output is zero, the quality of graduates from municipal schools is abysmal,' says Korde, who claims that on an average the BMC spends close to Rs 13 crore in a single academic year to provide students school uniforms, shoes, books and a one-time meal.

Yet, paradoxically, Korde is not in favour of private schooling. He believes that most private schools, particularly those in slums like Dharavi, are only marginally better than municipal schools. 'The answer is not private English-medium schools but putting our energies towards improving the municipal schools. In fact, we don't need more English-medium schools; what we need are good English-language teachers in vernacular-medium schools,' he says. He suggests a radical mass movement (also perhaps undoable) to shake up things wherein all kids under fourteen, including those of the middle class and elite, are put in government schools. 'Within two years, you will see a change in the system. Middle-class parents will not sit still; they will demand accountability from the government educational system and change it,' he chuckles.

Korde helped administer a private school in Sion for forty years, so he is well-versed in the challenges faced by government schools. For the last four years, he has helped with the implementation of the renovations at the Dharavi Transit Camp municipal school. This has included renovating the entire building and its premises, augmenting the school's resources, and upgrading the skills of its teachers and administrators. 'We found that children would go home to use the toilet because the ones in school were in such pathetic condition,' he says.

Korde understands the problems faced by government schools as being two-fold: the hierarchy and bureaucracy in the school system and the lack of accountability among municipal school teachers despite their earning more than average wages. 'The parents who send their children to municipal schools in Dharavi are poor and busy with making ends meet. So they don't have time to meet with the school authorities or follow up on school issues,' he says. 'As a result, these parents demand virtually no accountability from the school or from the teachers.'

However, teachers working in these schools face considerable challenges. Many of them are forced to teach large classes of 40–60 students and often two classes simultaneously. Usually a single municipal school class teacher has to teach all the subjects to his or her class. This happens not just at the primary school level but even in middle school (classes five to seven), where there are many subjects.

Another impediment to student learning is the standardized, rote teaching system which encourages memorization over innovation and does not take into account how students process knowledge. Arindam Bose, a researcher at the Homi Bhabha Centre for Science Education at the Tata Institute of Fundamental Research, has been doing his doctoral fieldwork at the DTC municipal school for almost a year now. In an attempt to understand the kids' everyday mathematical knowledge, he has been closely interacting with students from classes five, six and seven. 'While the number representation of many children may be flawed, several children have good number orality and practical mathematical skills. For example, they can count money very well,' says Bose.

Many of the children are sent out of the home from a young age to buy provisions from local shops, or made to sit at a neighbourhood store and do *dhanda*. Others work in a home-based industry or workshop part-time. As a result, their general numerical skills are often above the mark. Unfortunately, this out-of-the-classroom knowledge of the students is not harnessed optimally by teachers within the classroom. 'Instead of getting to know the children and the reality of their everyday lives and using that information to make their teaching more engaging, teachers end up only focusing on the set curriculum,' Bose points out.

To be fair, all the non-academic duties and engagements foisted on teachers by the municipal corporation leave little time for them to try innovative teaching techniques. 'So the focus remains solely on finishing the syllabi,' says Bose, who also makes regular forays into the homes of his students. Some of his students study in the school's morning shift (from 7.00 a.m. to 12.30 p.m.) and then work from 2.00 p.m. to 10.30 p.m. in a Dharavi karkhana. 'The learning they do there needs to be joined to the learning they do in school. If we can join those two streams of knowledge, we can change the quality of learning in municipal schools,' he says.[5]

[5]See A. Bose and K. Subramaniam, 'Exploring School Children's Out of School Mathematics' in B. Ubuz, (ed.), Proceedings of the 35th Conference of the International Group for the Psychology of Mathematics Education (PME35), vol. 2, Ankara, Turkey, 2011, pp. 177–84.

In the mornings, it is class five, division A. In the afternoons, it converts to class two, division A. But it is always the infamous 'Slumdog Millionaire' classroom. The only school scene that was shot in the Oscar-winning film was shot here on the first floor of the Bharatratna Dr Babasaheb Ambedkar Vidyalaya, a private, unaided English-medium school, in the heart of Dharavi.

In the film, when the young Jamal Malik and his brother Salim make a late entry into the crowded classroom—so packed-to-the-gills that blue-uniformed students squat all over the floor and even at the foot of the blackboard—the teacher throws a volume of *The Three Musketeers* at them. When Jamal is not able to even open the book properly, the teacher thrashes him with the same hardcover and sneers, 'What do you think of yourselves?'

Thayapa H. Santi, principal of the Ambedkar school since its inception two decades ago, is not particularly amused at the way schooling in slums has been depicted in the movie. On the one hand, there is the fame that comes with being in an internationally recognized award-winning film; on the other, the troubling portrayal of the school. Worst of all, 'they made our students don the blue uniforms of municipal school children for that scene', says Santi, who also acknowledges that the Danny Boyle film unit funded the benches and tables for the new second-floor classrooms in return for shooting space.

There is also the delicate matter of how slums in general have been portrayed in the film and slum kids in particular. Santi shrugs off the question, saying people in Dharavi don't take the image of the slum as depicted in the film seriously. 'They know for themselves what an industrious and hardworking place Dharavi is,' says the forty-five-year-old principal who gave up his dream of a job in the Indian Administrative Services to help run the school. 'And now by educating our children and that too in the English language, we are making them competitive and ready for the world outside.'

With 2,000 students on its rolls, the Ambedkar school is widely regarded as one of the leading private English-medium schools in Dharavi. It was established in 1990 by the Andhra Karnataka Dalita Varga Sangha, a non-profit community organization of Dalits mainly from the neighbouring districts of Gulbarga (Karnataka) and Mehboobnagar (Andhra Pradesh). It continues to receive funds from the group and its members. The idea was to offer English-medium education from kindergarten to SSC level to 'those groups who typically would not get access to an English-language education at the school level, namely poor lower-caste and minority groups in Dharavi,' explains Santi.

It has taken much time and sweat to see positive results. In March 1994, when the first batch of five students from the Ambedkar school appeared for the SSC examinations, not one of them cleared the state board. In 1996, five of the thirty-one students who appeared for the exams passed. The next year only one passed. 'Those early days were very rough,' recollects Santi.

To fix things, Santi implemented a system that met the students' needs. Many of the new kids at the school were coming with no English language skills. They couldn't follow the syllabus at all. For the first six months of the first term, Santi instituted the translation method of teaching wherein every subject was taught in an Indian language that the child understood and also in English. Extra remedial classes were added. Class ten students were required to stay in school till 4.00 p.m. to finish homework. They also had to attend special classes in the Diwali vacations.

Santi ensured the kids had a chance to do their homework. 'In Dharavi, the home atmosphere is often not conducive to studying. Houses are small or there is some home-based industry taking up the space,' he says. To help, he keeps some school classrooms open day and night and during all holidays for students, ex-students and even students from other schools to come in and study.

The accommodations worked. In March 2001, 80 per cent of the students sitting for the SSC board exams passed. But it was in March 2003 when they tasted true success—with a pass percentage of more than 95 per cent. Twenty-three students appeared for the SSC exams that year and only two failed. By 2011, many more students were sitting for the exams. Of the ninety-four students that gave the SSC exams in March 2011, seventy-eight students cleared the exam, with two students receiving a high score of 90.91 per cent. Even Bhau Korde admits, 'Santi's school is very good because of Santi's relentless push towards excellence.'

The parents of the children work as daily wage earners, manual labourers, BMC sweepers, railway employees and domestic labourers. But Santi is clear that family or linguistic background or caste status should not hold back Dharavi's youngsters. 'They should not have a small vision but a big vision for their lives and for that they need an English-language school education,' he says.

Santi did his initial schooling in the Telugu medium in

Mumbai and then went to an English-language college to study commerce. At first he found the technical-economic jargon confusing and frequently referred to the dictionary because he was too shy to raise his hand in class. But when he and his brother graduated from college in the late 1980s, they were the first ever graduates from their lower-caste community in their village of Aminpur in Mehboobnagar district.

Increasingly Dalit activists have argued that the access of lower castes to English education is an important step in their emancipation.[6] Not only does English open up job opportunities, but it also helps unify various lower-caste groups across the country and dismantles some of the caste and power hierarchies that arise when lower-caste members speak only their native language.

For Pappu Mandal, eighteen, English is the key to success at the next level. He graduated from the Ambedkar school in 2009 and is currently pursuing science at Khalsa College. 'That one skill gives one so much self-confidence,' says Mandal. 'I have a classmate in college who is a 90 per cent topper from a Hindi-medium school but he can't speak English, so he always feels left out. He does not understand the textbook, so he makes himself mug up the whole text.'

Unfortunately, various state and city governments across India have a confused response to English-medium school education. The Maharashtra state government, for example, does not offer financial aid any more to English-medium schools, but only to Indian-language schools. 'English schools are considered to be

---

[6]See Pallavi Singh, 'Dalits Look upon English As the Language of Emancipation', *Mint*, 8 March 2010.

schools for the richie-rich, so they refuse to fund them,' says
Santi, whose school is permanently unaided as a result. 'Never
mind that we are in a slum and cater to the poor. They expect
the poor not to study in English but in regional languages. That
is discriminatory.' The Ambedkar school has 160 students in a
Kannada-medium section from class eight through ten. They
receive government aid.

Lack of funding has not stopped the school from adding new
facilities, such as a fully air-conditioned compute centre with
twenty-five new computers, a new junior college for commerce
and a gym for the community. Such commitment translates
into student success, Santi thinks. In March 2011, the first
batch of thirty commerce students sat for the Higher Secondary
School Certificate (HSC) exam at the class twelve level and
only two failed. 'Our students are truly motivated not just to
pass SSC but to do something bigger and more meaningful
with their lives,' he says. 'Today we have ex-students who are
doctors, engineers and teachers.'

Pappu Mandal, for example, is keen to pursue further studies
in bio-technology. 'I like the idea of doing scientific research,' he
says. But college life, he admits, is tougher than he had envisaged.
In school, they were always being told what to do, being punished
if they did not do their best, and constantly being pushed to do
better. 'I now realize it was all about caring for our well-being.
We were told that we had to make Dharavi look good and that
if we did well, then Dharavi would shine. In college, no one says
anything. You have to be self-motivated to succeed in college.'
Mandal says he comes back to his old school from time to time
so that he can feel inspired to push himself.

Gillel Hemant and his friend Sheikh Akeel, both 2006

graduates from the Ambedkar school, also return to their old school almost every day. 'We use the open classrooms to study here every night—sometimes staying till 1.00 or 2.00 a.m. during the exams,' says Hemant, who studies at Guru Nanak College and stays in Subhash Nagar. Akeel, who studies at a college in Malad, says that when he speaks English in college his classmates tease him by saying, 'Arre, you don't look like you are from Dharavi.'

Another ex-student, B. Anita Krishnappa, who always dreamed of becoming a teacher, returned to her alma mater to teach social studies at the secondary level. She remembers a time when students did not aspire beyond the Secondary School Certificate. 'Now each and every child has a focused dream,' says this resident of Anna Nagar. 'And they are so confident as well. In my time, we hid the fact that we were from Mumbai pincode 17 [Dharavi]. The kids today don't feel a need to hide that so much now. And that is great.'

All kinds of people run schools in Dharavi. Baburao Mane, a former Shiv Sena MLA who led a raucous Sena rally in Dharavi that became known as the first violent incident of the 1992–93 riots, now presides over one of Dharavi's largest educational trusts, the Mahatma Phule Shikshan Sanstha.[7] The trust runs a primary (Raje Shivaji Vidyalaya) and secondary (Chh. Shivaji Vidyalaya) school as well as a junior college and degree college

---

[7] See Jyoti Punwani, 'Construct a Hospital on the Disputed Site', *The Times of India*, Sunday supplement, 26 September 2010.

(Manohar Joshi Mahavidyalaya) in the English, Hindi, Marathi and Urdu languages for about 4,000 students. In addition, each night there are evening classes for about sixty rag-picker children. These sessions start with a bath and a meal followed by a basic education class.

Mane says he is concerned not just with 'padhna-likhna' (reading and writing) but also with fostering an atmosphere in which teachers and students are free to express their religious beliefs and celebrate together within the framework of a secular educational structure. Urdu-medium Muslim students get a day off after badi raat during Ramzaan and two days off for Eid. All through Ramzaan the afternoon shift finishes an hour early. A joint Eid Milan–Diwali party is held and there are celebrations held for Holi and Makar Sankranti.

'What makes our celebrations different is that we ensure that Hindu students understand and participate in Eid festivities as do Muslim students in Holi and Ashadi Ekadashi celebrations,' says Mane, who himself studied at the Kala Killa municipal school in Dharavi. 'In all cultural and sports programmes, all the students and teachers participate collectively,' he continues. For this the school has one of the biggest playgrounds in Dharavi, a massive area of 5,500 sq. ft of open ground.

Muslim teachers and students say that coming to school here is easier as the school understands and respects their religious sentiments, such as the need to have a place to go and say namaaz and cultural observances such as having mehendi on the hands after Eid. These gestures, not common at other schools, likely help to limit dropouts among the Muslim students.

'In many cases family life is complex either with parents separated, or a second wife, or too many siblings, or a father who is an alcoholic,' says Veena Donwalkar, principal of the Marathi, Hindi and Urdu sections of the Chh. Shivaji Vidyalaya. 'Sometimes everyone in the family is working and the child comes to school hungry because no one was around to feed him.' That is when the big biscuit box kept in each headmistress's office comes in handy. 'Then, in the Urdu and Hindi-medium sections, we have parents marrying off their daughters in class nine or ten, and we spend a lot of time convincing the in-laws to allow the girls to sit for their board exams,' she continues.

Pinky Santepola Ashappa is a fifteen-year-old Dharavi resident with bright eyes and short plaits. Daughter of a railway employee, Pinky studies at the Ambedkar school, likes mathematics and computers, and is quite clear she wants to be a chartered accountant. 'We have more opportunities now than our parents ever did. Girls are also doing all kinds of big things now,' she says. 'But the competition is a lot tougher too.' For even with a Scheduled Caste certificate in hand, the contest for those few reserved seats is keener.

But that is not keeping students' dreams in check. Pinky's senior in school, Kaikashan Ansari, is pursuing science at the nearby SIES college with the hope of becoming a paediatric neonatologist. Pinky's classmate Kanimonni, whose father is a tailor, wants to be a software engineer. Another classmate, Karishma, wants to be a dentist and 'help poor people'. Suvarna Kotrik wants to be a teacher, while her male classmate, Kunchikoree Durgappa, whose father works in the BMC, wants to be the police commissioner of Mumbai and defend the city against terrorists. Pinky and her schoolmates on an average speak four languages in addition to English, and though they are poor, they enjoy the same things that wealthier children in Mumbai do—computer games, chatting with friends on Facebook, eating chips and watching television.

These kids don't like being called 'Slumdogs.' 'Slumdog is not a good way to refer to Dharavi and its people. It's also not an accurate description of the place which is developing so much day by day,' says an offended Kanimonni. For the children, Dharavi is a place that they stay and study in. For many of them it is the only home they know. They know it has much more going for it than outsiders (and certain film-makers) give it credit for.

As Pinky says, 'Dharavi has us. We are educated and we are going to change its image.'

17

FOOTNOTES

Mansi Choksi

BALLET IN THE *BASTI*

Dodging open nullahs and hanging sarees, hopping into someone's home to let a bicycle pass and getting used to people gaping at you through bed sheet curtains are not part of the usual shopping experience, especially for a professional dancer. But Jameel Shah's shoe store, a 100 sq. ft dim room tucked away in a crowded bylane of Dharavi, is the address that television starlets, assistant directors and anyone with a passion for dance heads to when scouting for sole mates.

Shah's shoe clinic is a sunless room with stacks of leather piled against chipping pink walls, unpolished shelves protruding at odd angles, Bisleri bottles filled with glue, and industrial scissors sitting atop an old tailoring machine. The room is occupied by five young Bihari men wearing greasy *ganjis* and squatting on the cold stone floor. One cuts, another carves, the third stitches, the fourth glues, and the fifth envelopes the finished shoes in plastic and tosses the consignment in a cardboard box. For hours they laugh and share tales of their hometown, all the while giving birth to a remarkable story of their own: a story that sums up the aspirational spirit of the neighbourhood. From tinsel-toed salsa stilettos and hip-hop pumps to tap dancing shoes and ballet flats, Shah's shoe shop is a professional dancer's fantasy. But for Shah, a twenty-seven-year-old from Darbhanga in Bihar who landed in Mumbai with fingers crossed sixteen years ago, it's the realization of a dream he almost never dared to dream.

Shah left home when he was only nine, and his memories of childhood are blurred by visions of abject poverty. He remembers scouting for discarded pens because he wanted so badly to study like the other motivated boys in the village. 'I would ask my father, who was a daily-wage labourer, for money to buy a pen refill,' he says. 'But we couldn't even afford that much.' One of eight siblings, Shah decided to try his luck in a big city. 'My father was hesitant to let me go at such a young age but he finally allowed me,' he says.

Shah jumped onto a train to Delhi and landed at Nabi Karim in the bustling Sadar Bazaar area of New Delhi, exactly where the villagers had advised him to go to. 'There's a lot of work for Biharis in the leather line there. I made wallets, mobile covers and bags for two years there,' he says. But Shah knew that something was amiss. '*Nabi Karim mohalla mein daal nahi galne wale thi*,' he says. (It wasn't going to work out for me there). So he packed his bags and landed in Dharavi, where his *khallu* (maternal uncle), Rafi Ahmed, lived. Shah's uncle introduced him to people in Dharavi's leather tannery where he was promptly employed thanks to his previous experience in Nabi

Karim. 'It was 1995 and the Cricket World Cup was on. I fell in love with Mumbai,' he recalls.

After two years of work, Shah saw the benefits of working in Mumbai. He was able to save roughly Rs 30,000 until a friend from the neighbourhood who was in desperate need of a loan borrowed Rs 25,000 from him. 'I know what it feels like when you are alone and broke, so I lent him the money,' Shah says. But the friend ran off to Bangalore. With a little help from the friend's family, Shah got hold of his Bangalore address and took off to find him. 'But when I reached Bangalore, he wasn't there. He had already left for Delhi,' says Shah.

Now alone and broke himself, Shah didn't have enough money to go back to his job in Mumbai. So he ambled about Bangalore for days and finally met 'his guardian angel' in the form of a 'Thomas aunty', a matronly figure who lived alone. She offered him a job as a watchman for a nominal salary and gave him meals and a place to stay. It was through Thomas aunty that Shah also landed a day job as a driver for a Life Insurance Corporation of India (LIC) agent and met 'Jacob Sir', a middle-aged man who rented a room in Thomas aunty's house. This person would introduce Shah to the experience that changed his life. As Shah remembers it, one evening, Jacob Sir called him to his room and said, 'Jameel, wear your best clothes, we are going out.'

The sight of mirrored walls, wooden floors, and men and women jiving and doing the salsa blew Shah's mind. 'The moment I stepped into the dance class, I knew I belonged there,' he said.

That dream, however, crashed right there. Shah couldn't afford the fees and the salsa teacher firmly refused to let him watch and learn.

He spent three more years in Bangalore but the memory of that night haunted him. He knew he needed to go back to Mumbai, where dreams like these could come true. At the Bandra railway station, Shah picked up a copy of *Mid-Day* and scanned the listings with help from a friend who could read English. He saw celebrity choreographer Sandip Soparrkar's workshop listing in Andheri and decided to take a chance.

In the beginning, he would go to the class for days but would invariably meet only Miss Soparrkar. Finally, when he got the chance to speak to Soparrkar himself, Shah told him he wanted to learn how to dance but didn't have the money. 'It's been eleven years since I've known him but I still remember the day he landed up at my house. The honesty, the genuine desperation of wanting to learn still brings tears to my eyes,' says Soparrkar. The celebrity choreographer agreed to enroll Shah at a fee of Rs 50 per month—the normal fee for his class was Rs 3,000 for two months—because Soparrkar felt that 'if one doesn't pay, one doesn't value it'.

For a few months, Shah helped out backstage and was occasionally caught inspecting special dancing shoes that needed to be imported for as much as Rs 15,000 per pair. 'I asked Sandip Sir if I could borrow his old pair of shoes. He looked at me and said, "*Main kyun doon*" (Why should I)?' laughs Shah.

Eventually Soparrkar did, and that night, says Shah, he sat in his tenement and performed a postmortem till dawn. He called on an old friend, the uncle from the leather tannery he worked for, and made a specimen to present to Soparrkar. The first one was stiff. 'Soparrkar Sir gave me honest feedback and I improvised further with the help of the dancers,' Shah says, rolling a supple ballet flat like a paneer wrap.

'He made almost fifteen pairs; the first few were terrible. But now I can safely say that Jameel makes the best dancing shoes in the world,' says Soparrkar.

Shah says that dancing shoes, especially for salsa and ballroom, need to have flexible soles which are lined with suede for firm grip. The inside also needs a lining to absorb sweat and cushioning for the moves that defy gravity. 'The dancer should feel the taps—that's why it's important to have heels made of fibreglass that are light, yet strong,' he adds.

To make the perfect shoe, Shah sources the resin from Nagpada, satin and suede from Dadar, and leather, glue and everything else he needs from Dharavi. 'This place is like a world of its own,' he says.

Shah still remembers the thrill of watching Dino Morea dance in the Bollywood film *Holiday* in 2006, the first Hindi movie in which his shoes were featured. He was only twenty-two. 'I took all my friends from the neighbourhood to watch the film and sent my relatives in Darbhanga news clippings of it,' he smiles.

With the star-studded clientele of Soparrkar's classes, Jameel's shoes were soon being worn by numerous celebrities. Model Jesse Randhawa was the first to try them, then model–actor Dipannita Sharma, then celebrity vocalist Sonu Nigam. These days Shah has so many famous clients he can barely keep their names straight. He's supplied shoes to stars like A-list Bollywood actresses Kajol, Neha Dhupia and Amisha Patel, Spanish actress Barbara Mori (for a shot in the film *Kites*) and Australian singer–actress Kylie Minogue (for the musical number in *Blue*). 'Kylie M'am's bodyguards wouldn't let me in when I went to deliver the shoes, but she came outside herself and placed another order of eight pairs for herself and her friends,' he says.

Thanks to Facebook and old-fashioned word-of-mouth endorsements, Shah now makes shoes (priced between Rs 1,500 and Rs 2,500) for dancers all over India and abroad. 'I'm not some big businessman but my small venture has grown. Earlier, I used to make roughly ten pairs a month and now I make at least hundred,' he adds. 'I have enough money to live happily and send money to my family in Bihar.' Business is also booming due to the spate of reality dance shows like *Dance India Dance*, *Jhalak Dikhlaja*, *Nach Baliye* and *Zara Nach ke Dikha* on Indian television channels. 'The other day, I got a call from the makers of *Zara Nach ke Dikha* for salsa shoes to be made overnight,' he says indifferently. 'I said yes, because at the end of the day, you have to see who is on the other end of the phone.'

Brushes with fame and pocket change aside, it is dance that is Shah's first love. He admits that when he bumps into celebrities he has made shoes for at parties, he asks them to dance with him. 'They must be thinking, how can they dance with someone who makes shoes? But some celebrities like TV actors Shweta Salve and Mona Singh have danced with me and even complimented me,' he says. Nothing gives Shah a greater thrill than showing off his skills. 'I have danced continuously for fifty-five hours and fifteen minutes at a dance competition in Goa and won a national Latin Ballroom Dancing Championship,' he boasts.

But family and friends in Bihar don't know anything about Shah doing the shimmy. 'They will think I am having multiple affairs. It's better that they think I make shoes only,' he says. His family's perception of Shah's parallel life in Dharavi, he admits, is best limited to newspaper clippings and money transfers. 'They need to see Mumbai to know what life is like here. They will not understand otherwise,' he says.

In Dharavi, Shah is happy because he gets the best of both worlds—a slice of home with his Bihari friends and privacy in the crowds of the city. 'This is why I will never leave Dharavi—it has made me who I am.'

TRIBAL INSTINCT: THE B-BOYS OF DHARAVI

A frail teenager in a Playboy t-shirt, baggy cargo shorts, and a Johnny Depp-esque beard carries a pile of plastic buckets on his back as he navigates the familiar bylanes of Sion Koliwada. The residents of the area are used to his throaty chants of 'bhaandi' which have, for the past four years, been luring thrifty housewives to their doorstep to trade old clothes for new utensils.

Lalu Ashok Khaura, better known as Ajay, is 'an eight class pass' from Dharavi and a member of the dwindling itinerant Bhangari tribe, a nomadic aboriginal group originally from the Sindh region of Pakistan. Traditionally, the Bhangaris traded farm produce for daily amenities, but now they often barter plastic housewares and sell off what they get in return. When he is not parching his throat on the sun-beaten streets of Mumbai, Ajay can be spotted capering across shaky bridges above open nullahs, tossing plastic *lotas* with rhythmic precision, bursting into a break dance in his one-room tenement, or performing a headstand in the common toilet line. 'My family thought, "This boy has gone crack"', smiles Ajay. 'One day a neighbour asked me if I had some problem. But I just tossed my hat and laughed madly.'

Mental health diagnoses from neighbours aside, Ajay's terpsichorean leaning has been cultivated over years of watching *Boogie Woogie, Dance India Dance* and other such shows that have equipped him with some impressive skills and moves.

He remembers the days when as a child he would be glued to the television as Javed Jaffrey (the host of *Boogie Woogie*) applauded, and even danced with, participants, many of them boys like him from humble backgrounds. 'If they could do it, so could I,' Ajay says. He watched intently as the young dancers set the screen ablaze, ignoring calls from family members and eating meals only before and after his favourite dance shows. Then he would practise one memorable move for days till the next episode was scheduled to be aired. With each episode, Ajay's skill-base widened until eventually he made a sequence that could be practised to pretty much any song, from a *bhajan* to a racy item number. Often he would injure himself, especially when he would try to copy twisted elbow stunts or headstands. '*Bolte hai na*, no gain without pain,' he says.

Ajay put his skills to use by forming a dance group with five other Bhangaris from Dharavi. Twins Naresh and Santosh, Babur, Pritam and Ajay are the core dancers, but anyone with a passion to learn is welcome to join. The boys say they can master any style from a video but they are best at locking and popping, a school of hip-hop dance that consists of rapid arm and leg movements and short pauses.

But since the Bhangari B-boys are more walk than talk, Ajay eggs on his friends to prove themselves as I watch in a sunny slum *anganwadi* in Khar. In this hutment, which faces a garbage dump and houses only a broken wooden cupboard, one of the boys in printed t-shirt, Converse sneakers and hat whips out a mobile phone that blares Punjabi rap, while the rest begin jerking their heads at the count of '*Ek, be, tan*' (one, two, three in their native Kutchi). They pinch their drooped collars and pull up their spines. Then one of them effortlessly does a reverse spin and starts to walk with his head on the ground. Instantly, a loyal audience of sleepy grandfathers, *lungi*-wrapped men and some giggly girls arrives.

The B-boys take their rehearsals very seriously, meeting every few days at the anganwadi to practise coordination and new moves picked up from shows. For hours they sweat it out in a small room where the sounds and smells of the neighbourhood are virtually zoned out for them. 'Once an accident took place on the road outside; everyone ran out to watch but we didn't even know,' says Santosh. When a sequence is ready, the boys test it at the Carter Road promenade where, according to Naresh, 'rich, educated and famous people walk'. 'Many people congratulate us and ask us where we are from and how we learnt it. It feels good,' he adds.

Lately, the Bhangari B-boys have started performing at weddings, religious processions and rallies. They are the stars and almost always attract a crowd. 'Nowadays, no wedding or celebration is complete without their dance,' says Manju Khaura (no relation to Ajay), a neighbour of the Khar studio who also belongs to the tribe and often leaves her kitchen to watch the boys rehearse.

When they are in form, a dance routine can run into hours, with improvisations from the dancers in response to the DJ's surprise selections. The kind of event determines the kind of music the DJ will spin. The B-boys usually practise on Hindi songs but they can adapt their moves to almost any genre. It's usually Naresh who takes the lead and introduces the new moves when the DJ changes the music. The other boys follow, repeating each new move as it is ushered into the routine. 'We all come up with steps, teach them to each other, and practise a lot. Of course, the routine really depends on the beat and tempo of the music,' says Naresh.

But whatever the tempo, the boys are tireless. 'Everyone in the wedding *baraat* (procession) or religious procession will get tired but these boys will go on and on. By the end of it, they will be dancing and a crowd will be cheering them,' Khaura says.

For the Bhangari B-boys, being tribesmen ensures that they won't have to take up dull nine-to-five jobs ('*gulaamgiri*', or slavery, as Ajay calls that life), which means they can follow their passion for dance while they earn a living. It's a good thing, too, because those reality shows that got them started not only instilled a love of dance in the B-boys, but also the desire for some notoriety. With each episode, it seemed that someone their age got famous. The idea that the same thing could happen to them one day is attractive. 'Dharmesh (a contestant of *Dance India Dance*) became a star overnight. I bet that we can also do every move he did,' says Ajay.

The boys plan to audition for dance reality shows in the coming season, and they may not be dreaming to think that something big could happen. Recently, at a religious procession near their hometown in Vadodara, the B-boys invited some shocked glares when they performed elbow spins in a red-roofed *shibir* (camp). 'At first people didn't know what to do but soon they started clapping. Even some religious leaders were there,' says Santosh, adding with a proud smile, 'We are called the Michael Jacksons of this area.'

Still, the B-boys are not ultimately in this for the money or the fame. 'We don't get paid to perform, we dance because we love to,' says Naresh. Dance is also an escape from daily worries. 'When I'm dancing I forget about how many hours I will have to roam the streets to get the next day's meal for my family,' says Ajay. He says a day's business, which can yield nothing despite hours of roaming, can also spring up some surprises. 'Once a woman exchanged an old *zari* saree, I pulled out the thread and traded it in the gold market for Rs 3,000. I could focus on my dance for a whole month after that,' he says. But a typical workday is a gamble. The best time for business is the late morning. Trying one's luck after sunset is practically a wasted effort. 'You could be roaming the streets for hours and even days but come home empty-handed,' he says. 'But on some days I'll be home before lunch also.'

For the boys' parents, too, there are rewards greater than national fame or money. To watch her children dance and win compliments from everyone almost always brings tears to the eyes of Naresh and Santosh's mother. 'When I hear that rich people in Bandra have complimented my sons, I can't explain what I feel,' she says. 'All these years, as I went from door to door in these very areas, I was made to feel like nothing more than a beggar. My sons have undone what our tribe has suffered for generations.'

18

THERE'S ALWAYS TIME FOR POETRY IN DHARAVI

Jerry Pinto

Poetry will not be denied. Nisar Ahmed Khan is fifty-three and writes his poetry in Urdu. He has written poetry all his life and has never seen any of it published. This does not stop him. He continues writing.

'In Dharavi, there is always time. There is always space,' he says.

We are standing in a *maidan* in which a group of priests and poets will sing praise to the Prophet Muhammad, peace be upon him. The man at the mike has a powerful voice, a full-throated voice, but he is too close to the microphone to make for a comfortable listening experience. No one seems to mind.

'Not to God, here it is clear, they will only recite praise to the Prophet,' says Khan. About a thousand young men are sitting on the ground, on tarpaulins. Traffic is directed by a bunch of young volunteers in heavy silk kurtas and jeans, a nicely wrought

212

combination of ethnicity and modernity. Women sit behind a screen, made of gunny sacking. Children punctuate the purdah, climbing in and out.

'They are not here for the poetry,' says Khan, a faint contempt in his voice. 'They are here because they do not have anything better to do. They come and they listen to theology that makes no sense to them. But for a couple of hours, they have something to do and they can go home and tell themselves that they have enjoyed the evening.'

He does not think much of the organizers or the event itself.

'Could they not have put in chairs? At least, chairs? Yes, this is Dharavi and it is free but how much money would it have cost to put in chairs?'

Nisar Ahmed Khan came to Dharavi thirty-five years ago. He married here and raised his seven children here. He went from cycling about selling soap powder to being the owner of a soap powder-making unit. But in his pocket, a poem.

'I write. I keep on writing. When something occurs to me, I park my scooter and scribble it on a piece of paper. Then I continue. Later, I may revise. Sometimes, if it has been a very busy day, I don't look at what I have written. I see the scrap of paper many days later, and I read it and think, "Did I write this?"'

I have no way of entering the poetic world of Nisar Ahmed Khan. He does not seem willing to recite for me. This, I understand. You cannot whip a poem out of hiding and recite it to someone who has arrived to interview you. You cannot expose a poem to that kind of harsh light and the many possibilities of misunderstanding and misrepresentation. Eventually, yes, every poem will go out and will stand naked in the marketplace. This is what you want most for it, the nakedness of standing in public, a slim column of words. This is what you fear most too, for it means you stand beside it and you must be judged, not just what kind of poet you are, but what kind of human being too.

So when Khan refuses to recite, I understand. And even if he did, I am not qualified to judge his Urdu poetry, were judgement called for. I have read some Ghalib, some Faiz, some Mir. I have learnt the script, and four years after my first encounter with the elegant splashes of ink, I can read slowly and haltingly. None of this will allow me to set myself up as an arbiter of what works and what does not in Urdu. I cannot tell you therefore whether Khan is a good poet. I cannot tell you much about his poetry. Or locate it in Dharavi for you.

Must it be?

Does Nissim Ezekiel's poetry get located in Belassis Road? Or Imtiaz Dharker's on Malabar Hill? Is mine a poetry of Mahim, kissing cousin to Dharavi? Is there such a thing as a Dharavi poet? Dharker herself has worked in Dharavi. She has written several moving poems about the space and the place it occupies in the heads of the visitor. Adam, in this case, visits from New Zealand.

> He wants a guided tour,
> to be fitted in his schedule
> between the film studio
> and a visit to Chor Bazaar.
>
> He doesn't understand
> why I refuse to take him
> like all the others, lugging
> cameras and microphones,
> sunguns, recorders, dictaphones.

('Adam from New Zealand' from
Postcards from God)

I have not been refused. Instead, I have been welcomed to *mushairas*. I have been asked to come and meet a Tamil poet, who has appeared on Sun Music, a television channel.

Vadivel Thambi is thirty years old but he has the bearing and demeanour of a sixteen-year-old. He seems to generate a moral climate around him, although this may simply be the way he surveys me, with a mixture of anxiety and confidence. He has reason to be confident.

'When he travels to Tamil Nadu,' says Rajesh Prabhakar, my guide to Dharavi, 'he has to stop at various stations in order to meet his fans. They bring him gifts. They garland him. He's a rockstar to them.'

Again, I have no idea what Thambi writes, although he gives me a list of the names of his poems and obligingly corrects my transliteration of them.

Prabhakar again: 'See that gold ring? He got it from a lady fan.'

'A lady fan?'

Thambi's face goes stern and forbidding.

'She was a lady in her seventies. She had withdrawn from life. She spent all her time in bed. And then someone showed her a mobile phone with Thambi's poetry on it. And she began to draw inspiration from it. She started coming out of her room. She began to take interest in things again. She recovered and she sent him this ring as a mark of respect,' says Prabhakar.

It is difficult to decode all this at once. We are sitting in a tiny milk bar in the middle of Dharavi at ten in the night. It is the only time that Thambi is free. In the morning, he goes on his rounds, delivering milk. In the evening, he must go on the same

rounds again, to collect the money. I don't know why he has to
do this twice but perhaps it has something to do with the
specificities of the Dharavi milk situation. I don't even know if I
can ask. I feel as if I have stepped into something like an
alternative reality here and even as I feel this, as I write it now, I
smell my own bourgeois discomfort at what Dharavi means. It
is terrible to admit it but I am Adam from New Zealand too.
Except that for me, this is not exotic, this cannot be Othered.
Everything is familiar, everything is different. I am talking about
Tamil poetry to a Tamil poet and the translation and
interpretation is in the hands of a Maharashtrian. I do not
know whether to respond to the notion of poetry as salvation,
poetry as a lifeline, or to talk about mobile phones. I choose the
latter. It seems safer.

Thambi seems to have worked a way out of the problem of
getting published. He simply sends a poem out as a text message.
His telephone company has a scheme which allows him to send
out five hundred short messages every day. I check his phone.
On the day we met, he has sent out four hundred and ninety-
seven.

There are messages on the phone too and he lets me read
them. 'U have 4got10 me, Thambi,' one man writes in. 'It is my
b'day 2day.' There's another from a woman: 'Gud nyt,' she writes.

Thambi has not bothered to send his poems to publishers.
He doesn't want to. When he began writing them in 2001, he
sent a poem out to a friend. The friend forwarded it. And when
the recipients asked him if there were more, the idea of a poetry
network was born.

'My poems are about love, about friendship mainly but I also
write about social issues, about poverty, caste problems, politics,

about the family. And nature,' Thambi says. 'My poems have something in them to make you think.'

Like Nisar, he does not want more time for poetry.

'I have enough time,' he says. 'When a poem comes to me, I park my bike and I note it down on the mobile.'

FIXING DHARAVI

The final section opens with a history of the redevelopment of Dharavi reprinted from Kalpana Sharma's *Rediscovering Dharavi: Stories from Asia's Largest Slum*, and covers the current Dharavi Redevelopment Plan, conceived by Mukesh Mehta in the early 2000s and approved in 2004. Sharma's work clearly demonstrates that all successful past redevelopment in the area had been achieved only by working closely with the residents of Dharavi. The ensuing chapters show that in the current plan, which has been stalled for nearly ten years, the builders and government officials have, by and large, neglected to create a solution in cooperation with the residents. Instead, they have promoted a scheme that would force many people out of Dharavi and cram the rest of them into high-rise buildings on a fraction of the land. Most activists agree that the plan cannot work.

The stories in this section bear that out. Shirish Patel's chapter, the second last in the book, and Dilip D'Souza's three articles, which were part of a five-part series published in *Tehelka* in 2007, provide a sober argument against the plan. As D'Souza shows, the numbers just don't add up. In order to turn a profit the developers would have to build more structures than is humanly possible. And even if they could build high-rises as they needed to, the property values would fall and they would have to keep building more and more residences to get their money back. If logic does not suffice, Mark Jacobson's article, first published in *National Geographic* magazine in 2007, shows how whimsical the plan really is. At one point while he is with

Jacobson, Mehta becomes taken with the idea of building a cricket stadium in Dharavi, but then confesses that he will need time to sort out the parking.

Nevertheless, despite the objections raised here, many people in Dharavi support the plan. For example, Hariram Dilliwala, who is featured in Rachel Lopez's story, looks forward to a cleaner, safer Dharavi, even if that means he'll have to move into a smaller apartment and that he may no longer be permitted to run his recycling business there. For Dilliwala, the parks, paved roads and new hospitals that have been promised compensate for the loss. And he trusts Mehta to deliver on his promises.

However, for many people opposed to the plan, Mehta has come to embody the greed that is driving the project. It is probably unfair to pile so much scorn upon him.

While Mukesh Mehta has been evangelical and myopic in his quest to transform Dharavi into a thriving business centre, I believe him when he says he wants to improve the residents' lives. Maybe I'm wrong, and he just wants to make a pile of money. But I think it is rather that he wants to improve people's lives *and* make a fortune. He sees no contradiction in this. If he gets his way, everyone ends up better off.

As I did the research for the book I heard a number of questionable things said about him. For example, on two occasions I went to a tannery owned by a father and son. The first time I interviewed the father. He told me that his son attended a conference at a posh downtown hotel at which Mehta told the crowd not to pay any attention to his public pronouncements. His real plan was to have all the residents out of Dharavi within five years. The father claimed to have heard this with his own ears. The son had called him and held his cell phone aloft so his father could listen to Mehta's speech.

Six months later I returned to the tannery to confirm the story with the son. He laughed it off, saying that his father could be a little daft once in a while. The son, however, proceeded to spin a couple of fantastic-sounding tales of his own. He claimed to be in the apartment of a high-ranking Shiv Sena official, whose party had gone on record numerous times as being against the Dharavi Redevelopment Plan, when Mehta telephoned with a bribe that the official accepted—on the spot with the son present. He then went on to tell me about one Xavier Castro, a French spy for the World Bank who lived in Dharavi for six months and collected reams of damning evidence against Mehta. Two weeks after this second visit to the tannery I received this text: 'Hi, u came to my office for information about dharavi leather industry and i told u about my friend who is in france. he has those tapes and is willing to trade for usd 3,000. let me know if u interested. he has 20 tapes near about 20 hours of data.'

On another occasion, when I was interviewing a Shiv Sena official, I was told that Mukesh Mehta had covered up the death of a crewman working on one of the buildings. As evidence, I was given an article from a Marathi newspaper. When I got the piece translated, sure enough the story was about a man who had been electrocuted on the job; however, Mehta's name was not mentioned and his business had no connection to the work site. Another person told me that Mehta had taken money from an entire community in Dharavi with the promise of building them a high-rise but had absconded with the funds and left the building half-finished. Again, this proved to be false.

What all of this tells me is that, regardless of the Dharavi Redevelopment Plan, the meaningful development work in

Dharavi is carried out by the numerous NGOs who try in less grandiose ways to help the people improve their lot. In the final chapter, for example, Judith Francorsi writes about the efforts of the ACORN India Foundation which has given the waste collectors identification cards and hosts art programmes for their children, among many other projects. Such efforts go significantly further than a housing plan that will likely never see the light of day.

19

A HOUSE FOR KHATIJA

Kalpana Sharma

Khatija lives in the Dargah Chawl of Dharavi's Social Nagar. Today, her house is typical of the incrementally improved structures you see around you. But thirty years ago, it was just thatch and bamboo. 'When we came here, there must have been hardly 5,000 people. It was all jungle. There was tall grass all around. There were snakes. We built the house with bamboo poles and *chatai* (coconut matting). It had to be replaced after each monsoon. I brought sacks of mud and filled this place,' recalls Khatija.

Now her house is made of brick and concrete. It has a phone, a TV, a fridge and a washing machine—the last of which she says she uses very occasionally. All the crockery is arranged neatly on a shelf on the wall of her spacious front room. There are two beds in the room, a couple of chairs, a table and a sewing machine. The kitchen is located in a room at the back and like most others in Dharavi, Khatija too has a loft the same size as her front room. She does not have piped water inside the house but a tap is located conveniently just outside. Khatija has a separate monthly meter and proudly shows me her bi-monthly bill for Rs 371.

When people like Khtaija first came to live in Dharavi, they had no electricity; now they have electric meters. For years they had to share community taps; now many of them have taps in their homes. For years the open fields were the only toilets; today, there are municipal toilets, albeit unusable on many days. Many things have changed, but much also remains unchanged.

There were two concurrent developments that marked the beginnings of Dharavi's transformation from a slum on a swamp to a settlement with a mixture of low-rise pucca houses like Khatija's and high-rise buildings built by the government and private builders. Both took place because as Mumbai expanded, Dharavi's location shifted from being at one end of the island city to almost the centre of Mumbai.

The first was a determined effort by the police to tackle crime and the criminal gangs that worked out of Dharavi. This brought about a change of attitude in the general public towards a place that was considered dangerous. It also allowed normal development work to proceed, something that reportedly could not be done earlier because of the criminal activity centered in and around Dharavi.

The second development took place in December 1985, when the Congress party's centenary celebrations were held in Bombay. On this occasion, Rajiv Gandhi, who had been elected prime minister following the assassination of his mother, Indira Gandhi, in 1984, visited the city. He was taken on a tour of Dharavi and some other slums.

Rajiv Gandhi was moved by what he saw and announced that

the Central government would release Rs 100 crore for slum redevelopment and other projects to improve life for the urban poor in Bombay. The scheme was christened Prime Minister's Grant Project (PMGP).

The grant, however, was not the consequence of sudden magnanimity. It grew out of the realization that Dharavi was ideally located and that its development would be profitable in many ways.

How valuable the real estate was in Dharavi would only emerge in the early 1990s when the concept of developing a new business district across the Mahim Creek was touted. This thinking coincided with the opening up of the Indian economy, with expectations that Mumbai would emerge as an important financial centre. It also led to a boom in property prices. Dharavi's location close to these new planned developments elevated its property status.

On receiving the Rs 100 crore grant from the Centre, the state government had to decide how to tackle Dharavi for the PMGP. In 1986, it commissioned a leading architect, Charles Correa, to head a committee which was asked to prepare a report on how Dharavi should be redeveloped. The committee began with a major handicap. It did not have data as no systematic survey of the structures and settlements that made up Dharavi had ever been done.

Rather than go through the painstaking and slow task of an actual physical enumeration, the Correa committee and the government asked the Hyderabad-based National Remote Sensing Agency to do an aerial survey of Dharavi. It is not surprising, therefore, that the numbers they arrived at—of an estimated population of 2.5 lakh—were so far off the mark, as more detailed surveys later proved. For given the way houses are laid out in Dharavi, with lanes merging into each other in a crazy and unplanned manner, it would require some extraordinarily high-precision cameras to identify where one house ends and another begins.

Despite this inadequate data, the Correa committee made some useful suggestions. It pinpointed the inadequacy of infrastructure, such as storm-water drains, as one of the main problems facing Dharavi. As a result, large parts of Dharavi would be flooded during the rains. Also, the water supply was far from adequate because the water mains, bringing in treated water into the city, did not extend to this area. And there was no underground sewerage system and practically no garbage collection. The committee also noted the huge shortage of toilets in Dharavi and stated that even where toilets had been built by the municipality, they were poorly maintained. According to one survey, 800 people were using one toilet in Dharavi.

The Correa committee recognized that although the structures in which people lived were unsatisfactory, they had not tried to improve them because they lacked a legal title to the land. Furthermore, existing regulations prevented them from making any substantial improvements in their homes. For instance, people were not permitted to buy a loft. Any change in the structure required permission from the local authorities. This gave petty officials the power to extort money from poor people already strapped for resources.

On the positive side, the report recognized that people in Dharavi were engaged in gainful economic activities that were useful for the rest of the city, and that the residents were genuinely interested in improving their settlements. The committee suggested that given these facts, the problem could be tackled at two broad levels. One was at the area level where deficiencies in infrastructure could be dealt with by the government. The second was at the block level where communities would be encouraged to form cooperative societies with about 100–150 members who would undertake upgradation if the state gave them land tenure, finance and related services. 'Given the enthusiasm of the residents for undertaking upgradation, if land tenure and finance are provided, the problems of shelter and related services can be solved,' stated the report.

The concepts were acceptable to people living in Dharavi. What was not so acceptable was the idea mooted in the Correa report of accommodating only 43,000 households out of an estimated 55,000—a figure that was at best a guesstimate— and shifting the rest so that there would be adequate open spaces for parks and other recreational facilities. Those that would have to be shifted included households living under high-tension power lines, close to the railway tracks and alongside roads that needed to be widened. To minimize the inconvenience to these families, the Correa committee recommended that land be allotted close to Dharavi for relocation.

The committee also suggested that all tanneries in Dharavi be shifted to Deonar in north-east Mumbai, thereby locating them closer to the abattoir. Relocating tanneries would free twenty-one acres which could be used for other purposes.

Another important concept articulated by the Correa committee was the need to set up a separate planning authority to deal with the redevelopment of Dharavi. Many plans had been tied up in bureaucratic knots because of the multiplicity of institutions dealing with questions of slum redevelopment and housing. For instance, land comes under the respective owner of the land on which a slum is located—the Central government, the state government, the railways, the airports authority, the municipal corporation or private owners. The planning needs of the area come under the Maharashtra Housing and Area Development Authority (MHADA). In addition, the municipal corporation has a certain set of powers and policies and the state government has another set. There is often an overlap between these different bodies which holds up implementation of schemes. One authority for slum redevelopment would simplify matters and accelerate implementation. This suggestion laid the grounds for the PMGP.

PRIME MINISTER'S GRANT PROJECT

At the time, a young IAS officer was posted to Mumbai after the mandatory stint in the districts. Gautam Chatterjee found himself placed in the unenviable position of having to devise a way to spend the Rs 100 crore that had come to Mumbai, and specifically how to use it in Dharavi.

Of course, not all of the money came to Dharavi. Inevitably, there was heavy bargaining from different interest groups. 'People asked why the entire amount should be given to Dharavi,' says Chatterjee. 'There was a pro- and anti-Dharavi group. It was argued that the major problem in Mumbai is not slums but old, dilapidated buildings. Rs 41 crore went for reconstruction of old, dilapidated, tenanted buildings. After deducting Rs 37 crore for Dharavi, the remaining was for slum upgradation in the rest of Mumbai.' But even Rs 37 crore was a generous amount, the kind of money that had never been invested in Dharavi before.

When the PMGP was launched, parts of Dharavi had already benefited partially from the slum improvement schemes in the past. But the benefits were limited to settlements on government or municipal land. The spatial layout of the settlements made the implementation of some of these schemes virtually impossible.

Chatterjee recalls, for instance, the difficulty of providing toilets to people living in parts of Dharavi. 'Because the slums in Dharavi are so dense, you are not in a position to give upgraded infrastructure. To give you an example, we were supposed to provide one toilet for thirty-five heads. But in actual practice, under the improvement programme, what we were able to achieve was one toilet per hundred heads. It was not possible to achieve the norm of thirty-five because of the density. You could not pull down existing residential structures in order to build toilets.'

The PGMP was the first scheme that actually considered slum redevelopment, that is, planning for entirely new structures where slum dwellers could live on the same site where they presently squatted. This was born out of a recognition that such reorganization was the only way to ensure real upgradation. Also, such redevelopment would free up land that could be used for other commercial purposes. The scheme also accepted the fact that people want to live where they can find work. Thus, the earlier concept of moving slum dwellers to distant suburbs was acknowledged as being unworkable as people would merely abandon those dwellings and find their way back closer to work. Many previous slum improvement schemes had failed because the authorities had not understood the crucial link between work and a place to live, particularly in the absence of affordable public transport systems.

Of the Rs 37 crore total, Rs 17 crore was used for infrastructure, such as laying sewerage lines and widening roads. But given the density of the settlements, even the roads that were widened were those on the periphery of Dharavi. The exception was the 90 Feet Road, which runs through the middle of Dharavi and links the south to the north. Such a road already existed, but it had been so heavily encroached upon as to be unusable.

Under the PMGP, the encroachers were moved to a transit camp on one side of the road and the road was widened to something approximating ninety feet. Today, encroachers have once again reduced the width of the road to much less. But at least it is a usable road at most times of the year unlike the Dharavi Main Road which remains narrow and highly congested.

Another Rs 2 crore of the PMGP was used to clean up the Mithi River which separates Dharavi from the northern suburbs of Mumbai. Since then, the river and the Mahim Creek have become silted and increasingly polluted with unchecked dumping of construction debris. And the remaining Rs 18 crore was allocated for slum redevelopment.

Chatterjee realized that there was room for some innovation as existing approaches had proved inadequate in dealing with the problem. One idea that emerged was of area development—to look at a cluster of settlements located in a particular part of Dharavi rather than individual settlements. An area adjacent to the newly widened 60 Feet Road, called Rajendra Nagar, was chosen. The majority of its residents had been relocated some decades earlier from Tardeo in central Mumbai.

Chatterjee decided to adopt a learning approach and began talking to the communities to find out what they really wanted.

'The people I spoke to argued that if dilapidated buildings could be repaired, why could there not be proper redevelopment of the slums. They wanted to get out of this so-called informal settlement syndrome and move to mainstream formal housing,' he says. 'This I thought was a brilliant idea because I would achieve my target of spending the money.

Fortunately for Chatterjee, he had the support of the then housing secretary, Dinesh K. Afzalpurkar (who coincidentally headed the committee which came up with the ambitious Slum Redevelopment Plan in 1995). Afzalpurkar issued a new government resolution which Chatterjee drafted. Under this, the beneficiaries would have to pay something towards their housing rather than getting it free as in the later scheme. The government recognized that the initial cost of redevelopment was outside the reach of poor people. 'So we developed a system by which we broke up these costs,' explains Chatterjee. The beneficiaries were expected to make an initial fixed contribution. A cross-subsidy was generated from commercial tenements which had to pay more. The difference between the two amounts was divided into monthly instalments which the beneficiaries were expected to pay over 15–20 years.

Additonally, these monthly instalments would increase telescopically. In other words, families would begin by paying Rs 100 per month and then gradually, the monthly contributions would increase up to Rs 250. The normal size of an apartment for the Low Income Group (LIG) was 180 sq. ft of carpet area, costing about Rs 37,000. People were expected to pay two instalments of Rs 5,000 each, one as down payment and the other on completion. Around Rs 5,400 per tenement would be generated as cross-subsidy from commercial tenements on the ground floor. The remaining Rs 22,000 would be recovered from people at 10 per cent rate of interest over a period of fifteen to twenty years.

On paper, the scheme sounded logical. In fact, it was not, for it created tremendous difficulties for the supposed beneficiaries, primarily because the state did not take into account the investment that people had already made in their existing structures, often going into debt in the process. Instead, it wanted them to accept a further burden of debt for the new house.

Secondly, the scheme did not accommodate the additional servicing costs of living in these new apartment blocks. Even if the residents paid a 'rent' to the municipal corporation, if they lived on municipal land, or to the local dada, if it was private land, the amount was far lower than what they would be expected to pay in the new PMGP buildings. As a result, the PMGP triggered off a panic sale of huts as people recovered the costs of improving their huts and moved to other slums.

Chatterjee grants that the difference between the PMGP and previous government schemes was that it had built-in community consultation and participation. But the extent of such participation was limited to the community forming a society and appointing its own architect. He says, 'Once that was done, the scheme was submitted to the PMGP. We would have to spend all the money and even the community's contribution would have to come to the PMGP. We would then proceed, through the transparent bidding mechanism for contracts. The contractor's work would then be supervised by the architect who would be accountable to the community. The PMGP would also monitor the work and pay out the money. At the same time we had to spend money in constructing transit camps.'

It is precisely this centralization of control with the PMGP that self-help groups found difficult to accept as it removed from their hands the control over the final construction of their buildings. Here Chatterjee differed with some of the community-based organizations already working in Dharavi. He admits that he had a different approach then. Since then, his views are more akin to those expressed by the non-governmental organizations in terms of what people want and need and how to ensure that their participation in slum redevelopment schemes is meaningful and sustainable.

PEOPLE'S WAY

In 1986, Chatterjee and his colleagues were working on a different set of premises than organizations like the National Slum Dwellers' Federation (NSDF) and Society for Promotion of Area Resource Centres (SPARC). NSDF/SPARC saw that the exercise to redevelop Dharavi was being done in the absence of a clear understanding of what Dharavi really is, or of what those who were expected to be part of the scheme really wanted. To obtain more accurate information about the settlements that together made up Dharavi and to ascertain people's views on the redevelopment plan, NSDF/SPARC launched an enumeration exercise.

The Dharavi survey involved communities in different settlements in the process so that the information generated would be 'owned' by them and they could use it in their negotiations with the state in the future. Too often surveys of such areas are conducted without involving the people concerned. As a result, they have no idea why the information is being collected and to what use it will be put.

In the course of doing the enumeration, NSDF/SPARC realized that although Dharavi was being looked upon as one slum even by the planners, the residents did not see themselves as part of one settlement. Instead, each settlement had a distinct identity. This was determined by the people who lived there—whether they had been relocated from another part of Mumbai, whether they were migrants from one part of India, or whether they were poor people involved in a common trade.

For the process of enumeration, people from each settlement were trained to gather the information. At the end of each day, the team of enumerators would collate the data and explain the process to the community so that the entire exercise was transparent and inclusive. The data was then cross-checked against the ration cards available at the local fair price shop and also the voters' list at the Election Commission's office, as well as the rent lists at the collectorate. Regularized slum households with a photo pass pay 'rent' regularly to the collector. This is an important document to establish their identity and the length of time they have lived in a particular slum.

As a result of this exercise, people were able to develop their own map of Dharavi which marked out all the main landmarks. The team also examined land records to determine the ownership of the land on which their settlements had been constructed. They found, for instance, that of the 175 hectares that made up Dharavi, 106 hectares belonged to the municipal corporation, private owners came next with forty-three hectares and the rest was state or central government land. It was in the course of the enumeration process that the Dharavi Vikas Samiti (Dharavi Redevelopment Committee), consisting of people interested in improving Dharavi, was established. It allied itself with the NSDF.

Even as the NSDF/SPARC team was involving communities in the enumeration and data collection process, the government decided to conduct its own survey for the PMGP scheme. Over 5,000 government representatives fanned out into the settlements to collect the information. In the end, there was a significant disparity between the numbers that NSDF/SPARC survey produced and that of the government.

According to the government survey, there were 55,000 households in Dharavi in November 1987. The NSDF/SPARC survey counted 86,000 structures housing 1,06,000 families with an average of 6.2 individuals per house. In addition, they counted sixty-two Pongal houses.

If one accepted the NSDF/SPARC data, the population would have been over six lakh in 1986. The PMGP was working on a figure of three lakh and the earlier Correa Committee had concluded that there were only 2.5 lakh people living in Dharavi.

Such a huge discrepancy in numbers underlines the inaccuracy of government-run surveys in areas like Dharavi, where people are not ready to tell you the full story unless they trust you. That is why the community-based approach to enumeration, so that the data would be in the hands of the community, made sense and was ultimately far more useful.

Unfortunately, the government continues to use its own inadequate and inaccurate data for all its plans without even looking at the reality. In Dharavi, you do not need to count each house to realize that the official numbers and the real numbers are vastly different.

WHERE THEY CAME FROM

One of the innovative aspects of the NSDF/SPARC survey was the 'historical trace'. They tried to locate original residents of Dharavi and put together a picture of how it had grown and developed. This process revealed that many migrants had settled in Dharavi from the early 1930s, when this swampy stretch was at the edge of the city limits. In the 1950s, '60s and '70s, many pavement and slum dwellers from the island city of Bombay were moved to Dharavi. The later migrants were those who came to join the existing trade activities in the settlements or to work in the city as the area was conveniently located between two major railway lines—Central and Western.

The survey also revealed the composition of Dharavi's residents. The majority, 36.76 per cent, came from Tamil Nadu, closely followed by 33.36 per cent from Maharashtra. Other groups were from Uttar Pradesh, Karnataka, Andhra Pradesh, Gujarat, Kerala, Rajasthan and Bihar, in that order. Of the Tamilians, over half came from Tirunelvelli district; the other big chunk, more than a quarter, was from Salem. The rest of the Tamil population included people from South Arcot, North Arcot, Ramanathapuram, Kanyakumari, Madurai and Coimbatore districts.

Of the Maharashtrians, over 20 per cent were from Ratnagiri, closely followed by 19.24 per cent from Satara. There were also people from Sangli, Solapur, Kolhapur and Pune districts. The original inhabitants of Dharavi, the Kolis, were less than 6 per cent of the Marathi-speaking population.

Although people from Uttar Pradesh comprised only 10 per cent of the population, according to this survey, they are certainly as visible a presence in Dharavi as the Tamilians. Indeed, a casual observer might be led to believe that their numbers equalled those of the Tamilians. However, this is not true. Their visibility has partly to do with the trades in which they are involved, like the leather business, and the fact that they live in large concentrations around Badi Masjid on Dharavi Main Road. One-third of the UP-wallahs come from Azamgarh district, another third come from Basti and the rest from Gonda, Jaunpur, Faridabad, Lucknow, Allahabad and Pratapgarh.

The survey documented all the income-generating occupations in Dharavi and came up with an astoundingly varied list. This ranged from 5,000 units churning out leather-finished goods to one of the largest plastic recycling industries in the country employing more than 5,000 people on daily wages. A thriving food industry produced everything—from idlis, to *chiki, gulab jamuns, channa* and papads—in the lanes and bylanes of Dharavi. And an estimated twenty-five bakeries sent out fresh *pav, khari* and *butter* to all parts of the city.

Also, according to the survey, while Dharavi had twenty-seven temples, six churches and eleven mosques, it had only 842 toilets and 162 taps for a population of six lakh. On completion of this exercise, and given the profile of Dharavi that emerged from it of a productive area where there were a large number of small industries, the NSDF argued that the PMGP should recognize that parts of Dharavi were industrial and should be granted that status instead of shifting out production units from the area.

The PMGP never got around to tackling the vast 13th Compound, the recycling centre of Dharavi, even though a fire in the area provided it with the ideal opportunity to start from scratch. At the same time, barring one instance where the NSDF was central to the formation of a cooperative society, it failed to accept the concept of housing that accommodates petty trades which provide sustenance to the majority of people living in Dharavi.

The PMGP concentrated instead on the periphery of Dharavi as these were the areas where the new sewer lines had been laid. As a result, it was feasible to build high-rises with toilets in the flats. Practically no work has been done since then to extend the sewer lines to the interior of Dharavi. High-rises have come up on all sides of Dharavi but the central part of the settlement remains dense, disorganized and unserviced.

Whatever its shortcoming, the PMGP scheme was a beginning. It marked the recognition of Dharavi as a potentially developable area. It also marked the start of an expansion phase in the city's development where an east–west axis was recognized as important. So far, most of the service sector had concentrated on the southern tip of the island city and the industry had been moved north under the development plan. Housing had increasingly grown in the northern suburbs with its proximity to employment. As a result, the transport services along this north–south axis were increasingly stretched and overused.

The idea of developing reclaimed land from the Mahim Creek area just north of Dharavi began to take shape around the time the PMGP buildings were being constructed. Although several government buildings, including the Maharashtra Housing and Area Development Authority, had come up in the area, the idea got a fillip when the Diamond Bourse was proposed on land across the creek and the Bandra-Kurla Complex of offices was planned. Suddenly, Dharavi's location became much more attractive.

FREE HOUSES

In 1996, Gautam Chatterjee found himself heading the Slum Redevelopment Authority (SRA) and was given the task of implementing a much more ambitious Slum Redevelopment Scheme (SRS) devised under the coalition government of the Shiv Sena and the Bharatiya Janata Party in 1995. In their election manifesto, these parties had promised free houses to forty lakh slum households in Mumbai. It was argued that most slum dwellers had already spent a substantial amount to develop the land on which they lived. Given the current value of that land, they ought to be given a free house in exchange for releasing some of the land for other uses.

The scheme, however, had to be fleshed out. The government set up a committee headed by Dinesh K. Afzalpurkar, who already had experience with the PMGP, and invited private builders and some non-governmental organizations to join in.

The result was a scheme that, at least on paper, appeared workable. At the time the scheme was launched, land prices in Bombay had gone through the roof. The SRS expected that private builders would be interested in redeveloping slums if they could gain something out of it. Thus, the scheme permitted private builders to get the consent of 70 per cent of the residents of any slum, move them to a temporary transit accommodation (which the government would build) and construct high-rise buildings on this land. These buildings would include those that accommodated the slum dwellers, giving them a free flat each, and also buildings with bigger flats which could be sold in the open market, thereby allowing the builder to recover his cost and more.

Each slum household was promised a 225 sq. ft area free in these high-rises with a built-in toilet. However, the height of the room would be just nine feet. As a result, those slum dwellers who had already invested in a loft in their existing structures as part of the slum upgradation project did not find the scheme attractive. The scheme had a commercial component but only for recognized businesses. As most slum dwellers conducted unrecognized businesses in their homes, they were not entitled additional space where this could be done.

It was assumed that because the slum dwellers were being offered a free house, they would jump at it. In fact, as the director of SPARC, Sheela Patel, argues, over a lifetime most slum dwellers would have spent up to over Rs 2 lakh to upgrade their existing dwellings. So the replacement was technically not free. Furthermore, the monthly outgoings for maintenance were often higher than what they presently paid by way of 'rent'.

The SRS failed to take off not just because of a lack of enthusiasm among some slum communities but also because of the fall in land prices within a year of the scheme being launched. When the plan was finalized in 1995, land prices in Mumbai were high. Dharavi's current location made it an especially attractive place for implementing the scheme. It is sandwiched conveniently between Western and Central Railways. And just across Mahim Creek, which cannot be reclaimed because it has been declared an ecologically important area, is the new Diamond Bourse which is being developed. A little further is the Mangaldas Goculdas Market that is eventually tipped to replace the centuries-old Crawford Market in south Mumbai.

It was assumed that once these two schemes took off, many a merchant would want living/office space much closer to these locations. Dharavi would be ideal, especially the areas running alongside the main Mahim–Sion link road. Dreaming of making a killing, builders moved into Dharavi as soon as the SRS was announced, quickly rounded up the slum dwellers, and got them to agree to form societies. Scores of redevelopment schemes were rapidly formulated and cleared by the authorities. Money passed hands, societies were registered, commencement certificates were issued, some of the old houses were demolished and the residents sent off to transit camps. And then nothing happened.

By the time all this had been done, the market had crashed. The development of the Bandra-Kurla Complex also slowed down. Suddenly, redeveloping Dharavi was not such a lucrative proposition for private builders. The profit margin was nowhere near the earlier calculations. Right across Dharavi you could find evidence of the greed of the private builders and the disappointment of the area's residents.

As a result, even genuine schemes were looked upon sceptically. According to Jockin Arputham, who as leader of the National Slum Dwellers Federation has fought for years for housing rights of the urban poor, 30–35 per cent of all societies formed on paper in Dharavi are dysfunctional.

One group broke through this scepticism and that was the Dharavi Vikas Samiti (DVS), which is a part of the NSDF. The federation's approach to the SRS is entirely pragmatic. They view it as an opportunity for communities to fight for the kind of housing they feel they need and, at the same time, take the entitlement that the state has given them. Rather than either spurning the scheme because of the many problem areas in it, or handing over their future housing to a private builder, members of DVS, with the help of NSDF, decided to negotiate with the government for some critical changes in the scheme.

An earlier attempt to do this had failed. The DVS had tried, when buildings were being constructed under the PMGP, to design and redevelop one area where their members lived. They designed a building which accommodated the needs of the families for a loft by getting the government to agree that the rooms would have a height of fourteen feet even though the regulation height is only ten feet. Consultations with members of the community revealed that the majority were happy to have a community toilet as they did not want to waste precious space in their rooms. Under the PMGP schemes the houses were only 180 sq. ft for the low-income groups. And most people did not want a building of more than ground plus one as they were concerned about how far they would need to walk in the eventuality, or the inevitability, of water shortage. These were practical points that had emerged from detailed consultations with the community.

Unfortunately, in the 1980s, when DVS and NSDF attempted this intervention, they had not mastered the system of housing finance. As a result, a scheme that was billed to take no more than two years dragged on for ten, adding to costs and the frustration of members of the society. The building was finally completed, but it did not resemble its original plan because the society had to make changes to accommodate many more households to recover costs.

The experience of what is called Markandaya Society under the PMGP had prepared the Dharavi Vikas Samiti to deal with the Slum Redevelopment Scheme. P.S. Shanmuganand, originally from Tirunelvelli district, is the chief developer of the Rajiv Indira Cooperative Housing Society. Located off the main Mahim–Sion link road in Kalyanwadi, this building has become the cynosure of all eyes in Dharavi.

The reasons are simple. DVS first got all the fifty-four

residents of the plot to agree to form a society which they themselves would manage. Then they found a contractor who would do the work. They were lucky. They found four brothers, who own and run Falak Construction Pvt. Ltd, who readily agreed to take on the task.

The DVS negotiated with the Slum Redevelopment Authority, under which all schemes are managed, for a special dispensation; they wanted to construct flats of 225 sq. ft, as required under the scheme, but with a height of fourteen feet which would permit a half loft. They argued that this would ensure that all those with workshops in their homes could continue their work and even those who did not do so at present would find an additional source of income.

The permission was granted and today Markandaya Society, on the south of Dharavi on 60 Feet Road, and Rajiv Indira Housing Society on the highway have this arrangement. A three-plus-ground building will accommodate fifty-four families. In the additional area, freed by removing their huts, another building will be constructed of seven floors with the regular nine feet high, 225 sq. ft flats. This will accommodate another forty-two families from an adjoining slum. This scheme, in turn, will free up space near the road, give Rajiv Indira Housing Society better access to the main road, and allow them to develop the roadside property as commercial premises which can be sold at good prices.

The scheme is innovative because it accommodates people's needs and also recognizes the commercial possibilities that this location can yield. The Rajiv Indira Housing Society example has now been accepted as a feasible plan that any group of slum dwellers can adopt as part of the redevelopment scheme.

LESSONS FOR THE FUTURE

There are several lessons from the Rajiv Indira Cooperative Society experience that are relevant for future slum redevelopment schemes in Mumbai or elsewhere. First, if a community is consulted, and assured that its views will be taken seriously, there is the possibility of coming up with housing solutions that people want and will maintain. In the past, government-designed and -funded housing schemes for the urban poor have been deemed failures because the 'beneficiaries' have sold their allotted flats and moved back into slums.

The assumption from this was that such people prefer to live in illegal, informal housing rather than in formal housing. It was never considered that the kind of structures the government built for the poor were inappropriate. Most of these buildings are not just badly designed but are also poorly constructed. If you have four-storey-high buildings without an adequate water supply and built-in toilets, how are people supposed to survive? Without water, flushes do not work. And no one, not even a poor person, will voluntarily want to carry water up four floors just for the joy of living in a pucca building which looks as if it is about to collapse. Furthermore, as it is mostly women who have to bear the burden of collecting water, they are hardly going to be enthusiastic about such structures. They would much prefer living in their incrementally improved ground-level slum structures.

Dharavi today has several buildings which are either unfinished or which have been caught up in disputes, lying empty and unused, while their neighbourhoods are teeming with people waiting for a pucca house. These are the buildings constructed under various schemes including the PMGP. They were supposed to be 'sold' to raise additional finance for low-cost housing. But neither did buyers rush to purchase flats which were so poorly constructed, nor were they allocated to people in Dharavi looking for a place to live.

This is a pity, as unlike many other areas, people living in Dharavi wish to continue living there. This is evident from the composition of people living in the high-rises built on private lands like the Nagri and Diamond apartments as well as Vaibhav. Most of the residents of these buildings are people who had always lived in Dharavi. This shows a certain level of identification with the area which you do not necessarily find in other slums. It also suggests that if buildings meet the needs of people who plan to live in them, irrespective of whether they are poor or rich, they are more likely to remain occupied, and will even be maintained, than unimaginative concrete blocks constructed in haste to solve a 'problem'.

The Dharavi experience also shows the limitations of seeing areas as 'slums' without recognizing the variegated nature of land use and structures. People live in Dharavi, but they also work there. In the absence of separate areas for production units, the two are merged. While this might not matter much for home-based industries, it is a real health hazard in the case of other units. There are units, for instance, that have furnaces built into the rooms. Men work and breathe vast quantities of carbon monoxide day and night. In other parts, bakeries light their wood-fired ovens in the early hours of the morning and the entire area is enveloped in choking smoke. And the filthy work of treating leather hides, which includes washing off the blood and flesh and later removing the hair, is conducted in open spaces in close proximity to where people live. All this muck flows down open drains, past people's homes.

Under the present scheme, the high-rises will provide places for people to live and there will be some commercial spaces, mainly for shops. But there is no plan for the small-scale industries that are such an integral part of a place like Dharavi.

There are two strategies that can be adopted. One is to close down all hazardous units, regardless of where they are located, and move them out of Dharavi. In the past, such a strategy did not work in the oldest industry of Dharavi, leather processing. It will be even more difficult in the case of small production units which are hidden deep inside the dense settlements. But a systematic effort could be made. The new location need not be in a distant suburb. There are several plots of land along the Mahim–Sion link road which could be developed into mini-industrial areas. In fact, 13th Compound, which is a vast recycling area, is ideally located for such a purpose.

For the non-polluting units, a separate strategy needs to be devised. These businesses run on very low margins. Often all the members of a household are employed in the work. Such businesses cannot survive if people are required to pay additional costs for a place where the work is done. A more pragmatic approach is to accept the argument put forward by the Rajiv Indira Cooperative Society, that is, to permit a loft to be constructed as part of the 225 sq. ft room in some buildings. People have expressed their willingness to pay for this additional space. In the long run, a genuine and sustainable redevelopment of a place like Dharavi is only possible if the working needs of the people are fully accommodated.

And, finally, what Dharavi shows is that the needs of settlements vary greatly. Therefore, a uniform approach to redevelopment is not feasible. The potters of Kumbharwada, for instance, will not be satisfied with a high-rise building, even if their rooms have a half-loft, because their trade requires space at ground level for their potters' wheels and their kilns.

Therefore, instead of treating all of Dharavi like one slum and imposing a uniform policy, flexibility and real community consultation needs to be built into the policy. This will ensure that people will take some initiative in solving their housing problem instead of sitting back and waiting for the government to deliver.

Dharavi is already greatly transformed from the days when people spoke of it as a *khadi* (swamp). 'Now it is *sona* (gold),' says Khatija, remembering her early days in Dharavi. 'Then there was no electricity. We used to live on that khadi and there, day and night, *daru ka bhatti* (illegal liquor still) would be burning. When I first saw it, I thought the entire hill was on fire!'

At the end of 1999, Dharavi had moved a long distance from the days of burning hills and swamps. But Khatija continues to live in Dargah Chawl, Social Nagar, albeit in a greatly improved structure. She still dreams of a pucca house.

20

THREE PIECES

Dilip D'Souza

THREAD OF A SUBSIDY

Madhukar Gurav welcomed me to his apartment, airy and bright. Its 225 sq. ft houses a family of four. Yet this modest home is several levels up from where he lived before, and not just because it is on the top floor of the building. Until Gurav scraped together the five lakh rupees (then about $12,500) to buy this flat two years ago, he lived in a Mumbai slum in a shack made of plywood and tarp.

But Gurav's new quarters are also in a slum—the most famous in Mumbai, in fact—which he shares with about one million other people. In a typically Indian paradox, his neighbourhood of Dharavi, notoriously known as 'Asia's largest slum', has suddenly turned desirable. Builders, developers and politicians all eye the square mile of prime real estate that it occupies and hatch plans to put it to use. That, and Gurav's step up, says things about this city. And it's no wonder. With sixteen million people squeezed into 240 sq. miles, Mumbai is one of the most densely populated cities in the world. Housing, in perennially short supply, is wildly expensive. I am by no means rich, yet my suburban 1,100 sq. ft flat was recently appraised a few years ago at Rs 3.25 crore (then about $800,000). I own it only because I inherited it from an uncle; I could not have afforded to buy it when he died in 1998, and I could not afford it today. Like Gurav's apartment, mine is pleasant but not particularly sumptuous. It's an ordinary Mumbai flat built in the 1970s, but it has made me almost a millionaire.

Because housing is so expensive, about two-thirds of Mumbai's population live in slums or in the streets. This has been true for decades and, yes, it remains true in ready-for-boom-time India. Indian politicians have concocted countless schemes over the years to 'redevelop' slums, which they consider eyesores. For a variety of reasons, they've never managed to deliver on their promises. But one idea that took off decades ago still fuels the construction boom in Dharavi and throughout Mumbai. It explains a lot about this dizzying, maddening city.

The concept, called 'cross-subsidy', is simple. The government invites developers to build flats to be sold to slum dwellers at subsidized prices. In return for their participation, the government loosens zoning regulations, usually in the same area, so that the developers can build other larger and plusher apartments to sell to middle- and upper-class people at the market rate. The profit developers make on these sales will pay for the subsidized units—a nice marriage between government policy and private profit-making. Or so the theory goes.

Take the cross-subsidy principle to its logical conclusion, and you have free housing for slum dwellers. In 1995, a new government rolled into power in the state of Maharashtra promising just that: free homes for four million slum dwellers in Mumbai, the state capital, over its five years in office.

Consider the arithmetic. Divide four million by five. That's 800,000 homes, assuming five people live in each one. Divide by five once more. That's 160,000 subsidized flats to be built in each year of the government's term. Quick calculations showed that, given construction costs then, profits made from the market-rate sale of 560 apartments would finance 1,000 free homes for slum dwellers. So, to give away 160,000 homes, developers would have to sell almost 90,000 full-priced homes. In total, they would have to build 250,000 each year. (The numbers have changed since then, but the reasoning hasn't.)

These figures are clearly unattainable. As the government report that established this policy noted in 1995, developers were building only 40,000 housing units per year, not including the units for the cross-subsidy deal. Today, that number is up to about 60,000, but it remains well short of the annual demand.

Like everything, the price of housing follows supply and demand. Say builders manage to build 90,000 additional for-profit units in a single year. What will that do to a market already fat on a supply of 40,000? Easy. Prices will go into free fall. The foundation of the cross-subsidy plan implodes.

Not surprisingly, the scheme was a spectacular failure. By 1997, slum dwellers should have moved into 320,000 free flats. That year, I asked the Urban Development Department how many homes had actually been built. The answer: 1,146. It's a Catch-22. Mumbai's soaring real estate prices made this idea conceivable. Executing it made it impossible.

Today, back in Dharavi, the cross-subsidy theory fuels the

transformation of the neighbourhood's tenements into apartment buildings. Developers are frenetically building middle- and upper-class homes there and across the city, while millions of slum and lower-class residents don't have proper housing.

That's where people like Gurav enter the picture. In one scheme, a group of slum residents band together and invite a builder to raze their shacks and build new apartments, some to turn over to them and some to sell at the market rate. There are now several such buildings in Dharavi and elsewhere in Mumbai.

The interesting thing about Gurav is that he didn't belong to such a group. He hoarded his money and bought his flat from the original owner, who knew its value and couldn't resist the temptation to sell. With the money from the sale, he was able to buy another home and still come out ahead. The owner has moved back to a shack, Gurav explained to me during our visit. 'In that slum over there,' his daughter piped up, pointing out of the window to an expanse of rooftops like so many matchboxes in the distance.

And that's one more twist in the cross-subsidy tale. If you build at the rate the housing crisis—or an election promise— demands, the market crashes, making a cross-subsidy unworkable. Therefore, you build slowly, so that housing prices remain high. But when prices remain high, some of the former slum dwellers will sell their flats and move back to the slum. Sometimes, that was their plan all along.

I have a vicarious personal interest in this whole tangle. Among other interesting jobs he held in the Indian bureaucracy, my late father was Mumbai's municipal commissioner—the equivalent of a mayor—from 1969 to 1970. Low-cost housing was always his great interest, and for the last fourteen years of his life, he

ran a low-cost project in Mumbai's northern suburbs founded
on the cross-subsidy principle. It has about 5,000 subsidized
flats, plus about 1,100 others and commercial space for sale at
market rates.

My father died in September 2007, and the veteran socialist
leader P.B. Samant, one of the moving spirits behind the project,
died about a year later, but the project goes on. Why does it
work? Because the subsidy is small, residents pay close to market
rates for their little flats, and because it has taken so long to
complete—nearly twenty-five years. The slow progress troubled
my father and his colleagues greatly.

But they understood that in the convoluted world of Mumbai,
this remains the only workable way to provide livable, sustainable
housing for the poor. And yet the dilemma remains that those
who are worst off can't afford even the subsidized flats.

As I downed a cup of tea with Gurav and his family in
Dharavi, I found myself reflecting on the final, yet perhaps
simplest, lesson in all of this. Anyone seeking to solve Mumbai's
housing crisis must recognize the enormity of the problem and
proceed accordingly. Ponderously, even. Anything else is a band
aid. Just ask Madhukar Gurav. Two years after he bought it, his
flat is worth more than twice what he paid. Naturally, he thinks
he might sell and move. Where to? 'To another slum,' he says
and smiles. 'Where else?'

'KITNA PALTI KIYA!': DHARAVI, VIA THE LINGO*

The view from the terrace is dominated by, of all things,
staircases. Ladders, really. Dozens of metal ladders on terraces,

---

*Perhaps best translated as 'What a flip-flop!'

spindly things that lead to water tanks on top of buildings, flimsy things that you would hesitate to trust your weight to. One rising beside me too. In a sea of clearly cheaply made buildings, these rooftop adornments look especially cheap. Yet they fit where I am. Dharavi: climb out of the morass, sky's the limit, watch your step on the flimsy stair . . . OK, I should not stretch the metaphors too far. But they come to mind anyway.

It's been four years or more since I last set foot here. Today I'm amazed by how different the place looks since that visit. The view is no longer a sea of roofs of matchbox-like shacks, though there are those too, but of seven- and eight-storeyed buildings like the one I'm atop. Certainly Dharavi is still teeming, still a feast for every one of your senses, still arguably the country's finest tribute to enterprise and verve—but physically, it is swiftly transforming itself from a long-held image. Something is emerging from that chrysalis of rooftops. Maybe not a butterfly, but something.

Dharavi has been in the newspapers recently, and not just for being Asia's biggest slum. Via ads placed in publications around the globe at the end of May 2007, the Maharashtra government invited tenders for a Dharavi makeover. Those who paid Rs 100,000 for the tender document include Reliance, DLF and Hiranandani, and a clutch of firms from Dubai, Hong Kong, Israel and elsewhere. The estimate for the so-called Dharavi Redevelopment Project (DRP) is astonishing: over Rs 9,000 crore. That's nearly one lakh rupees for every child, woman and man in Dharavi. And what's the vision behind that unimaginable sum? Well, Dharavi is arguably the city's last large tract of land that's not been commercially exploited. For years nobody cared much about it, so Dharavi grew much like moss on a rainy day.

But now there's the nearby Bandra-Kurla Complex, and BKC has plenty of smart new corporate offices, and the people in those offices need housing and entertainment and shopping . . . suddenly, Dharavi is a large tract of rupee signs. Forty million square feet of commercial and residential space will hit the market if the DRP goes through. In a city perennially short of real estate, that prospect alone is already starting to push prices down: one developer in an interview in the *Mint* (5 June) said that BKC prices are down 'by as much as 15–20 per cent'. Schools are coming up, industrial units will be rehoused (polluting ones at the outskirts of the city), and there will even be an SEZ.

But as with any large project, there is substantial and growing opposition. On 18 June, Dharavi shut down and many residents joined a procession to the nearby office of the Slum Redevelopment Authority. They were not consulted about these plans, and they are unhappy about the snippets they hear about them. For example, that they will be re-housed in 225 sq. ft flats. Often, that is smaller than what they have now. Besides, it's an old fact of life in Dharavi that people run small businesses— shops to tailoring to workshops—out of their homes. How will that happen from 225 sq. ft?

Besides, too, there are already signs of how this development will happen: buildings like the one I'm atop.

This is the Jai Kalimata society, and I've just been speaking to several residents. Twenty-odd families who used to live in *jhopadpattis* (mud huts) on this very tract of land; about seven years ago a builder offered to house them in flats in a building he would erect there. The result is this seven-storey affair, where twenty-three-year-old Sharada and her mother Vimal live on the fifth floor.

On their wall is a garlanded portrait of Shirdi's Sai Baba, and a red-rimmed Air India clock inscribed to 'Shri Chandkiran A Yadav, 25-01-07' (no idea who that is, but it's neither Sharada's brother nor her 'chulta'—father's brother—the two men of the house, both away on security guard jobs). In the other room of the 225 sq. ft flat, every possible receptacle—bucket, cooking vessel, small plastic tank, mug, bottle—is filled with water, for, says Vimal, 'we get municipal water for only an hour each day'. For that one hour, it flows into a pump outside the building, pumped from there to the tank on the terrace. Enough to last the residents the whole day, confirms Vimal, but even so, she feels she must hoard in her flat. A lingering habit from the jhopadpatti days, maybe?

Our conversation turns into an education, for me, in the arcane argot of development in a great slum.

First up, of course, is that Sharada works in a 'garment'—one of the nearly infinite number of tiny Dharavi sweatshops that turn out clothes, in her case jeans. Why has she not gone to work today? She giggles. 'Garment is closed,' she says.

Then it's 'maintain'. In the little shack they used to occupy, their outgoings were a monthly rent ('bhada', they say) of Rs 20 and the electricity bill, usually about Rs 200 a month. They agreed to the move up because water was a constant problem, involving a trek to a communal tap, and because they had to use a public toilet, also a trek. Move, said the builder, and you'll be in a building with just three flats on a floor, water and toilet in your home, electricity bill about the same, and you'll only have to pay about Rs 300 a month as 'maintain'. That last, meaning the fees in a building like this, to pay for lift, watchman, trash collection—general maintenance, hence the word.

Seemed like a bargain.

After the jhopadpattis were torn down, they lived six years in a building in Kurla, then moved to their new flat late last year. Came some shocks. Four flats per floor, first. Electricity bills are higher, second—anywhere between Rs 350 and 550 a month. And third, the 'maintain': not the promised 300, but Rs 600. That is, monthly outgoings have risen about five-fold since jhopadpatti days. But incomings—two security-guard incomes plus Sharada's 'garment' take-home add up to about Rs 6,000 a month—have not risen five-fold. Oh no.

It's an airy, bright flat, and the two women are grateful for the private toilet and water. But it no longer seems such a bargain. '*Builder kitna palti kiya, dekh!*' ('See how the builder flip-flopped!') is Vimal's wry but annoyed comment, and she follows it with: 'We should get capacity for the money we give, yes or no?' She means '*paisa-vasool*', value for money.

At least a few of the families saw all this coming—they took money from the builder and moved somewhere. About ten more families sold their new flats—at an incredible Rs 12 lakh today, a tempting cash cow—and moved out too. 'Capacity' indeed.

There's more to the 'palti'. Jai Kalimata is actually only half the building. Just a wall divides it from Jai Bajrangbali, home to over a hundred families. They were also in jhopadpattis here, so they got the same deal from the builder. But Vimal points down at the gate. 'See that? Same gate for both societies. We told the builder, give the Bajrangbali people a gate at the back of the property. But what did they do? *Palti kiya!* Yes, just one gate to both buildings that are really just one building. And the Bajrangbali people park their motorbikes on the short drive leading to the gate. And there are so many of them. And they are different people, says Vimal, they are 'Mohammedans'.

Something makes me steal a look at her portrait of the Sai Baba of Shirdi.

From another window, Sharada points to more buildings. Those are, she says, 'shell' buildings. It takes a few tries, but I finally understand this word too: it's 'sale', meaning that flats there were sold, not just given to residents. The old cross-subsidy idea: builder uses the land he gets to build market-rate flats that subsidize the flats he also builds to offer residents.

Sharada wants me to know, and report, that the 'maintain' in 'shell' buildings is lower than in 'society' buildings like hers. Why? 'Builder said our society is set back from the road.' Which it is—remember the short motorbike-laden drive—but that's the explanation? Really? 'Really', she says.

It's been a confusing few hours, especially as I come to grip with the lingo. But that's Dharavi: confusing even as it mutates. For me that's epitomized in the small wooden sign on a nearby edifice. It says 'BM Enterprise Vinay Coating', and below that 'BM Jaiswar, Advocate'.

Only in Dharavi will you get an aluminium coating workshop and an advocate's chambers, both in the same tiny room.

And if you want to consult the advocate, or get some aluminium coated, you have to negotiate—what else—a spindly, cheaply made ladder. Dharavi is moving up. But watch for the 'palti'.

KICK IN THE STOMACH

There's a sudden gap in the conversation, a momentary but noticeable frostiness. Just when I am about to ask what the

matter is, Vinod speaks. Not really angry, but quiet and
reproachful, these are his words as near as I can translate: 'We
believe he is God. How can you refer to him as a man?'

I make some sheepish apology—'you're right, I'm sorry, of
course he is a God to you' is the gist of it—and only then does
Vinod relax.

Genial Vinod Narkar and I have been standing outside his
brother Pramod's tiny phone booth in Dharavi, chatting about
all that's happening in the area. Earlier, I noted idly that the
door to the booth had a small 'Art of Living' poster with a
picture of Sri Sri Ravi Shankar. Now Vinod has just told me
what that's about, and that's ended with me putting foot in
mouth.

But first: Dharavi is changing, he says; the jhopadpattis are
turning into multi-storeyed buildings. He points to the one that
looms above us, where he and Pramod live. He doesn't like the
current official plans for Dharavi, a departure from the tested
and government-originated Slum Redevelopment Authority
path that produced his building (which is prominently marked
'SRA'). In the old way, a group of residents could get together
and approach a builder, who would place them in a temporary
accommodation (a 'transit camp'), demolish their shacks and
erect blocks of flats there, some of which would be given to
them and some sold for a profit. But now the buzz is that
Dharavi will be divided into 'sectors', each to be handed over to a
private developer who will decide how to develop the sector.

Whatever the truth is in this buzz, many people dislike it, and
for various very valid-sounding reasons. Pramod points out
that what they've heard is that there will be much taller 'towers'—
15–20 storeys—built in these sectors, and the resultant 'maintain'

charges will be much higher than in the 6–7 storey SRA buildings.

Maybe, but what about the well-known plan to reserve the ground and first floors of these towers for small businesses? If a man like Pramod could live just above his shop, wouldn't that justify the higher outgoings?

Well, across the road from Pramod, Murtaza Ali runs a small *kabadi* business from a ten by twelve feet room crammed with rusting bicycles, old paper and plastic bottles. Listening intently to us, he pipes up to say the sector plans will ruin small businesses like his, several up and down this road and thousands all over Dharavi. Even if they move to such buildings, their rents will be higher; but more importantly, they will be cleared off the road. By itself, that would mean an immediate drop in customers.

Around the corner, general store owner Mohammed Iqbal Suleiman Parekh, his shop also fronting the road, echoes this point. He points to the shop on the ground floor of the SRA building 'Shivneri' opposite. It is a tall step up from road level and set back a few feet. 'If I were there,' he says, 'I would be doing 50 per cent less business just because of that step. People today just want to take what they need'—here he grabs a *gutkha* (a mixture of tobacco, betel nut and palm nut) packet hanging above us—'and go. And if this sector comes, they will put me in a shop like that.'

Mangesh Roge, who used to run a printing press but now contracts out orders, starts by saying it's good that Dharavi will change. 'Should we live in a slum all our lives?' he asks, 'and after all, doesn't everyone have dreams of a better life?' But with the sector plans, Dharavi will become a magnet for 'high-class' and 'middle-class' people, which will eventually drive out the 'low-

class' people like him. Because they won't be able to afford the
higher costs of living that are coming. It's like 'slow poison'—
Roge says those two words in English to underline his point—
'because you don't need to push people out. You don't need to
tell them to go. They will themselves leave.'

After conversations with several owners, like these, of small
Dharavi businesses, the overriding impression is one of gloom.
Sectors, says Pramod, are a kick in the stomachs of the poor.
'*Garib marne wale hain* (the poor are going to die),' he says, then
points to his own stomach. '*Mere pet pe bhi laath padega* (my
stomach will be kicked too).'

In Vinod's case, the gloom and dislike for the sector plan may
have an added edge that has to do with politics: Vinod is an
office-holder with the Shiv Sena, and the state government that
is pushing the redevelopment plans is a Congress/NCP coalition.
More than once, I've heard about how the protests against the
plans for Dharavi are 'just' an anti-Congress platform. Though
why that alone should invalidate the protests is a mystery to me.

That apart, Vinod has one major beef with the way Dharavi is
redeveloping, and he specifically asks that I write it down,
twisting his head to look into my diary to satisfy himself that I
am doing so. 'When they put up these buildings,' he says, 'the
builders don't care about space for three things we need. A
temple, a hall with a stage, and a garden. Do you know, when
our kids want to play, they come out of the buildings right onto
the road!'

And this is where Sri Sri Ravishankar enters the story, in
particular because of the third of those three things: a garden.
One year ago, Vinod tells me, the heart and soul of 'Art of
Living' came to this very Dharavi neighbourhood. 'I invited him

here,' says Vinod proudly, 'in fact, I went and brought him here. And it's because of him that we have this small garden.'

Here he points behind and to his left, to a little fenced-in enclosure that is part grass, part slush and dirty rainwater after the morning's downpour. Painted on a wall at the other end is a graceful swan, with the words 'ART OF LIVING' blazoned below. Sri Sri Ravishankar came here to inaugurate the spot.

Just outside the entrance at that end of the garden is a huge, noisome pile of garbage. It so constricts the road that a passing jeep has actually to drive over it to get through. As Vinod explains, the garden used to be an empty plot strewn with garbage. Following Sri Sri Ravishankar's direction, Art of Living turned it into what we now see, the garden that everyone in the area now uses. Nice. But does that mean garbage is now simply flung on the road?

In any case, this part of our conversation is where I inadvertently offend genial Vinod. 'You met him, so what is Sri Sri Ravishankar like?' I ask, 'What kind of man is he?'

For a few minutes after Vinod's frosty reaction, I feel like I've had a small kick in my stomach too. Metaphorical, but painful nevertheless.

21

MUMBAI'S SHADOW CITY

Mark Jacobson

All cities in India are loud, but nothing matches the 24/7 decibel level of Mumbai where the traffic never stops and the horns always honk. Noise, however, is not a problem in Dharavi. By nightfall, deep inside the maze of lanes too narrow even for the putt-putt of auto rickshaws, the slum is still as a verdant glade. Once you get accustomed to sharing 300 sq. ft of floor with fifteen humans and a countless number of mice, a strange sense of relaxation sets in—ah, at last a moment to think straight.

Dharavi is routinely called 'the largest slum in Asia', a dubious attribution sometimes conflated into 'the largest slum in the world'. This is not true. Mexico City's Neza-Chalco-Itza barrio has four times as many people. In Asia, Karachi's Orangi Township has surpassed Dharavi. Even in Mumbai, where about half of the city's swelling twelve million population lives in what is euphemistically referred to as 'informal' housing, other slum pockets rival Dharavi in size and squalour.

Yet Dharavi remains unique among slums. A neighbourhood

smack in the heart of Mumbai, it retains the emotional and historical pull of a subcontinental Harlem—a square mile centre of all things, geographically, psychologically, spiritually. Its location has also made it hot real estate in Mumbai, a city that epitomizes India's hopes of becoming an economic rival to China. Indeed, on a planet where half of humanity will soon live in cities, the forces at work in Dharavi serve as a window not only on the future of India's burgeoning cities, but on urban space everywhere.

Ask any longtime resident—some families have been here for three or more generations—how Dharavi came to be, and they'll say, 'We built it.' Stay for a while on the three-feet-wide lane of Rajendra Prasad Chawl, and you become acquainted with the rhythms of the place. The morning sound of devotional singing is followed by the rush of water. Until recently, few people in Dharavi had water hook-ups. Residents such as Meera Singh, a wry woman who has lived on the lane for thirty-five years, used to walk a mile to get water for the day's cleaning and cooking. At the distant spigot she would have to pay the local goons to fill her buckets. Deprived of public service because of their illegal status, the slum dwellers often found themselves at the mercy of the 'land mafia'. There are water goons, electricity goons. In this regard, the residents of Rajendra Prasad Chawl are fortunate. These days by DIY hook or crook, every household on the street has its own water tap. And today, like every day, residents open their hoses to wash down the lane as they stand in the doorways of their homes to brush their teeth.

Mornings at Rajendra Prasad Chawl are hectic. With the eight furniture makers to whom she rents part of her apartment gone for the day, Meera Singh combs the hair of her grandchildren: Atul, seven, Kanchan, ten, and Jyoti, twelve. Soon the apartment, home to fifteen, is empty, save for Meera and her twenty-something son, Amit, he of the dashing moustache and semi-hipster haircut. A couple of years ago, the Singh family, like everyone else in Dharavi, sat in front of the television to see local singer Abhijeet Sawant win the first Indian Idol contest. But now Meera is watching her favourite TV personality, the orange-robed yoga master Baba Ramdev, who demonstrates an anti-ageing technique: rubbing your fingernails against each other at a rapid pace.

'Why listen to this fool?' dismisses Amit.

'You know nothing,' Meera shouts back. 'His hair is black, and he is more than eighty years old.'

'Eighty? He is no more than forty. Don't fall for these cheating tricks.'

Meera shakes her head. She gave up trying to talk sense to Amit long ago. 'His head is in the clouds,' she says. She wishes he'd get a job as did his brother Manoj, who sews jeans in one of Dharavi's *karkhanas*, or factories. But this is not for him, Amit says. A thinker, he sees life in terms of 'a big picture'. Central to this conceit is the saga of how the Singhs came to Dharavi in the first place. Kshatriyas, regarded only second to Brahmins in the caste system, Amit's great uncles were zamindars, or landlords, in the service of the British. Stripped of privilege after independence, the family moved from Uttar Pradesh to Mumbai, where Amit's father worked in the textile mills. The collapse of the mills in the late 1970s landed the family in Dharavi. 'A hundred years ago, we would have been bosses,' Amit muses.

It is this story of chance and fate that spurs Amit's outsized sense of self. He's always got a dozen things going. There's his soap powder pyramid scheme, his real estate and employment agency gambits. New is his exterminator firm, for which he has distributed hundreds of handbills ('No bedbug! No rat!'), claiming to be Dharavi's 'most trusted' vermin remover, despite having yet to exterminate one cockroach.

Also on Amit's agenda is the *Janhit Times*, a tabloid he envisions as a hard-hitting advocate of grassroots democracy. The first edition featured a story about an allegedly corrupt Dharavi policeman. Amit's headline: 'A Giant Bastard, a Dirty Corrupted Devil, and Uniformed Goon.' Cooler heads, pointing out that the policeman wielded a *lathi* (a lethal bamboo nightstick), suggested a milder approach. Reluctantly, Amit went with 'A Fight for Justice.'

Even though the paper has yet to print its first edition, Amit carries a handsome press pass, which he keeps with his stack of business cards. This leads his mother to remark, 'That's you, many cards, no businesses.' Looking at her son, she says, 'You are such a dreamer.' It is an assessment that Amit, who has just decided to open a rental car agency in hopes of diversifying his portfolio in the mode of 'a Richard Branson of Dharavi' does not dispute.

'Talk about doing something about Mumbai slums and no one pays attention, talk about Dharavi, and it is Mission Impossible, an international incident,' says Mukesh Mehta as he enters the blonde-panelled conference room of the Maharashtra State Administration Building. For nine years, Mehta, a fifty-six-year-old architect and urban designer, has honed his plan for 'a sustainable, mainstreamed, slum-free Dharavi'. At today's meeting, after many PowerPoint presentations, the plan is slated for approval by the state chief minister, Vilasrao Deshmukh. Dharavi is to be divided into five sectors, each developed with the involvement of investors, mostly non-resident Indians. Initially, 57,000 Dharavi families will be resettled into high-rise housing close to their current residences. Each family is entitled to 225 sq. ft of housing, with its own indoor plumbing. In return for erecting the 'free' buildings, private firms will be given handsome incentives to build for-profit housing to be sold at (high) market rates.

'All that remains is the consent,' Mehta tells Deshmukh, a sour-looking gentleman in a snow-white suit sitting with his advisers at the forty-feet conference table.

Normally it is required that 60 per cent of Dharavi residents approve the plan. But Deshmukh announces that formal consent is not needed because Mehta's plan is a government-sponsored project. All he must do is give the residents a month to register complaints. 'A thirty-day window, not a day more,' Deshmukh says with impatient finality. Later, as his driver pilots his Honda Accord through traffic, Mehta is smiling, 'This is a good day,' he says. 'A dream come true.'

At first glance, Mehta, resident of an elegant apartment building on swank Nepean Sea Road, a long-time member of the British Raj-era Bomby Gymkhana and Royal Bombay Yacht Club, does not appear to be a Dharavi dreamer.

'You could say I was born with a golden spoon in my mouth,' he remarks at his West Bandra office, overlooking the Arabian Sea. 'My father came to Bombay from Gujarat without a penny and built a tremendous steel business. An astrologer told him his youngest son—me—would be the most successful one, so I was afforded everything.' These perks included a top education, plus a sojourn in the US, where Mehta studied architecture at Pratt Institute in Brooklyn.

'For me, America has always been the inspiration,' says Mehta, who made a fortune managing his father's steel business before deciding to develop real estate on Long Island's exclusive North Shore. 'Great Gatsby's country,' he says, detailing how he built high-end houses and lived in Centre Island, a white community with 'the riches of the richest'—such as Billy Joel, who recently listed his mansion for 37.5 million dollars.

'The slums were the furthest thing from my mind,' Mehta says. This changed when he returned to Mumbai. He saw what everyone else did—that the city was filled with a few rich people, a vast number of poor people, and hardly anyone in the middle. This was most evident in the appalling housing situation. The city was split between the Manhattan-priced high-rises that dotted the south Mumbai skyline and those brownish areas on the map marked with the letters ZP for *jhopadpatti*, aka slums.

Downtown business people railed that the slums were choking the life out of the city, robbing it of its rightful place in the twenty-first century. After all, India was no longer a post-colonial backwater famous only for the wretched people of the earth and the gurus who appealed to gullible Beatles. Now, when a computer broke in Des Moines, the help desk was in Bangalore. Economists were predicting exactly when the Indian GNP was likely to surpass that of the United States. If Mumbai was going to achieve its stated destiny of becoming a world-class metropolis, a rival to China's soaring Shanghai, how could that happen when every bit of open space was covered with these eyesores, these human dumps where no one paid taxes?

For Mukesh Mehta, if India was to become the ideal consumer

society, it would have to develop a true middle class—and housing would be the engine. The slums would have to be reclaimed. But which slums? There were so many of them. Then it jumped out, as clear as real estate's first axiom, location, location, location: Dharavi, right in the middle of the map. It was a quirk of geography and history, as any urban planner will tell you (the American inner city aside): Large masses of poor people are not supposed to be in the centre of the city. They are supposed to be on the periphery, stacked up on the outskirts. Dharavi had once been the northern fringe, but the ever-growing city had sprawled towards the famous slum, eventually surrounding it.

It didn't take a wizard to see the advantages of Dharavi's position. Served by two railway lines, it was ideally situated for middle-class commuters. Added to this was the advent of the Bandra-Kurla Complex, a global corporate enclave located across the remaining mangrove swamps, as close to Dharavi as Wall Street is to Brooklyn Heights. Sterile and kempt, the BKC was the future, right on the doorstep of the jhopadpatti.

'I have approached it as a developer. In other words, as a mercenary,' says Mehta, satellite images of Dharavi spread across his desk. 'But something happened. I opened an office in Dharavi, started talking to people, seeing who they were, how hard they worked, and how you could be there for months and never once be asked for a handout.'

'It was then,' Mehta says, 'I had an epiphany. I asked myself if these people were any different from my father when he first came from Gujarat. They have the same dreams. That was when I decided to dedicate the rest of my life to fixing the slums. Because I realized: The people of Dharavi—they are my genuine heroes.'

Back on Rajendra Prasad Chawl, news of the plan's approval was met with a decidedly mixed response. Meera Singh barely looked up from Baba Ramdev's lecture. She had heard often the stories about Dharavi's supposed transformation. Nothing much ever happened. Why should Mukesh Mehta's scheme be any different? Moreover, what reason would possess her to move into a 225 sq. ft apartment, even if it were free? She has nearly 400 sq. ft. 'Informal housing' has been good to her. She receives Rs 1,100 a month from the furniture workers and another thousand from renting her basement. Why should she give this up for a seven-storeyed apartment building where she'll be saddled with fees, including 'lift' charges? She doesn't like to ride in elevators. They give her the creeps. Amit Singh was more outspoken. Mehta's plan was nothing more than 'a scam, a chunk of fool's gold'. Amit was already drafting an editorial in the *Janhit Times* demanding a citizen's arrest of 'the gangster Mehta'.

In a place with one toilet for every few hundred people, the prospect of having one's own bathroom would seem to be a powerful selling point for the plan. But even if a stir broke out the previous summer when gurus declared the waters of Mahim Creek, the slum's reeking unofficial public toilet, had miraculously turned 'sweet' (leading to much gastrointestinal trauma), many Dharavi locals were unmoved by the idea of a personal loo.

'What need do I have of my own toilet?' asks Nagamma Shilpiri, who came to Dharavi from Andhra Pradesh twenty years ago and now lives with her crippled father and thirteen other relatives in two 150 sq. ft rooms. Certainly, Shilpiri is embarrassed by the lack of privacy when she squats in the early morning haze beside Mahim Creek. But the idea of a personal flush toilet offends her. To use all of that water for so few people seems a stupid, even sinful waste.

Everyone in Dharavi has their own opinion about how and why the plan was concocted to hurt them in particular. The nuanced assessment came from Shaikh Mobin, a plastics recycler in his mid-thirties. Mobin has lived his whole life in Dharavi, but he'd never called himself a slum dweller. His recycling business, started by his grandfather, passed to his father, and now to him ('the post-consumer economy, turning waste into wealth,' he says), has made Mobin a relatively rich man. He and his family live in a marble-floored flat in the thirteen-floor Diamond Apartments, 'Dharavi's number one prestige address.'

Mobin is a supporter of development in Dharavi. Change is necessary. Polluting industries like recycling have no business being in the centre of a modern metropolis. Mobin was already making plans to move his factory several miles to the north. But this didn't mean he was happy with what was happening in the place of his birth.

Much of his critique is familiar. The government's failure to create housing for middle-income people was responsible for the existence of slums, Mobin contends. Many people in Dharavi make enough money to live elsewhere, 'a house like you see on TV'. But since no such housing exists, they are doomed to live in the slum. Mobin doubts Mukesh Mehta's private developers will help. All over Dharavi are reminders of developmental disasters. Near Dharavi Cross Road, members of the L.P.T Housing Society, their houses torn down in preparation for their promised apartment, have spent the last eight years living in a half-finished building without steady electricity or water, at the mercy of the goons and the malarial Mumbai heat.

But when it comes down to it, Mobin says, Dharavi's dilemma is at once much simpler and infinitely more complex: 'This is our home.' This is what people like Chief Minister Deshmukh and Mukesh Mehta will never understand, Mobin says. 'Mukesh Mehta says I am his hero, but what does he know of my life? He is engaged in *shaikchilli*, which is dreaming, dreaming in the day. Does it occur to him that we do not wish to be part of his dream?'

Such sentiments cause Mukesh Mehta distress. 'If someone calls me a dreamer, I plead guilty,' he says, finishing his crème caramel at the Bombay Yacht Club. To be sure, Mehta has made some fanciful statements regarding Dharavi's future. His idea to install a golf driving range was met with widespread guffaws. 'Golf? What is golf?' asked Shilpiri's crippled father. The other day Mehta was fantasizing about constructing a 120,000-seat cricket stadium in the slum. Asked where the fans would park, Mehta looked stricken.

'Parking! Oh, my God,' he exclaimed. 'I'm going to be up all night trying to sort that one out.'

But being a dreamer doesn't mean he is 'unrealistic', Mehta says. He has been around the block of India's bureaucracy. He has learned hard lessons along the way. One is that 'sometimes the last thing people in power want is to get rid of slums'. Much of what Mehta calls 'slum perpetuation' has to do with the infamous 'vote bank'—a political party, through a deep-rooted system of graft, lays claim to the vote of a particular neighbourhood. As long as the slum keeps voting the right way, it's to the party's advantage to keep the community intact. A settlement can remain in the same place for years, shelters passing from makeshift plastic tarps to corrugated metal to concrete.

But one day, as in the case of Dharavi, the slum might find itself suddenly in the 'wrong' place. Once that happens, the bulldozer is always a potential final solution. A few years ago, the Maharashtra government, under the direction of Chief Minister Deshmukh, in a spasm of upgrading supposedly aimed at closing the 'world-class' gap, demolished 60,000 hutments, some in place for decades. As many as 300,000 people were displaced.

This, Mehta says, is what his plan is devised to avoid. 'No one wants to be that unhappy guy driving the bulldozer.' Preferring 'the talking cure', Mehta says if anyone, anywhere, doesn't think his plan is the best possible outcome for Dharavi, he will sit with them for as long as it takes to convince them.

A few days later, at Kumbharwada, he got his chance. To many the Kumbhar potters are the heart and soul of Dharavi. Their special status derives not only from their decades-long residence but from the integrity of their work. While Dharavi is famous for making use of things everyone throws away, the Kumbhars create the new.

The Savdas family members have been Dharavi potters for generations, but Tank Ranchhod Savdas once imagined another kind of life. 'I had big dreams,' he says. 'I thought I would be a lawyer.' But Tank's father died in 1986, and 'as the oldest son I took up his business.' Not that he has any regrets. 'During busy times, I make hundreds of pots a day, and I get pleasure from each one,' he says.

Recently, however, the fortyish 'Mr Tank' has begun to fear for the future of Kumbhars in Dharavi. An increasing number of the community's young men have become merchant sea men or computer specialists at the Bandra-Kurla Complex. Kumbharwada is full of teenage boys who have never used a potter's wheel, unthinkable only a few years ago.

And now there is this plan. Just talking about a 'slum-free Dharavi' is enough to make Tank shake with anger. How dare anyone claim that Kumbharwada is a 'slum' in need of rehabilitation! Kumbharwada is home to working people, men and women who have always made their own way. If Mukesh Mehta was so enamoured of the US, couldn't he see that Kumbharwada was a sterling example of the American dream? 'Look at my house,' Tank demands, showing off his 3,000 sq. ft home and the workshop he built and now shares with his two brothers and their families. Why should we move from here to there?'

By 'there' Tank means the Slum Rehabilitation Authority high-rise under construction behind Kumbharwada. Freshly painted, the building has a sprightly look, but soon lack of maintenance will turn it into a replica of every other SRA building: a decaying Stalinist-styled pile, covered with Rorschach-like mildew stains. Inside is a long, dank hallway with eighteen apartments on either side, which Amit Singh calls 'thirty-six rooms of gloom'.

'That is a slum,' says Tank, 'a vertical slum.' Told that Mehta says he's willing to talk to anyone unhappy with the plan, Tank says, 'Then bring him here. Tomorrow.'

On his cell phone from Hyderabad, Mehta, 'not risk averse', says 'ten o'clock'. But he is sceptical the meeting will accomplish much. He's spoken with the potters many times. Proposals allowing them to keep the majority of their space have been rejected, as was his idea to maximize the potters' profits by adding ornamental ceramics to their traditional vessels and religious objects. 'I've offered them the moon and been repaid with crushing indifference,' Mehta bemoans. Plus, he never knows which alleged leadership group represents whom. It's a frustrating situation that one afternoon causes the Americanized Mehta to shout, 'Your trouble is you have too many chiefs and not enough Indians!'

Yet, when ten o'clock rolls around, there he is, impeccably attired in a tan suit, cuff links gleaming in the sunlight, in the courtyard in front of Tank's house. Perhaps a hundred people have assembled, sitting on plastic chairs. Most are potters, but there are others, too, such as Amit Singh and several colleagues from the *Janhit Times*. After politely listening to Mehta's short form of the plan (he has brought his PowerPoint presentation, but sunlight prevents its deployment), the objections begin. It is outrageous that this was even being discussed, people say. 'We have been making pots for 130 years,' one man shouts. 'This land is ours.'

Mehta is sympathetic to the Kumbhar position. But there are a few 'realities' they must understand. First, the assumption that the community owns the Kumbharwada grounds by virtue of the British Raj-era Vacant Land Tenancy Act is incorrect. Mehta says the Kumbhars' long-term lease ran out when the Act was repealed in 1974. Also, there is the pollution issue. Every day the potters' brick kilns send huge black clouds into the air. It's gotten so bad that the nearby Sion Hospital is complaining that the smoke is aggravating patients' pulmonary ailments.

The Kumbhars are vulnerable on these issues, Mehta says. Chief Minister Deshmukh would be within his rights to send the dreaded bulldozers rolling down 90 Feet Road. The Kumbhars should trust him, Mehta says. His very presence proves his sincerity. 'People said if I came here I should wear a hard hat. But you see me bareheaded.' At the very least, the

Kumbhars should allow him to conduct a census of the area. That information would help him fight for them, get them the best deal.

With the return of the monsoon rains, the session breaks up. Mehta goes back into his chauffeured car feeling upbeat. 'A good meeting,' he says, driving off through puddles.

Back at Kumbharwada, Tank is asked what he learned from the meeting. Surrounded by perhaps twenty potters, Tank says, 'We have learned that Mukesh Mehta's plan is of no use to us.' Would they participate in the census? 'We'll think about it,' says Tank. In any event, there is no time to talk about it now. The meeting has taken almost two hours. With orders piling up there is work to be done.

Mukesh Mehta's plan is scheduled to be implemented sometime this year, not that Dharavi is excessively fixated on it during the holiday season, a time to, as a sign in the window of Jayanthian fireworks store on 90 Feet Road says, 'Enjoy the festivals with an atom bomb.' Today is Ganesh Chaturthi, and much of Dharavi (the Hindus, anyway) are in the streets beating giant drums and blaring Bollywood-inflected songs on car-battery-powered speakers in celebration of Lord Ganesha. Ganesha, the elephant god, has special significance in Dharavi, being considered the deity of 'removing obstacles'.

One such obstacle is in evidence at the outset of the parade marking the end of the ten-day festival for which people make *murtis*, or idols. These effigies are borne through streets to Mahim beach and then tossed into the water. One group has constructed a ten-foot high Ganesh from silvery papier-mâché. They have not, however, bothered to measure the width of the narrow lane through which Ganesha will need to pass to reach

Dharavi Main Road. After much discussion and a torturous fifty-metre journey during which many 'Dharavian obstacles' including ganglia of illegally connected electric wires, needed to be removed, the murti makes it through with a quarter of an inch to spare. Not a bit of the god's silvery skin is nicked.

As the Ganesha idol is lifted onto a flatbed truck for its journey to Mahim beach, one resident turns and says, 'You see Ganesha is undamaged. This is our talent. We deal with what is.'

22

TROUBLE STARTS WHEN YOUR DREAMS COME TRUE

Rachel Lopez

It's a cool Sunday evening and four-year-old Ritu has just given her grandparents a very convincing performance as a teddy bear. She's turned around, touched the ground, polished her shoes and is 'off to school' just like the teachers at her English-medium school have taught, prompting her doting grandfather Hariram Tanwar Dilliwala to forget the pain in his back and applaud furiously. It's a good day in the Tanwar household. Ritu's sisters, the slightly older Priti and Heemani, have also sung and danced to a Bollywood hit song and for a few moments, everyone had forgotten where they were: squeezed into the ground-floor area of their shanty house in Dharavi, with a rolling shutter for a main door, and a cot, a moulded plastic chair and a rickety metal stool leaving only standing room for the children's performances.

Hariram, sixty-five, and his family of seven—the children's

parents also live with them—live in a two-storey dwelling on a 280 sq. ft plot just off Dharavi's busy 60 Feet Road. It's close to the recycling units of the neighbourhood's 13th Compound and is close enough to Mahim railway station for the family to hear the incoming trains. But it's in an area so densely packed with houses that often the only sounds that penetrate are those from the busy street immediately outside and the chatter of neighbours passing by Hariram's open doorway, unashamedly peeking in on their way to their homes or the corner-shop next door.

Hariram is a scrap sorter and raw-material supplier and his house is part workplace, part home. The ground floor is at once living room and warehouse for mountains of plastic and metal scrap. A steep ladder leads to the first level, on which are the kitchen, a store room and a central area for TV viewing, studying, sleeping and eating. The TV is a new model, space-saving flat screen. But there's no room to put a refrigerator, so the Dilliwalas make do without one.

The roof is part of Hariram's workplace too. It's the drying area for all his sorted and cleaned plastic. Hariram has been living here for thirty years, but there's no toilet in his house. Everybody uses the pay-and-use latrines at the end of the street, shelling out Rs 2 for every use and, for no apparent reason, Rs 5 on public holidays. Not that the money ensures clean facilities. 'The people who manage the *sulabh shauchalaya* (toilets) do nothing,' Hariram said. 'We often end up cleaning the place ourselves.'

The house is the Dilliwalas' biggest asset and their biggest headache. Their family is spread across north India. Hariram's other sons have apartments in Delhi and his brothers in Haryana own fields that are bigger than his entire street. But because he owns a house in Mumbai, even if it's in Dharavi, his family counts him as the wealthiest of them all. 'The money we've made here is more than anyone could have made in Punjab or Delhi,' said Hariram. 'Everyone thinks that we're sitting on a land of gold.'

They're sitting uncomfortably. As the state's committee of secretaries approves the sector-wise development through the Rs 15,000-crore Dharavi Redevelopment Project, the first move towards a new Dharavi since redevelopment bids were cancelled in August 2009, Hariram is worried about his house all over again. He's lived in the same place for thirty years, making him easily eligible for resettlement in the new plan, which allots housing to those who have lived in Dharavi before the year 2000. But he's not sure that being housed in a multi-storey tower will actually improve life for his family. 'Residents who live in rooms that measure less than 60 sq. ft will benefit the most,' he explained, referring to the fact that they will have proportionally the largest lodgings. Commercial plots will also lose little, he believes, since they'll be housed on the ground or first floor of the new buildings. 'But my house is commercial and residential,' he said. 'We have the most to lose.'

The house is in a residential neighbourhood too. This means that the government sees his property only as a 280 sq. ft ground-floor tenement, ignoring the top floor and the drying roof above. So the Dilliwalas won't be entitled to a 840 sq. ft slice of the new Dharavi. They'll have only a 225 sq. ft flat in a high-rise, no warehouse in which Hariram can store his scrap aluminium, no roof on which to dry his washed plastic chips, and no office in which to continue his business.

'The trouble starts after all your dreams have come true,' Hariram said. 'I'll have a house with a bathroom but I won't have a livelihood.' His recycling business employs ten people, all of who also stand to lose their jobs when Hariram moves from his residence—warehouse to an apartment. His only solution is to somehow turn his home from residence to commercial plot on paper. That way he'll be allotted 280 sq. ft of ground floor space when redevelopment comes, and if the builders keep their promise of providing the shops with 14-ft-high ceilings, he'll be able to fit in a mezzanine, house his family, and do business on the ground floor as usual. 'It's the same situation as it is now,' he admitted. 'But there'll be roads, a playground, schools, hospitals and a post office. That's the life we need.'

It's also the life that the Dilliwala, like so many others in Dharavi, deserves. A school headmaster in his hometown in Punjab, he moved to Mumbai from Haryana in 1972 after parents made repeated attempts to secure their children's grades by bribing him with kilos of ghee. He settled in Dharavi in 1980, a time when the suburb lacked even basic amenities like public toilets and electricity and a home cost Rs 5,000 even if you had to build it from scratch. But Hariram saw it as a place of opportunity, a locality that housed everyone from 'diamond merchants to needle makers'.

In the years that followed, he learnt enough about the sorting trade to see three kinds of valuable plastic where others could only see a discarded mobile phone. He kept abreast of new plastic compounds by reading their names off the sides of packaging boxes and learning to pronounce them phonetically. He even learnt to set prices for his raw material, and travelled as far as Indore in search of new markets for his sorted, cleaned, recyclable material. He has made a quick buck on the weekend by catching a Cool Cab to Pune and cutting deals with recyclers there. He has been exposed to enough toxic fumes to detect if the awful smell comes from the melting of polyurethane, polycarbonate or polypropylene.

It's the kind of job that Hariram says the government hasn't the first clue about. 'Five per cent of India is involved in waste management or in recycling metal, paper or plastics in some way,' he claimed. As a scrap supplier, he makes Rs 15 for every kilo of cleaned and sorted plastic bags, so that a recycler can make sheets of raw plastic that can be moulded into shapes. 'But I have to pay 4 per cent VAT and 12 per cent excise to move my goods,' he complained. 'There are no subsidies in power, no tax waivers on selling waste material for re-use, and we still have no industry status.'

As a Dharavi resident, Hariram has had a long history of worrying over the security of his house, his livelihood and his family. He was fighting for them years before stories about the neighbourhood's redevelopment hit the headlines. He recalls sparring, in 1987, with G.R. Khairnar, the Brihanmumbai Municipal Corporation's ward officer who became the BMC's deputy commissioner the following year and eventually earned the nickname Demolition Man for his action against illegal construction in the city. 'His people came here with their bulldozers and tried to raze this part of the neighbourhood,' he said. 'They stopped just short of my door. They only retreated when a group of us walked up to the MHADA office and demanded the right to live in the city.'

Hariram has made it easier for other residents to live in

Dharavi, too. He actively works with a thirty-one-year-old civic group PROUD (People's Responsible Organization for a United Dharavi), serving as its chairman for land and housing. The organization has helped legitimize old and new locals by applying for their ration cards, connecting their homes to the water and electricity supply, and protecting residents from eviction. Hariram was among those who fought for the removal of a tar factory that had been set up in a residential part of Dharavi in the early 1990s. 'We kept telling them to move but they wouldn't listen,' he said. 'So a group of us went to their office one day and began smoking, blowing air into their faces and strewing litter around their clean work stations. They were furious, of course. But we explained that this was exactly how they were polluting our houses. They got the message and moved. No bones were broken.'

More recently, in 2010, Hariram joined PROUD's fight when hutments near the pipeline area were given only twenty-four-hour notice before their shanties were broken down. 'The timing was so insensitive,' he said, explaining that the order came two days before the Muslims celebrated Ramzaan Eid and the Hindus began the ten-day Ganesh Chaturthi festivities. PROUD not only secured a fifteen-day extension from the government, allowing celebrations to continue peacefully, it also brokered an agreement with the authorities that allowed for a longer notice period for eviction.

A Hindu resident in a predominantly Muslim section of Dharavi, Hariram played a part in the anti-Muslim riots that broke out in 1992–93 as well. When the police began firing at a peaceful gathering of Muslims on 7 December 1992, killing one and injuring two locals, it was at his house that locals gathered, defying the curfew to plan a course of action. 'We'd been a unified community for decades,' Hariram recalled. 'It could only have been an outside force which was trying to separate us.'

The group decided to keep an eye out for strangers, bar outsiders from entering the locality and take turns to patrol the neighbourhood every night. Hariram, like his Muslim neighbours, went on rounds too, making as many as five rounds of tea a night to keep his fellow sentries fuelled. He'd chat with patrolling policemen on those nights and recalls meeting one, a Hindu 'three-star officer' who let it slip that Dharavi's Tamil Hindus had asked him to look the other way while they planned to eliminate the neighbourhood's Muslims. 'I managed to convince him that avoiding deaths was actually good for him—that he'd get promoted faster,' Hariram said.

His neighbours rallied to his defence in return. 'They'd found that a Muslim boy, renting a room in the area, was planning to annihilate all the Hindus, starting with me,' he said. 'My neighbours told him that they would cut the finger of any hand raised against their Hindu brother and that if he had any sense he'd leave the area, fast.'

His cosmopolitanism faced its biggest test a few years after the riots, when his son broke tradition and married his Muslim neighbour. Hariram wasn't opposed to the match, but still worries about what his family back home thinks of him today, even though the couple has moved to Delhi.

Hariram, who is given to wearing sharp safari suits and polished loafers, and sticks a gold-plated Cross ball-pen into his breast pocket (just one of the many gems he's found in the trash he sorts), is proud of what he has achieved in the city. But he doesn't know if there will ever be a time when people outside

Dharavi will see the area as more than a slum full of unhappy, desperate people. 'When I travel, people from outside the city ask me where I live,' he said. 'I tell them I'm from Mumbai, but I say I live in Mahim East.' He's quite certain that he won't see a new, improved Dharavi, one that even the rest of Mumbai and India will be proud of, in his lifetime.

He describes an incident in late 2009 in which a man running a fake deodorant business had employed local children, locking them up in his warehouse so that they could fill aerosol cans. There was an explosion and four children, including the son of an acquaintance, died. 'Stories like that don't make the papers,' Hariram said. 'But the people who are in the fake-goods trade make a lot of money in Dharavi. They have the most to lose from redevelopment because all their activities will be forced to be legitimate and above board. They'll do all they can to oppose redevelopment.'

It's to rid Dharavi of businesses like these that Hariram is looking forward to zoned development, even if the current project pencils his livelihood neatly out of its plans. Unlike many civic-minded residents in the area, he trusts Mukesh Mehta's plans for a new Dharavi and is deeply suspicious of government agencies like MHADA and the government-approved expert committee that has criticized the plan for being unfair to businessmen like him. He believes that private developers are more likely to keep their promises, bring new building technologies and international levels of quality, while any construction by a government 'who only chooses the cheapest bid' is likely to be ill-designed and unstable even if its promises are bigger. 'It's easier to approach a private builder if I have a problem,' he explained. 'But if there is a trouble with a government structure, there are no faces, only offices and officers who pass the buck.'

Mukesh Mehta, on the other hand, 'has never hidden any part of his plan,' he said. 'In 1996–97, when he first started thinking of redeveloping Dharavi and had set up an office here, we would see him walking through the neighbourhoods, conducting surveys himself.' He also sees Mehta as being on the side of the people, not the profiteers, recalling that the architect quietly but persistently refused to meet local residents intending to talk him or bribe him into giving them a better deal.

The expert committee, in contrast, appears flawed to him. 'Too many people represent the same interest groups,' he said, explaining how two people on the eleven-member panel belong to the same organization (Jockin Arputham and Sheela Patel from the Society for the Promotion of Area Research Centres or SPARC), and a husband-and-wife team (architects Arvind and Neera Adarkar) takes up two more positions. 'Few of these people have actually lived in Dharavi. How can we trust their judgement?' he asked.

He even refuses to trust Arputham, the president of the National Slum Dwellers' Federation, on account of corruption and nepotism charges that date back to even before Arputham moved to Dharavi. 'He's been a thief ever since the time his shanty home in Deonar was demolished and he bagged himself three flats in exchange,' Hariram alleged.

With PROUD, Hariram is currently working towards ensuring that every resident of Dharavi, regardless of when he made his home there or which part of Dharavi he currently calls home, gets an apartment when the suburb is redeveloped. 'If the government cannot make homes, it has no right to destroy homes,' Hariram reasoned. 'Every home made in Dharavi, old or new, symbolizes a failure on the part of the government to provide housing for its people.'

But regardless of whether Dharavi is redeveloped, Hariram believes that the future of his little grandchildren lies outside Dharavi. He wants each one to complete her schooling and get into college, something that not too many Dharavi parents, Hindu or Muslim, expect of their girl children. 'They have to be prepared for the future,' he said. 'Mumbai is that kind of city where you just have to keep up. Change comes like a big wave here. You can either be prepared for it to take you places or you can drown in it. It has no patience with the undecided.'

23

DHARAVI: MAKEOVER OR TAKEOVER?

Shirish B. Patel

Dharavi is an extraordinary conundrum: a happy, thriving, prosperous place with the most insanitary, inhuman and degrading working and living conditions imaginable. No one will contest that its most disgusting aspects need to be improved. And no one will deny that in many ways it is an inspiring place, with a strong sense of community, negligible crime, and a great deal of cheerfulness and vigorous hope. It is obvious that the abominable aspects are a consequence of official denial—no sewerage or safe water supply, drains open, insanitary and chemically contaminated—and the admirable aspects have been brought about by the people themselves, who live and work there and have built, without subsidy or support, whatever it is they have. How can Dharavi's ugly aspects be changed?

There is enormous pressure for the redevelopment of Dharavi from forces whose primary interest is not the welfare of Dharavi's people, but the hunt for profits, where the Government of Maharashtra is a declared partner. For the government, any plan must involve a peaceful transition—that is, not too much blood on the streets. Residents must somehow be enticed to accept redevelopment that will generate huge profits for developers (of the order of tens of thousands of crores— government alone expects Rs 9,000 crore as its premium). Essentially, this means that the residents, already living at densities among the highest in the world, must be persuaded to move into part of the land area they currently occupy, in high-rise buildings packed closely together. The remaining land area, rather more than half, will be freed for construction of high-value apartments, offices and malls. Some of the profit will finance the re-housing of existing residents, free of cost to themselves. They must be persuaded that for years they have been living as illegal trespassers, and that their homes can be bulldozed. But if they agree to the new arrangements they will own spanking new apartments, much larger than their present homes, in high-rise buildings, something they highly prize as a symbol of middle-class respectability, far above the indignity of living in a shack. The resulting crowding and loss of community spirit are not easily understood.

No one is asking whether the final densities, several times anything seen so far anywhere in the world, will be livable. By the time it is discovered that such crowding is in fact not viable, the original promoters will have made their money and vanished.

Alternatively, if we start with the welfare of the residents as our primary concern, a completely different set of possibilities emerges. If one wants to undertake 'redevelopment', for whatever reason, there is much in Dharavi that is precious and at risk of being lost if the intervention is clumsy or insensitive. One should hesitate to endorse any particular approach, however carefully thought through, without first testing it on a pilot scale. The urgency of intervention, much touted by the profit-seekers, thus seems a consideration that is adverse to uncovering the solutions that offer the best long-term advantages for the residents of Dharavi.

Before searching for solutions let us first understand Dharavi's many complexities and the attendant limitations and constraints that these impose.

GEOGRAPHY

In relation to Mumbai Dharavi is remarkably well located, at the heart of the city, a triangle of land served by railway lines on two sides and bounded by the Mahim Creek and its mangroves on the third. It is just south of the important new business district, the Bandra-Kurla Complex (BKC), an emerging alternative to the old Central Business District (CBD) in south Bombay. BKC is just south of the airport, so in many ways it is more convenient to reach than the CBD. Any location adjoining BKC would naturally be highly prized. That Dharavi rubs shoulders with BKC, and that it is exceptionally well served by mass transport, makes it of huge interest to real-estate promoters and developers.

LAW OF ADVERSE POSSESSION

There is something in India called the doctrine of 'legitimate expectations', according to which 'a person may have a legitimate expectation of being treated in a certain way by an administrative authority even though he has no legal right in private law to receive such treatment'.

Another doctrine, particularly interesting from the point of view of Dharavi, is expressed in the Law of Adverse Possession. This is where someone claims his own title to a property to which the title of another is not disputed: what is alleged is only its extinction. In regard to property, we note that the law distinguishes between ownership and possession. They are not the same. Ownership is pre-eminently a right. Possession is good title against all but the true owner. Possession is prima facie evidence of ownership, and the prima facie evidence becomes absolute if the right of the real owner is extinguished under Section 27 of the Limitation Act, 1963. Under this Act, the period for adverse possession to become a right is twelve years. If for twelve years, reckoned from the time adverse possession first occurred, the owner has not taken legal steps to recover possession, then the occupier can claim title to the property. In the case of government lands the period is thirty years, not twelve. What is interesting is that there are many residents in Dharavi who have been there for more than thirty years.

APPRECIATION OF LAND VALUES

When land appreciates in value, to whom does the appreciation belong? To the commons or to the private landholder? The private landholder may or may not have done much to contribute to the appreciation in its value. Appreciation is just as likely to have arisen from a range of external factors, such as growth in the city, or improved amenities in the area, or the construction of a nearby mass-transit station, or the introduction of new, high-profile activities that elevate the tone of the district. If someone has acquired property in the district much earlier, but done nothing with it except wait for land values to appreciate, surely we can say the appreciation should not go entirely to him? We need more sophisticated ways of apportioning appreciation between the commons and individual land owners.

MIXED-INCOME HOUSING

In large and dense urban agglomerations, there is a definite value in having high-income communities intermixed with middle- and low-income communities, as compared with a pattern of high-income residents at the centre diminishing to lower and lower incomes as one moves towards the periphery. Among the many advantages, one is that transport demands reduce. High-income residences will almost invariably have high-value employment locations close by. Both the residential and the business areas will require services from the middle- and low-income groups. Having them close by, and not far-flung, will reduce both the cost and the time of travel for everyone.

Another advantage is more qualitative, hard to quantify: it comes from the mixing of people from different income groups in activities of common interest. This may be walking in a park, haggling for vegetables, eating at moderately priced places, or watching street theatre. There is more to be learnt from variety in the people one encounters than one could learn from interaction with people 'just like us'. A widened awareness of others can only be beneficial for society as a whole. There is thus a sociological gain from the intermingling which is lost when you divide communities into gated enclaves of the rich and ghettos of the poor. It is equally lost when you divide communities along religious lines, or along linguistic lines. In fact, much of the value of living in an urban area is lost when you divide the area into communities segregated in this, or in any other way—you might as well return to your village for all the difference the urban area is making to the widening of your mental horizons.

One additional reason for not segregating low-income groups is that their localities, when isolated, become black holes from which everyone wants to escape. They become derelict, if not abandoned. No worthwhile activity will move there—no shops, no gyms, and no other decent facilities. Such areas, and the families that live in them, are consigned to a world of hopelessness. They cannot wait to get out and move to a more upmarket locality.

DENSITY

Dharavi fits squarely in the SRA model of the in-situ redevelopment of slums by adding, in the same location, new for-sale areas, to generate profits as well as finance free *pucca* (permanent) housing for all Dharavi's residents. This will unquestionably crowd Dharavi more than it is crowded already. Can such further crowding work?

Let us compare the densities proposed in Dharavi with existing settlements elsewhere in the world. Barring a small number of even more crowded localities, the population density in the most crowded areas of Hong Kong hovers around 2,500 persons/hectare. These are localities covering an area of 3–8 hectares, all served by an underground transport system, something that contributes significantly to making the area workable. The densities in the most crowded parts of Mumbai are slightly lower.

To understand densities in Dharavi we really need to look at larger sizes of concentrated urban development. Dharavi is about 214 hectares in size, so comparing it with localities of 3–8 hectares when looking at densities makes no sense—when you look at the smaller areas you are leaving out the relatively low-density spaces such as recreation grounds, schools, hospitals and other public facilities, even access roads, that are essential to the larger development. These less crowded areas bring down the overall density figures significantly. If we look at some of the most crowded areas in the world, of a size comparable to Dharavi's, we find that nowhere in the world, except in some of the wards in Mumbai, do we have densities larger than 1,000 persons per hectare—and let us not forget that every one of these locations, other than in Mumbai, has an underground railway system which is a dramatic aid to mobility.

Now let us look at what is proposed for Dharavi. The total area is 214 hectares. Scattered throughout the area are plots where developments have already occurred. These areas cover seventy hectares and are not part of the redevelopment project. There is no exact count of the population residing in the seventy hectares, but a rough estimate is 10,000 families. That means 50,000 people, at an average density of $50,000/70 = 714$ persons per hectare, a perfectly reasonable number.

On the remaining 144 hectares, to be taken up for redevelopment, we have 57,000 families, a number obtained by a detailed survey where each dwelling has been uniquely identified and its occupants given identity cards. Significantly, occupants on upper floors have been deliberately ignored: they are not to be rehabilitated at all. The logic for this is not clear, and is probably open to a successful challenge in the Bombay High Court (what the Supreme Court will say, however, as we have seen, is unpredictable and another matter altogether). We can only guess at the numbers of families living on upper floors, but they must be at least 10,000. That gives us a total of 67,000 families. At five persons per family, that means a population of 3,35,000 occupying 144 hectares. The density works out to 2,326 per hectare. This is already far above anything that exists anywhere else in the world, including elsewhere in Mumbai.

The proposal prepared for Dharavi redevelopment is that the existing population be re-housed on 43 per cent of their existing land area, with the remaining 57 per cent area turned over for commercial or other development. The new development will attract additional population, and even if it is no more than half the existing population it will take densities to three times what exists anywhere else in the world. The scheme is, on the face of it, unworkable. Neither transport capacities nor the quality of life within the settlement will allow such packed living to be sustainable. The most likely outcome is that most of the present 67,000 resident families will be bought out, will move elsewhere, and Dharavi will become a high-value, high-class area at reasonable densities. It behooves us to see through the chicanery and recognize the true intentions of the scheme for what they are. Our loss will include a thriving, prosperous, mixed-income area and its sociocultural values; a valuable hub of enterprise and economic activity; and a portal for new migrants whose aspirations and energy can contribute to the city.

REDEVELOPING DHARAVI

As with any urban planning exercise, let us begin by setting out our objectives. We need to agree on these before we start any work of preparing physical layouts or drawing up rules that will govern the redevelopment. A suggested set of objectives is the following:

1. Do not densify Dharavi any further; that is, do nothing that will add more occupants to the area.
2. Improve infrastructure, in particular sanitation and water supply. Improve powered transport if possible but never at the cost of the free and easy movement of pedestrians throughout the area.
3. Let the residents of Dharavi determine when and how redevelopment should take place. They have done an outstanding job in bringing the settlement up to the conditions in which it finds itself today, despite the most adverse conditions of infrastructure supply. We should seek mechanisms by which they can continue this kind of contribution in future.
4. Profit-making has no place in the redevelopment plans for Dharavi.
5. To the extent possible, encourage low-rise redevelopment that retains the community character of the locality.

How do we justify these objectives? In particular, what do we do about the fact that the underlying land is owned by other agencies, some governmental, some private, but definitely not by the people of Dharavi? The simplest is to invoke the Law of Adverse Possession and say that the ownership rights of the original owners have been extinguished, with time, and now vest in the present occupants. Do we give the current occupants title, and if so, in what size lots?

One way to proceed would be to subdivide Dharavi into plots of a size that can be managed by a cooperative society. Experience with these in the past suggests that the number of families in a single society should be around 100, certainly never more than 200. The boundaries of the plot should preferably be existing natural boundaries, such as roads or pathways or nullahs. These families should form either a cooperative society, or better still, something in the nature of a Community Land Trust (CLT) where profits arising from sale are shared between the individual property owner and the CLT (the Cooperative Societies Act as it stands does not currently envisage any such sharing). Questions that immediately arise are, first, who will be the members of the cooperative society—owners or tenants or both? And second, what safeguards are there that the entity does not rapidly fall into the hands of a commercial developer?

These are not easy questions to address. On the matter of who owns a hutment, the simplest is not to disturb the current pattern of ownership: owners remain owners and tenants remain tenants, with the original owner (who may not be a current occupant) retaining ownership. This hands-off approach at least has the merit of peaceful acceptance by all, since it does not interfere with any existing rights. As to whether developers will succeed in taking over properties or not, once again this is probably best left to the hutment owners to decide. The best one could do would be to build in safeguards regarding transfer of trusteeship of the CLT to ensure that the rights of the residents are not snatched away, and whichever way the project moves forward it does so with their genuine and uncoerced consent. In any case the implementation of this or any other process should be phased, so that a few early projects are first tried out, and the results observed, before implementation is extended to a grander scale.

Water supply and sanitation lines are not hard to lay down,

even in an area as densely built-up as Dharavi. There are access lanes everywhere, and the drainage and water supply lines can follow existing alignments without, as far as possible, cutting through any of the CLT plots. This is a matter of careful layout and planning.

Improved access is more intractable. Movement, especially with powered transport, whether public or private, requires space and that is one commodity that is in desperately short supply in a densely crowded settlement. The logical response is layering: add a layer of transport which is distinct from the layer on which life goes on. In Hong Kong or Shanghai or other crowded cities the extra transport layer is an underground railway network, used only for travel. In Dharavi, where an underground railway would be too expensive to afford easily, layering could be achieved by insisting that all redevelopment takes place with a podium at about second-floor height above the ground. The ground area would then be laid out to manage transport; and the podium level would be a pedestrian-only area, extensive enough to enable walking on it from one end of Dharavi to the other. On the podium would be a level of shops and above them the living units; below it, and with access to motorized transport from the ground level, could be the industrial and warehousing activities that are today so much an integral part of the functioning of Dharavi. To enable this kind of layering of transport and living activities it would be necessary to draw up a set of building regulations that govern the way each CLT can redevelop, if it chooses to go in for pucca reconstruction. But it should be equally open to the CLT to choose not to rebuild in this way: to retain instead the current character of its area, but now with improved and functioning water supply and sanitation systems in place.

24

TALKING TRASH WITH
VINOD SHETTY

Judith Anne Francorsi

For over twenty years Advocate Vinod Shetty has been a fixture in Mumbai's Civil Liberties movement. He has worked with the International Campaign for Justice in Bhopal, the Textile Workers Union, FDI Watch India, and the Indo-Pakistan Seeds of Peace programme. In 2005 Shetty fought to keep retail giants out of the country. He remembers the battle against Walmart as his biggest victory to date. Shetty's been lathi-charged and imprisoned many times.

Since 2008, Shetty has led the Dharavi Project of the ACORN Foundation of India. The group represents the interests of rag pickers, the men and women who sort through the waste strewn about the city and bring the recyclables back to Dharavi. For four decades Dharavi's rag pickers have supplemented municipal waste-collection by recycling 80 per cent of Mumbai's recyclable waste. They have saved the city millions. Shetty fears that one day soon the government will deploy highly priced imported technologies in the recycling sector and take scores of jobs away from the rag pickers. While he understands that recycling cannot be left in the hands of informal workers, Shetty also argues, 'the future lies in community-based programmes because we need to keep people employed'.

Shetty has petitioned the government to set up a fund that pays rag pickers a proper wage and provides medical insurance. So far he has not been as successful as he was against Walmart. 'It is not easy working with people who are not protected under any labour regulation,' he sighs. 'It's like going into a gun battle without ammunition, I guess.'

In April of 2008, Shetty assembled hundreds of rag pickers at the Jesuit-run Xavier's Engineering Institute in Mahim. ACORN founder Wade Rathke flew in from New Orleans to present them with ACORN ID cards. Each card displayed the member's photograph and gave his name and approximate address. Below the photo, Shetty listed the person's mobile number. The waste collectors could reach him anytime they needed help. If the person presented the card to the police or at a clinic, a representative could call Shetty to verify the bearer's membership in ACORN. The cards gave the rag pickers access to ACORN's free medical clinics. Lotus Eye Hospital gave cardholders free eye examinations in an ambulance made available by Impact India. Those who needed them were given glasses. Lotus referred cataract cases to other participating city hospitals for free surgery. In the days leading up to the inaugural card ceremony over 150 people had their eyes checked, many for the first time.

The cards made most of the people gathered at Xavier's proud.

A short, old man leaning on a stick considerably taller than he was, stayed on stage long after he received his card, flashing a toothless smile. The room burst into song. The crowd gave Rathke and Shetty a standing ovation. Then a young woman shouted above the clamour, 'It's not cards we need, it's houses', and stormed out of the room.

An ID card is no house, but it does help. Often rag pickers come from migrant families and proof of address is difficult to come by. Without it, their applications for basic amenities covered by the government's schemes for the urban poor are turned down. 'Grain is rotting away in warehouses or being sold in the black market, yet the most deserving candidates go hungry, only because they are without a ration card, which they can't get without an address,' Shetty says.

ACORN ID cards can give the rag pickers a foothold in society. At one of the union meetings, Laxmi Kamble, making her first public speech, told the crowd, 'In our country, if you go to a shop and they give you a higher rate for the grain, you don't question. You just accept whatever they say. You go to admit your child into school and they tell you, give me Rs 25,000, you don't question. How long are we going to continue like this?' Explaining her outburst, Laxmi told me, 'If you are part of an organization, you have the strength to question. All I want is to show my children and the children of others that whatever rights we have, we have to fight for them.'

In 2009, ACORN established a Sunday school on the Xavier grounds for the children of the waste collectors. Anil Sawant, ACORN's lone full-time staff member, runs the programme. Volunteers from the American School of Bombay, the Finnish and British consulates and the India People's Media Collective teach most of the classes. After her first computer class, students had a special request for volunteer instructor Nupura Hautamaki. 'They saw me driving off, so they wanted a ride in the car with the air-conditioning on. For them it was such a thrill, to sit in a car that is not a Fiat taxi, to play with the music system, to press the buttons for the windows,' Nupura said. When her classes first started, about ten children attended regularly, but after a few weeks a couple of them stayed away. 'The problem I see is that the parents are not very keen on them leaving work to go for classes,' Nupura explained to me. Today Nupura offers rides in her car as an incentive for the children to continue to attend classes. 'The drives are conditional on attendance and test performance, as well as completion of homework,' Nupura said. So are other perks the volunteers have planned for the kids, like visits to the planetarium and the aquarium.

Shetty tries especially hard to expose the kids to the arts and put them in touch with the glamorous side of Mumbai. In April 2010, he established a relationship with Blue Frog, Mumbai's upscale jazz club, that brings touring artists to Dharavi. Invariably, the kids would take over the stage by the end of every show. Taufiq Quereshi and his Mumbai Stamp group invited the children to join him on stage to play their own drums made from old bins, cans and buckets sourced from Dharavi. Blue Frog's Emma de Decker began two campaigns with Shetty—'Artists for a Cause' and 'Dharavi Rocks'—to raise funds for a music school. De Decker's dream is to start a band with the children playing instruments made from recycled materials. 'Who knows, one day they may need a manager in New York,' she says. Proceeds from a concert featuring a mix of singers and music bands that included Bombay Bassment, Agnee, Suneeta Rao, the Mavyns, Ayush Shreshtha, Adrian D'Souza and the Colour Compound were donated to the project.

Every year ACORN hosts a concert at Dharavi's Maharashtra Nature Park as part of their Eco Fair. Popular singers Shankar Mahadevan and Suneeta Rao are regulars at this event. Over the years there have been a number of impressive acts, including British jazz saxophonist and rapper Soweto Kinch, Columbia's Banda la Republica, hip-hop royalty Apache Indian, Austrian beatboxers Bauchklang and the Australian band Aurora Jane, as well as locals Ankur Tewari and Something Relevant. All agree that the Dharavi kids are the best crowd to play to in Mumbai.

When I asked twelve-year old Guddu what he did before he joined Shetty's programme, he said, 'I used to be an entrepreneur. I sold things.'

'What things?'

'I used to sell other people's stuff. But Vinod sir told me that that won't work, so now I play football and dance,' he told me.

ACORN also works with wealthy students, to make sure they see a little of the life they have been spared. Every month Shetty takes children from Mumbai's most prestigious private schools—'tomorrow's little leaders, so to say'—deep into the recycling centres of Dharavi. I accompanied him on one such trip. As we were standing on Mahim bridge overlooking the 13th Compound, Shetty pointed to the approaching busload of students. 'These children have unlimited access to the homes of the powerful. If they start nagging about all the waste and the conditions rag pickers work in, my job will become this much easier,' he told me. The school bus came to a grinding halt near us. 'Here they are—our new recruits, our agents of change,' he said. Two plastic bottles tumbled down the steps as the doors opened. 'For now, they are our primary waste generators,' Shetty joked and went off to greet the teachers and students.

Sure enough, at the end of the tour, when the kids made their way back to the bus, one student picked up the plastic bottles that had announced their visit so unceremoniously. Many of the children will stay in touch with Shetty long after their field visits and return every year to attend the ECO Fair. Back at school they will speak to their peers about the rag pickers and the importance of recycling. They will appoint energy directors to ensure air conditioners and lights are switched off when a class leaves a room. They will segregate their dry waste and send it straight to ACORN's recycling shed, thus saving children their own age from having to rummage through their waste on toxic landfills.

A NOTE ON CONTRIBUTORS

Jeb Brugmann

For the past twenty years, Jeb Brugmann has developed strategies for governments, corporations, international agencies and non-governmental organizations to tackle global issues at the local level. From 1990 to 2000, he served as founding secretary general of the International Council for Local Environmental Initiatives, the international environmental agency for cities, counties and towns. His initiatives have involved thousands of cities in more than fifty countries. A strategy consultant to organizations and leaders internationally, he also serves as a faculty member of the Cambridge University Programme for Industry.

Mansi Choksi

As a journalist for *The Times of India*, Mansi Choksi has covered civic issues, social justice, terrorism, shipping, environment and society. Her work chronicles Mumbai as a society in transition and her stories lie at the intersection of the new and the old, of urban and rural, of hope and despair. She is currently a Fulbright fellow at Columbia Journalism School.

Dilip D'Souza

Dilip D'Souza is a writer, though there was a time when he wrote software in the US. He has won several awards for his writing, including, most recently, the Newsweek/Daily Beast Open Hands Prize for Commentary (2012). He has written four books, including, most recently, *Roadrunner: An Indian Quest in America* (2009) and *The Curious Case of Binayak Sen* (2012). He lives in Bombay with his wife, their son and daughter, and two cats.

Anna Erlandson and Stina Ekman

Anna Erlandson is an artist educated at Umea University College of Fine Arts. Stina Ekman has been working as an artist for over a quarter of a century. She has taught for over ten years in Stockholm and northern Sweden. Her work has been exhibited in seventeen countries. Erlandson and Ekman have contributed to *Dharavi: Documenting Informalities,* a collection of writings and photographs.

Sonia Faleiro

Sonia Faleiro is an award-winning reporter and the author of a novel, *The Girl.* Her new book, *Beautiful Thing: Inside the Secret World of Bombay's Dance Bars,* has been published worldwide and translated into numerous languages. She lives between San Francisco and Mumbai. You can read more about her work at www.soniafaleiro.com.

Judith Anne Francorsi

Judith got her first stint in journalism working as a broadcast journalist with SBS Radio and Triple R in Melbourne, Australia. In 2006 Judith moved to Mumbai where she continues to collaborate with media networks in Australia and Europe. She is married to music producer Tino Francorsi and they have a daughter.

Mark Jacobson

Mark Jacobson is an American author and writer. His books include his debut novel and cult classic *Gojiro* (1992); the autobiographical Jacobson family travel saga co-authored with daughter Rae Jacobson, *12,000 Miles in the Nick of Time—a Semi-Dysfunctional Family Circumnavigates the Globe*; the critically acclaimed compendium *American Monsters* co-edited with Jack Newfield; and *American Gangster*. Jacobson was awarded the 2001 Humanitas Prize for his screenplay work on *The Believer*. He is currently a contributing editor to *New York Magazine* and a frequent contributor to *The Village Voice, National Geographic, Natural History Magazine, Men's Journal* as well as other publications

Sharmila Joshi

Sharmila Joshi is a researcher, writer–journalist, editor and occasional teacher. She has worked in the media and in academics. Her areas of interest include development, globalization, gender, inequality and labour. She lives in Mumbai not far from Dharavi.

Sameera Khan

Sameera Khan is a Mumbai-based independent journalist, writer and researcher. A former assistant editor with *The Times of India*, she teaches journalism at the School for Media and Cultural Studies at Tata Institute of Social Sciences. Most recently she co-authored the book *Why Loiter? Women and Risk on Mumbai Streets*.

Aditya Kundalkar

Aditya Kundalkar was born and raised in Bombay. After completing the diploma course in journalism at Xavier Institute of Communications, and a short stint at *Business India*, he joined *Reader's Digest*. A position as music editor with *Time Out Mumbai* followed and currently he is associate editor at GQ *India* magazine.

Rachel Lopez

Rachel Lopez has been a Mumbai resident all her life and would rather move into a Dharavi tenement than live anywhere else. In the ten years that she's been a journalist, she has chased cattle smugglers, walked around with a fake pregnant belly, interviewed Manipuri Jews studying Hebrew doctrine in English from Marathi-speaking teachers, and received acid-attack threats over a profile of Mariah Carey. She has worked with *Time Out Mumbai* and is currently with the *Hindustan Times*.

Freny Manecksha

Freny Manecksha is an independent journalist from Mumbai who is interested in issues related to urban poverty and displacement. She has travelled widely, and has studied issues of land displacement in Chhattisgarh and Odisha and militarization in Kashmir. Her work has appeared in 'Crest' (*The Times of India*), *The Hindu* and *India Together*.

Meena Menon

Meena Menon is the chief of bureau at *The Hindu*, Mumbai. She has worked with the United News of India, *Mid Day* and *The Times of India*. She has co-authored with Sharmila Joshi *The Unseen Worker: On the Trail of the Girl Child* (1998). She is also the author of *Riots and After in Mumbai: Chronicles of Truth and Reconciliation* and *Organic Cotton: Reinventing the Wheel*. She has received fellowships from the National Foundation of

India, Centre for Science and Environment, London, and SARAI-CSDS. She writes on politics and development issues including environment, women, human rights and health.

Leo Mirani

Leo Mirani is a journalist. He has worked as a reporter with *Time Out Mumbai*, been a Mumbai correspondent for *Tehelka* and is a frequent contributor to *The Economist*.

Shirish B. Patel

Shirish B. Patel is a civil engineer by training, and an urban planner by accident, experience and passionate interest. The civil engineering consultancy he founded and ran for over forty years is considered one of India's best. He was one of the three original authors who suggested the idea of New Bombay, a new 350 sq. km city across the harbour from the old city. He currently devotes his time to urban affairs on issues principally relating to Mumbai.

Priyanka Pathak-Narain

Priyanka Pathak-Narain is an award-winning journalist with *Mint*, where she belongs to a small group of features reporters and covers the business of religion in India and rural and urban development issues. She won the CNN Young Journalist award for her series on the unviability of a government-proposed sea channel around the southern coast of India. Prior to *Mint*, Priyanka worked with *The Times of India*, All India Radio and the investigative journalists' team at ABC News (New York). She lives in Mumbai with her husband and two daughters.

Jerry Pinto

Jerry Pinto lives and works in Mahim West. As far as the island city goes, Mahim is on the wrong side of the tracks. Except when Mahim East comes into the picture and then Mahim West becomes the right side of the tracks. His city's geographic snobberies continue to fascinate him.

Saumya Roy

Saumya is a journalist who has written for different publications including *India Real Time*, *Mint* and *Vogue India*. She was earlier with *Forbes India* and *Outlook*. She also co-founded and runs Vandana Foundation, which works on supporting livelihoods for urban poor in Mumbai and widows of cotton farmers in Maharashtra's Vidarbha region. She has a master's degree in journalism from Northwestern University, Illinois.

Amartya Sen

Amartya Sen is Thomas W. Lamont University Professor and Professor of Economics and Philosophy at Harvard University. He has also taught at the University of Calcutta, the Delhi School of Economics, the London School of Economics and the University of Oxford. He served as Master of Trinity College, Cambridge, from 1998 to 2004. In 1998, Sen won the Nobel Prize in Economic Sciences. His many publications include *Development As Freedom* and *The Idea of Justice*.

Kalpana Sharma

Kalpana Sharma is a Mumbai-based journalist, columnist and editorial consultant with *Economic and Political Weekly*. In four decades as a journalist, she has worked with leading Indian newspapers including *The Hindu*, *The Times of India* and *Indian Express*. Her writing has focused on environmental, developmental and gender issues. She is the author of several books including *Rediscovering Dharavi: Stories from Asia's Largest Slum.*

Suhani Singh

Suhani Singh is a journalist based in Mumbai. She writes for *Time Out Mumbai.*

Annie Zaidi

Annie Zaidi is the author of *Known Turf: Bantering with Bandits and Other True Tales,* a collection of essays that was shortlisted for the Vodafone Crossword Book Award for Non-fiction, 2011, and the co-author of *The Bad Boy's Guide to the Good Indian Girl.* Her work has appeared in various anthologies including *Mumbai Noir, Women Changing India, India Shining, India Changing,* and literary journals including *Pratilipi* and *Desilit.* Her first Hindi play *Jaal* opened in 2012 as part of Writers Bloc, in Mumbai. Her collection of short stories *Love Stories # 1 to 14* was published in 2012.

S. Hussain Zaidi

S. Hussain Zaidi is a journalist, a veteran of investigative, crime and terror reporting in the Mumbai media. He has worked for *The Asian Age, Mumbai Mirror, Mid Day* and *Indian Express.* He is the best-selling author of *Dongri to Dubai: Six Decades of the Mumbai Mafia,* the first ever chronicle of the Mumbai underworld. His previous books include best-sellers like *Black Friday: The True Story of the Bombay Bomb Blasts* and the *Mafia Queens of Mumbai.* His *Headley and I* was published in 2012. S. Hussain Zaidi was also associate producer of the HBO movie *Terror in Mumbai,* based on the 26/11 terror strikes.

ACKNOWLEDGEMENTS

My deepest gratitude goes to the people of Dharavi who shared their stories and made this book possible. May their homes and their livelihoods remain intact.

I also owe a great debt to Vinod Shetty, Director of the ACORN Foundation India, who first conceived of this book and trusted me to put it together. Vinod showed great patience throughout the four years it took to complete the project. Rajesh Prabhakar, my guide on numerous visits to Dharavi, helped me arrange the interviews, introduced writers to the residents of Dharavi, translated for them when necessary, suggested ideas for chapters, and made himself available at all hours of the day and night to accommodate the writers' schedules. Rajesh's enthusiasm for the project carried us through a number of lapses and his inexhaustible knowledge of the place and the people were an inspiration to everyone who worked with him. There would be no book without Rajesh.

Thank you to each of the writers. They took time out of their work lives and their weekends to conduct interviews and write their articles. They came back to Dharavi when scheduled meetings fell through. They returned again when I asked them to follow up or to take their stories in new directions. I've not met a group of people who has been so generous with their time and their talent. Special thanks is also due to Anand Shinde who oversaw much of the photography for this book.

I am also grateful for the support and assistance of the following people and institutions: Manjeet Kripalani, Anand Shinde, Indira Chandrasekhar, James Brunner, Paul Folmsbee, Naresh Fernandes, Sheela Patel, Jockin Arputham, Jane Swamy, Paul Fochtman, Craig Johnson, Jane McGee, Barry Raut, the Xavier Institute of Communications and the American School of Bombay.

Krishan Chopra, Publisher, HarperCollins, and Debasri Rakshit, my editor, for their close reading of the text and guidance in arranging the chapters.

Mary Ann Gibney, Joan Luangpakdy, and Mike and Paul Campana—my siblings—as well as Ray and Sue Caso, and Jack Kenny, Matt Hellerer, Tim Lennon, Mike Diggins (may he rest in peace), Bob Butler, Mick Cochrane and David Costello— my teachers—all of who have showed me how to work hard and persevere.

My daughter Estelle, a relentless debater and the most determined person I know, and my wife, Jillian, who always believed, despite evidence to the contrary, that this book would come together. They are the two best travel companions a person could hope for.

CITATIONS

'Prologue: The Perspective of Freedom' by Amartya Sen
This first appeared in *Development As Freedom*. New York: Alfred A. Knopf, 1999.

'The Making of Dharavi's "CitySystem"' by Jeb Brugmann
This first appeared in a slightly modified form in *Welcome to the Urban Revolution: How Cities Are Changing the World*. New York: Bloomsbury Press, 2009.

'The Kadam Family' by Anna Erlandson and Stina Ekman
This first appeared in *Dharavi: Documenting Informalities*, edited by Jonatan Enquist and Maria Lantz. New Delhi: Academic Foundation, 2009.

'Footnotes' by Mansi Choksi
Shortened versions of both pieces first appeared in *The Times of India*.

'Ballet in the *Basti*.' *The Times of India*, 15 June 2010.

'Tribal Instinct: The B-Boys of Dharavi.' *The Times of India*, 17 April 2011.

'A House for Khatija' by Kalpana Sharma
This first appeared in a slightly longer form in *Rediscovering Dharavi: Stories from Asia's Largest Slum*. New Delhi: Penguin, 2000.

'Three Pieces' by Dilip D'Souza
All three articles first appeared in *Tehelka*.

'Thread of a Subsidy.' *Tehelka*, 21 July 2007.

'"*Kitna palti kiya!*": Dharavi, Via the Lingo.' *Tehelka*, 7 July 2007.

'Kick in the Stomach.' *Tehelka*, 14 July 2007.

'Mumbai's Shadow City' by Mark Jacobson
This first appeared in *National Geographic*, May 2007.

'Dharavi: Makeover or Takeover?' by Shirish B. Patel
This first appeared in a slightly longer form in *Economic and Political Weekly*. 45.24 (2010): 47–54.

It was written specifically for this volume. However, the author requested if he could publish it first in *Economic and Political Weekly*.